If . . . Then . . . Curriculum: Assessment-Based Instruction, Grades 3–5

Lucy Calkins with Colleagues from the Teachers College Reading and Writing Project

Photography by Peter Cunningham

Illustrations by Marjorie Martinelli

HEINEMANN ◆ PORTSMOUTH, NH

Heinemann
361 Hanover Street
Portsmouth, NH 03801–3912
www.heinemann.com

Offices and agents throughout the world

The authors and publisher wish to thank those who have generously given permission to reprint borrowed material:

Cataloging-in-Publication data is on file with the Library of Congress.

ISBN-13: 978-0-325-07739-0

Series editorial team: Anna Gratz Cockerille, Karen Kawaguchi, Tracy Wells, Felicia O'Brien, Debra Doorack, Jean Lawler, Marielle Palombo, and Sue Paro
Production: Elizabeth Valway, David Stirling, and Abigail Heim
Cover and interior designs: Jenny Jensen Greenleaf
Photography: Peter Cunningham
Illustrations: Marjorie Martinelli
Composition: Publishers' Design and Production Services, Inc.
Manufacturing: Steve Bernier

Printed in the United States of America on acid-free paper
19 18 17 16 15   VP   2 3 4 5

Contents

A Letter to Teachers of Grade 3 • v

A Letter to Teachers of Grade 4 • x

A Letter to Teachers of Grade 5 • xiv

A Word about Assessment • xvii

Third Grade

Learning through Reading: Countries around the World • **1**

Bend I: Learning about a Country Using a Variety of Texts and Lenses • 5

Bend II: Researching a Different Country • 10

Bend III: Learning and Thinking across Countries: Exploring Similarities and Differences to Grow Ideas • 12

Bend IV: Learning about Countries and Cultures through Literature (Folktales and Fairy Tales) • 14

Third Grade and Fourth Grade

Nonfiction Book Clubs: Author Studies • **20**

Bend I: Investigating Nonfiction Identities and Setting Out to Make Those More Powerful • 24

Bend II: Investigating Beloved Authors and Deepening Understanding of Nonfiction Techniques • 26

Bend III: Expanding Nonfiction Experiences • 30

Third Grade or Fourth Grade

Solving the Mystery before the Detective: Inference, Close Reading, Synthesis, and Prediction • **34**

Bend I: Mystery Readers Read for Clues • 39

Bend II: Reading across Mysteries • 44

Bend III: Mystery Readers Learn Life Lessons from Books • 48

Third Grade or Fourth Grade

Biography Book Clubs • **54**

Bend I: Biography Readers Use All They Know about Reading Stories • 59

Bend II: Biography Readers Use All They Know about Informational Texts • 63

Bend III: Biography Readers Not Only Follow a Life Story, They Also Grow Ideas • 69

Third Grade, Fourth Grade, or Fifth Grade

Little Things Are Big: Making Meaning from Poems and Poetic Craft in Literature • **74**

Bend I: Discovering Poetry in Poems and Prose • 78

Bend II: Reading for Deeper Comprehension • 84

Bend III: Looking at Life and Literature through the Lens of Poetry • 88

Fourth Grade or Fifth Grade

Social Issues Book Clubs: Applying Analytical Lenses across Literature and Informational Texts • 94

Bend I: Reading between the Lines to Interpret Issues in Texts • 100

Bend II: Analyzing the Way Different Authors Address and Craft Similar Social Issues in Both Literature and Current Events • 106

Bend III: Bringing Our Reading Lenses to the World—And Making Our Thinking More Complex • 111

Fourth Grade or Fifth Grade

Author Study: Reading Like a Fan • 117

Bend I: When Readers Read More Than One Book by the Same Author, They Come to Know That Author • 122

Bend II: Reading Many Books by a Beloved Author Means Apprenticing Oneself to That Author's Craft • 126

Bend III: Becoming an Author Expert • 129

Bend IV: Readers Explore the Deeper Connections that an Author Inspires in Them • 132

Fifth Grade

Historical Fiction Book Clubs and Related Informational Reading: Tackling Complex Texts • 136

Bend I: Deep Comprehension and Synthesis of Complex Story Elements • 145

Bend II: Interpreting Complex Texts • 150

Bend III: Becoming More Complex Because We Read • 155

Fifth Grade

Learning through Reading: Westward Expansion • 165

Bend I: Reading Nonfiction about Westward Expansion and Summarizing with Structure in Mind • 170

Bend II: Learning about an Aspect of the Westward Expansion through Reading • 177

Bend III: Building Theories and Reading Critically • 187

Online Digital Resources

Intellectual Independence: An Ambitious Workshop for Experienced Readers

Launching the Readers Workshop with Young Readers

A Letter to Teachers of Grade 3

Dear Teachers of Third Grade,

Thanks for turning to this book and for the time you are willing to spend planning your yearlong curriculum. I hope you and your grade-level colleagues are able to read this brief letter, to look over the tables of contents and front matter for the four Units of Study books we've written for third grade, and to plan out your year together, because a little bit of shared planning goes a really long way.

The most important thing I have to suggest is that you and your colleagues make plans that allow you to teach in synchronization with each other. Something really magical happens when curriculum is shared enough that you can support each other. Any one teacher's teaching becomes buttressed by the knowledge and resources that others have to offer.

I know that you'll want to plan a year that includes not only the four Units of Study books but also other units as well. We've helped tens of thousands of third-grade teachers think through those decisions, so I'll weigh in on choices that I think you could make, but of course I am mindful that you need to take into account local resources, pressures, and passions.

I'll discuss the writing units from Units of Study in Information, Opinion, and Narrative Writing as well as the reading units you have in hand, as most of you will probably be interested in the interface between reading and writing. Of course both reading and writing Units of Study can be taught without links to the other.

Start with *Building a Reading Life* and *Crafting True Stories*.

My first clear suggestion is that you will want to begin the year with *Building a Reading Life* and, alongside it, the writing unit *Crafting True Stories*. Those units both support the foundational work you need to do in order to establish productive, well-managed reading and writing workshops, assess your readers

and writers, help children to develop identities as readers and writers, and show your students how to begin to use the foundational tools that will be essential across the upcoming three years. The thought collective that comprises the TCRWP regards grades 3–5 as something of a unit, and there are fairly different expectations for grade 3 than for grade 2. So these first two opening units in reading and in writing are especially critical at your grade level because they launch the entire grades 3–5 span of work.

My other suggestion for you is that you plan, from the start, for the date on which those units will be completed, making sure that you don't devote more than five weeks to them (I can live with six weeks—but not more, please!). The units are not written to sustain two months of reading and writing. If you find that some of the sessions take you more than a day to teach, begin now to tackle that problem without stretching all the sessions across two days. You can look over a minilesson and decide, based on your kids and on that particular lesson, what part of it can be trimmed. Perhaps you can crop the Connection so that you start right in with the Teaching Point. Perhaps you can do the Teaching and the Link and either skip or shorten the Active Engagement.

You should know, however, that all of the minilessons in this series can be given in 10–12 minutes, so if they are taking much longer than that for you, it might help to watch a video tape of a minilesson being given, and think about ways that you could increase the pace of your teaching. On the Teachers College Reading and Writing Project website, we have a number of videos of minilessons, including "Whole Class Instruction to Teach Students to Reread Their Information Texts with an Eye Toward Logical Structure and Then Use This to Guide Revisions (3–5)," "Whole Class Instruction in Opinion Writing: Teaching for Transfer as Students Move Between Persuasive Speeches and Petitions (3–5)," and "Second-Grade Information Writing (Forces and Motion)."

In any case, we strongly suggest you begin your yearlong reading work-shop with the unit, *Building a Reading Life*. This unit not only helps you to establish a well-run workshop and to conduct your initial assessments, it also helps your students develop the habit of reading with stamina, of monitoring for comprehension, of envisioning as they read, and of reading in such a way that they can retell a story (using story elements to do so). The unit has a foundational skills bend in which it especially supports the vocabulary work that third-graders need to be doing, including working with prefixes and suf-fixes and words in context.

Decide whether *Reading to Learn: Grasping Main Ideas and Text Structures* or *Character Studies* comes next.

We recommend you move next to the foundational nonfiction unit—*Read-ing to Learn: Grasping Main Ideas and Text Structures*—so that you can shift between fiction and nonfiction units. This unit channels kids to read large chunks of a nonfiction text before pausing to recap what they have read, using the text structure to help them glean the main ideas and supporting details. It helps readers read expository and narrative nonfiction texts differently, and to read in such a way that they can not only summarize but also think about the texts they are reading.

However, you could teach *Character Studies* prior to *Reading to Learn: Grasping Main Ideas and Text Structures*. Why might you do this? The one most important reason that you might reverse the sequence is if your school has a limited supply of nonfiction books, and you decide that the school can't sustain nonfiction reading in too many grade levels at one time. Perhaps you gather nonfiction books from hither and yon and channel them to the grade level that is teaching nonfiction—a good idea—in which case, you could switch the sequence of the next two published units for third grade. That is, the second book across all the grades in the reading series is a nonfiction book, and that could be an unsustainable plan. So if you wonder whether *Character Studies* and *Reading to Learn* could be reversed, the answer is yes.

At least for your first year working with this series, if you were to teach *Character Studies* as your second unit and if many of your students are below benchmark, you could borrow some minilessons from the second-grade Units of Study, looking especially at *Bigger Books Mean Amping Up Reading Power* (Unit 3) and at *Series Book Clubs* (Unit 4). If this is your school's first year working with the reading Units of Study, your third-graders will never have experienced those second-grade units. Unit 3 of that grade begins and ends

with work on fluency and comprehension, and Unit 4 supports readers read-ing series books at levels I–M. Those books would be a terrific resource for third-grade teachers whose students are operating below benchmark levels.

But either way, a second unit on fiction is an entirely reasonable go-to in third grade.

Just a word about the reciprocity between your writing and reading cur-riculum: You'll note that the second book in the writing Units of Study is a book on writing information books, *The Art of Information Writing*. If you worry that it would be a big mistake to teach the *Character Studies* unit while your children are writing information books, there are a few ways to think about this. First, you could solve that by teaching a second narrative writing unit—"Writing Gripping Fictional Stories with Meaning and Significance" from the *If . . . Then . . . Curriculum* book is a terrific option.

But more importantly, *The Art of Informational Writing* is *not* meant to support your students in doing a reading research unit. At this point in the year, we don't think it is a good idea for third-grade readers to inch through a few nonfiction books or articles, copying down tons of facts so they can insert them into their own information books. The push in *Reading to Learn: Grasping Main Ideas and Text Structures* is for children to read high-interest nonfiction on an array of topics, looking for the main ideas and the supporting information. You'll push your kids to read large chunks of text before pausing, and then, when pausing, to glean the main ideas and supporting points and to resist the temptation to record cool facts. Channeling early third-graders to copy down bits and pieces of random information so they can insert those facts into their information writing books would be a big mistake.

Therefore, if you *do* teach the writing unit, *The Art of Information Writ-ing*, alongside the reading unit, *Reading to Learn: Grasping Main Ideas and Text Structures*, try not to link those two units together too closely. There are important reasons why the reading unit does not ask students to research a single topic in order to write a nonfiction book about that topic. Please do not push students to read just about one topic and then to also write about that topic. This doesn't mean that children who are reading and writing nonfiction alongside each other won't make important connections—they will. They can look over the structure of their reading books, noting text features and adding these into their own writing. They can also do a few days of targeted research on the topic on which they are writing, but that'd be the sum total of what we recommend. This is not a good time for close alignment between the topic of their reading and the topic of their writing. There will be a time for that later in the year (see the unit in this book titled "Learning Through Reading: Countries Around the World").

Your third unit: *Character Studies* or *Reading to Learn: Grasping Main Ideas and Text Structures*?

We expect that your third unit will come before the winter holidays. If you have taught the first two books in the series, you will probably want to progress to the third, *Character Studies*. This all-time favorite unit for third-graders teaches essential skills for fiction reading. Also, we assume that you won't want to teach two nonfiction units in a row.

Character Studies builds on the character work described in *Building a Reading Life*, and it references the story element work described in the narrative nonfiction bend of *Reading to Learn: Grasping Main Ideas and Text Structures* (though your instruction in story elements doesn't depend on prior instruction in *Reading to Learn*). *Character Studies* is designed to give third-graders a solid foundation in the sort of work that they will do with increasing sophistication in similar units in grades 4 and 5. Children will learn how to go from making observations about characters, to growing ideas, to deepening those ideas and then turning them into evidence-based theories. The unit then shifts gears to a focus on the way in which characters tend to progress across a story—that is, to a focus on story structure—and the role of story elements, including problem, setting, and theme. Then, in the final bend, children will do some cross-text comparison work that incorporates the instruction of the first two bends. This unit also introduces third-graders to clubs, which they will revisit in *Research Clubs: Elephants, Penguins, and Frogs, Oh My!*

If you teach *Character Studies* now, we imagine you'll have two really terrific choices for the writing unit that you want to teach alongside it. First, *Changing the World: Persuasive Speeches, Petitions, and Editorials* was written to follow *The Art of Information Writing*, and to introduce third-graders to opinion writing, which can set them up for a subsequent unit on writing literary essays (another kind of opinion writing). If your students do this writing unit now, they'll become different kinds of school and global citizens, and you'll live in the reflected glory of this unit for the rest of your year. They also use the skills they learned during *The Art of Information Writing* to bring a lot of information into the writing they end up doing to support causes such as recycling, saving the whales, and so forth.

On the other hand, *Character Studies* gives students a language for talking about fiction books. This unit helps them to think and write about a character's traits, about the life lessons a character learns or the ways a character struggles and changes, and, of course, about the importance of setting. All of that work can go very nicely into literary essays.

You may decide to teach the unit, "The Literary Essay: Equipping Ourselves with the Tools to Write Expository Texts that Advance an Idea about Literature" from the third grade *If . . . Then . . . Curriculum* book. (You should know, by the way, that most of us refer to this unit, affectionately, as "Baby Literary Essays.") That unit is a lovely complement to *Character Studies*, and if your high-stakes test includes any writing about reading, this will set students up well for that later expectation. Of course, you can also move this unit into Unit 4, when it is closer to those tests and can help students transfer what they learned during *Character Studies* into units on reading mysteries or series books. I discuss those options in the upcoming section.

If you already taught *Character Studies*, then it is absolutely clear to us that you'll want to switch to *Reading to Learn: Grasping Main Ideas and Text Structures*—that unit teaches essential skills of nonfiction reading. Again, if you decide to have students writing informational books while reading this unit, please read my earlier comments on that. You would then teach the writing unit, *Changing the World: Persuasive Speeches, Petitions, and Editorials*, alongside it.

Surveying your many options for the fourth unit.

Your fourth unit will presumably come just after the children return from winter holidays. This is a beautiful time for a substantial unit—test pressure is still far off the horizon, and your children are growing older and more capable. You may, then, decide to teach the last of the four Units of Study books: *Research Clubs: Elephants, Penguins and Frogs, Oh My!* Then again, for third-graders, this is a good time to help kids make major strides in moving up levels of text complexity—and that actually is some of the most important work you can do with your third-graders. In order to support that progress, you may decide to teach a unit that supports fiction book clubs. Remember that book clubs are, in a sense, the perfect forum for guided reading. If you decide on a fiction unit, you will probably teach the unit, "Solving the Mystery Before the Detective: Inference, Close Reading, Synthesis, and Prediction." You essentially tell kids that their goal when reading mysteries is to try to solve the mystery before the detective does. To do this, mystery readers need to first figure out what the mystery is in the story, and then collect clues themselves, reading suspiciously (and closely) to try to figure out the culprit. Almost every fiction book that third-graders read is actually a mystery, and this unit helps your third-graders create a through line in a text, seeing cause-and-effect relationships, and predicting outcomes. This requires close, attentive, influential reading and lots of thinking about what the clues suggest.

This unit supports third-graders in reading a great volume of increasingly complex fiction with high levels of engagement and attentiveness, using sticky notes and reading entries to do increasingly amounts of writing about reading during reading time (the presence of a club provides an audience for that writing). Because the "Solving the Mystery" unit involves book clubs, it provides great opportunities for students to become more accustomed to citing the text, providing evidence for their ideas, and then not only mentioning the evidence but discussing it. Another advantage to this unit is that there are countless books available for readers at a variety of levels, from Nate the Great and Cam Jansen (level K) for earlier readers, to Sammy Keyes (level T) for more advanced readers, and, of course, the entire range in between. Also, because children will be reading in tandem with their peers, either in partnerships or book clubs, they will have the support of another reader or readers, as well as the benefit of reading the same books. Both of these things support reading with increased volume, stamina, and engagement. Many of the mystery books your students will be reading are also part of a series, and reading in a series positions them to tackle harder and harder books. If high-stakes tests are now on your students' horizons, this work sets them up well for the hoops they'll need to jump through. The unit is both wildly popular with kids and easy to teach.

As I mentioned earlier, you may decide to teach the final book-length unit, *Research Clubs: Elephants, Penguins, and Frogs Oh My!* If you teach this unit, you could conceivably revisit *The Art of Information Writing* in your writing workshop, this time teaching that unit with a strong writing-about-research spin.

On the other hand, for your writing workshop you could choose either *Changing the World: Persuasive Speeches, Petitions, and Editorials* or "The Literary Essay: Equipping Ourselves with the Tools to Write Expository Texts that Advance an Idea about Literature" (see *If . . . Then . . . Curriculum*) if you haven't yet taught one of those units. Both of these are units on opinion

writing, but it is also conceivable that you'd decide to return to either an old favorite narrative unit, "Writing Gripping Fictional Stories with Meaning and Significance." That, too, is in the *If . . . Then . . . Curriculum* book in the writing series.

Your fifth unit.

If you do not teach *Research Clubs: Elephants, Penguins, and Frogs, Oh My!* in the previous month, this may be the time for that unit. It is the penultimate of the third-grade books. That unit provides kids with a lot of instruction in main idea, use of text features, accumulating information across texts, comparing and contrasting, and vocabulary. It invites your youngsters to experience the process that researchers undertake when they engage in research. Your children work in clubs to research first one animal, then another, and to compare and contrast those animals. When reading up on an animal, they learn to try the easiest and broadest texts first in order to give themselves an overview of the terrain. Then they read a few texts to learn about a single subtopic (their animal's habitat, for example), synthesizing information from across multiple texts on that habitat or on whatever else they are studying.

The other option we can well imagine for now is that you might decide to teach a unit on biography. The unit on biography that is described in this book, "Biography Book Clubs," channels students to focus for a time on reading a biography about a single person, which allows them to compare and contrast the information and discuss the way the biography is written. Students are also encouraged to read about the era in which the person lived and made his or her contributions, thereby reading across expository as well as narrative nonfiction texts and using their skills to synthesize. In addition, today's standards increasingly emphasize a need for students to be "intertextual," to connect what they are reading with other print and media sources. A reader who is tackling the biography of Martin Luther King Jr., for example, may pair this reading with audio clips of King's historic speeches or with photographs and videos of King leading a civil rights march. Standards also call for children to be able to negotiate multiple perspectives, for example, reading King's biography, which was written by a historian, versus reading or hearing his actual speeches. This unit is designed to enable readers to compare, contrast, and ultimately integrate information gleaned from multiple sources, both print and media.

Your sixth unit.

This time of the school year is a particularly exciting time for third-graders. They are spreading their wings now and able to do so much more than they could do in the fall. You can teach higher-level comprehension skills, which often involves them working with text sets and with clubs. Energy should be high.

You have lots of choices open to you. If you haven't yet taught *Research Clubs*, you will certainly want to do so now. You could easily do some related information writing. However, think about how to do that as the children cycle through a study of first one kind of animal, then another kind, and whether kids would write about just one animal or multiple animals.

But then again, the energy that you'll tap into with a unit on "Solving the Mystery" will dazzle you. That unit is absolutely tailor-made for third-graders, and it will support the volume of reading that perhaps matters more than anything else at this point. To make your decision, think a bit about the books that you have available, and make sure you choose a unit that allows kids to make choices among high-interest books.

Finally, in many schools, teachers take this time for a cross-disciplinary unit on a topic that is important in your social studies curriculum. This book includes an overview on a unit on "Learning Through Reading: Countries around the World" that can give you a sense for how to bring together your reading workshop and your social studies curriculum. In this unit, students study one country, then another, and then they compare and contrast the two countries. They learn to read maps, to relate chapters on geography to those maps, and then to think in cause-and-effect ways about the relationships between geography and culture and economy. In many ways, children do similar work with their studies of countries as they did earlier with studies of animals. The reading unit aims to work hand-in-hand with the content area unit to create an in-depth study of a country that ranges across the curriculum. The hope is for students to be transferring and applying their learning from one subject to another seamlessly. This is a unit rife with cross-curricular connections, which will deepen content knowledge and teach students how to read to learn.

Your seventh unit.

For your final unit of the year, you could go back to any of those that you didn't teach from earlier, or you could decide to author an entirely new unit for yourself. Presumably your children will be writing fairy tales; *Once Upon a Time: Adapting and Writing Fairy Tales* is a great favorite from the Units of Study in Opinion, Information, and Narrative Writing, and you could decide to devise your own fairy-tale unit. Then, too, you might decide to end the year with a unit on poetry. This volume contains an overview of such a unit, "Little Things Are Big: Making Meaning from Poems and Poetic Craft in Literature." That unit is angled a bit high for third-graders, but by now you should be comfortable with these units, and you can revise it with your colleagues.

A Letter to Teachers of Grade 4

Dear Teachers of Fourth Grade,

Thanks for taking the time to look over the optional units that are overviewed for you here, in *If . . . Then . . . Curriculum: Assessment-Based Instruction*. My letter is meant to help you find your way among all the alternatives that are laid out in this book, and to help you imagine yet other possibilities. We've been helping literally thousands of fourth-grade teachers construct yearlong curricular plans for decades and have some advice to offer based on that work. In the end, of course, I am fully aware that decisions depend on local contexts. You will have passions, knowledge, resources, and pressures that are unique to your setting and to you, so know that I offer only suggestions and am glad the decisions will be yours to make.

I'll also outline ideas for writing units, as I know many of you will be teaching from Units of Study in Opinion, Information, and Narrative Writing and looking to establish reciprocity.

One thing I do recommend, however, is that the decisions not be yours alone. Experience has shown me that something really magical happens when teachers across a grade level plan a curricular path together, teaching in ways that are in synchrony with one another. If your curriculum is shared enough that you can support your colleagues and lean on them, too, then the teaching that any one of you offers can be buttressed with the knowledge and resources that others have to offer. Few things matter more than that your school is a place where you and your colleagues plan and teach in collaboration. For that to happen, establishing a shared calendar with dates on which units will be completed is critically important.

If you find that sessions are taking you two days, that minilessons are taking you twenty minutes, please know that's not the way things should go. Watch the minilessons on the Teachers College Reading and Writing Project website to imagine ways to speed them up, and feel comfortable cropping parts of a minilesson that feel as if they won't be necessary for your kids. Each session should take a day, each minilesson, 10 to 12 minutes. You can extend a few sessions, absolutely, but don't let your units drag beyond five weeks.

Your first unit: Launching your year.

I recommend that you begin your year by teaching *Interpreting Characters: The Heart of the Story*, as that book does a yeoman's job of carrying your students into the interpretive work that is essential as they move toward fourth-grade expectations for reading fiction. The first bend of the unit supports the work that is essential at the start of the year. You'll get help rallying your children to invest in their reading and to establish the habits, rituals, structures, and tools that will be essential throughout the year. The next two bends support high-level work with character, setting, theme, and literary language.

This unit fits beautifully with *The Arc of Story: Writing Realistic Fiction*, if you are teaching the writing units of study alongside reading.

If you worry that your kids need some more basic information, you might borrow a few minilessons from the third-grade book, *Character Studies*.

Your second unit: *Reading the Weather, Reading the World* or alternatives.

You will probably want to shift from fiction to nonfiction for this next unit, and our suggestion, of course, is to follow the sequence in the fourth-grade Units of Study books, teaching *Reading the Weather, Reading the World* next. You should know that this unit comprises three bends. The first bend supports students reading high-interest nonfiction books of their own choice while learning essential skills such as reading for the main idea and supporting details, reading with an alertness to text structure, tackling unfamiliar vocabulary, and so forth. The second two bends of that unit channel readers into some very exciting work around a unit on extreme weather.

It is possible that you don't have the resources to support the final two bends of that unit just yet. You may say to yourself, "I could get together some books, articles, and videos on hurricanes, tornadoes, and the rest but not in time to teach this unit at this point in the year."

If that is the case, you could still teach Bend I of that unit, perhaps transplanting some minilessons from *Reading to Learn: Grasping Main Idea and Text Structures* (grade 3) to support students doing more work with those high-interest nonfiction books. You could add another bend to the unit if you decide to do so, channeling students to work for one portion of the unit on biographies that students choose to read. If you make that choice, the third-grade unit, *Reading to Learn: Grasping Main Ideas and Text Structures* has a bend on biography, and you could borrow some sessions from that bend. That bend, combined with the unit on biography, "Biography Book Clubs," in this *If . . . Then . . . Curriculum* book, could work together to help you extend the first bend from *Reading the Weather, Reading the World*, if you decided to postpone the inquiry into extreme weather until later in the year.

You could, of course, also disconnect minilessons from the content of the weather cycle and use some of them within a unit supporting high-interest nonfiction books. But know that the weather inquiry that is supported in Bends II and III of *Reading the Weather, Reading the World* are very popular, and that cycle of work does a lot of essential teaching, so you'll probably want to return to those bends later in the year, once you have had time to gather your resources.

Although I've discussed those options at some length, I expect that most of you will teach *Reading the Weather, Reading the World* as the book stands, and you will wonder about the writing unit to teach alongside it. We recommend *Boxes and Bullets: Personal and Persuasive Essay*, even though it seems disconnected to the reading unit. The reason for this is that the fourth-grade writing units require that students have that foundation in essay before they proceed into literary essay. That is, your writers need the foundational knowledge they will glean from *Boxes and Bullets*.

I also hope you will refrain from encouraging your students to write information books about the weather during *Reading the Weather, Reading the World* unit. At this early point in the year, you need to help your students read expository texts with a focus on reading fluently and reading to understand and think through main ideas. That is, the goal for now should be for your fourth-graders to read increasingly complex nonfiction texts in a manner that resembles the way you read nonfiction magazine articles, the newspaper,

and high-interest nonfiction texts. Your goal in nonfiction, for now, is *not* to channel your kids to inch through nonfiction books, recording all the facts and transporting them to their own information book. *Reading History: The American Revolution* is a time for your kids to read and write on the same topic, but we do not recommend that for your second unit of the year. Of course, in the end these decisions are yours to make.

Your third unit.

By now, you will have taught units in both fiction and nonfiction, so you may want to return to nonfiction (in which case the obvious choice is *Reading History: The American Revolution*) or shift to fiction, and if so, you have a variety of options for how you might do so. "Historical Fiction Book Clubs and Related Informational Reading: Tackling Complex Texts" is a heavy-hitting unit that teaches students to read interpretively, to make cross-text connections between fiction and nonfiction texts, and to wrestle with questions around perspective. Your students work in clubs, which gives them a reason to increase the amount of writing they do about reading.

If you have many readers who read below benchmark, you could consider teaching the unit, "Solving the Mystery before the Detective: Inference, Close Reading, Synthesis, and Prediction," an all-time favorite unit. If you made that choice, you could then teach "Historical Fiction Book Clubs and Related Informational Reading" in May, when more of your students will have moved up another notch or two in the level of text complexity they can handle and may, therefore, be more ready to embrace the complexity of historical fiction. "Solving the Mystery before the Detective" supports stamina in fiction, moving up levels of text difficulty, thinking about cause and effect and other within-text relationships, reading closely, and comparing texts. Students learn to accumulate text so that they see that what happens in one chapter ties back and relates to what happened earlier. The unit also helps students to read closely and alertly, to be active and engaged enough that they are predicting wisely. The unit is wildly popular among both teachers and students. You presumably won't want to teach that unit at the same time for both third- and fourth-graders in your school because you will need multiple copies of mystery books—but I expect this unit will be Unit 4 for third-graders, allowing you to sneak it into fourth grade before then.

There is one other option for a fiction unit you could teach at this point in the year. If your students are reading easily and quickly but aren't doing the high-level intellectual thinking that you want them to do, if they are too apt to be plot junkies and are not talking and thinking about their books as much as you'd like, you could decide that another unit that accomplishes goals similar to those of "Historical Fiction Book Clubs and Related Informational Reading" is "Author Study: Reading Like a Fan." That unit is well described in this book and is detailed in the write-up on the fifth unit. "Author Study" supports students in becoming more skilled at talking about the choices that authors make and the reasons for those choices and thinking about the relationship between particular parts of a text (places where the author has done something) and the whole text, which is a big part of analytic reading.

For your writing unit, I imagine you choosing between two good options. First, if your students are reading historical fiction and you just completed an essay unit, you could "run to the other side of the boat" and invite students to do what they most want to do, which is to write historical fiction of their own. This will work only if they have been studying history during social studies and know something about a time in history in which to set their own story.

Many of you will likely decide instead to teach *The Literary Essay: Writing about Fiction* from Units of Study in Opinion, Information, and Narrative Writing. This book channels kids to write literary essays around short texts, so your students need not be reading novels and working to interpret them, but the work on interpretation in "Historical Fiction Book Clubs and Related Informational Texts" will surely support this.

Your fourth unit.

If you didn't teach nonfiction during your third unit, you'll want to do so now, and you'll want to choose *Reading History: The American Revolution* and another nonfiction unit. *Reading History: The American Revolution* will be a great favorite, and it will allow you to synchronize your teaching in writing, reading, and social studies. If you make that choice, launch the reading unit a few days before you launch the companion writing unit, *Bringing History to Life*, because children need to have studied the topic before they write about it.

You may decide that this unit comes at a time when much of your teaching is compromised because of the oncoming high-stakes tests. If that's the situation, you probably will move *Reading History: The American Revolution* to another time in the year so the unit is given its due.

An alternative is teach the second two bends from *Reading the Weather, Reading the World*, if you didn't teach that portion of the unit earlier in the year. Your children essentially study first one and then another form of extreme weather, then work on compare and contrast and on studying bigger themes that pertain to the larger topic.

Your fifth unit.

We are assuming this is the time of year when you can put high-stakes tests behind you and go for the gold. If you haven't taught "Historical Fiction Book Clubs and Related Informational Reading" or *Reading History: The American Revolution* you'll want to do so now, as this is a great time for a heavy-hitting unit.

There is one more enormously popular unit—"Social Issues Book Clubs: Applying Analytical Lenses across Literature and Informational Texts"—that teachers often schedule at this juncture as it can bring new energy to the curriculum. This unit involves cross-genre work including fiction, nonfiction, and poetry. In this unit you will harness the energy of unabashed teaching toward social justice. Get ready for it by wearing your own passions on your sleeve. All of us know that sometimes when we read a wonderful book, we find ourselves welling up with a passionate commitment to everything we believe. Stories remind us that we care very much about justice and injustice and about living meaningful lives. In this unit, you will teach children to take their books and their lives seriously. As you prepare, think about how books have affected you—the choices you make, the kind of person you try to be, the issues you care about—so that you can talk about these particular books and your life with your students.

Your sixth unit.

We imagine that either now or in your final unit, you will want to teach a unit on author studies. In "Author Study: Reading Like a Fan," you'll stretch your arms wide and gather *all* your students into the inner circle. Whatever their level and previous success with reading, in this unit, your students will articulate their identities as readers. Specifically, they will identify one book or one writer, who speaks to them, and then become experts and insiders on everything this author has written and everything the author stands for. It is a powerful thing for a child to be able to say, "Oh, my favorite author is so-and-so." Name-dropping alone is a way to hitch oneself to the literary world. It is even more powerful for this child to be able to tell you precisely *why* his favorite author is special, to list titles by the author, and to comment on how the author has changed this student's way of living in and seeing the world. This unit taps into the power of studying an author's work closely, of eagerly anticipating reading another book by this author, and of becoming enriched by the craft and life lessons this author's books provide. This work will pull students firmly into forging a unique personal literary identity by attaching their own name with that of an author who speaks to them. With your help, this is work that *all* students—not just the strongest ones in the room—can do.

Your seventh unit.

Think about the big celebrations in your life. Chances are good that those will be times when poetry is brought forward. At the inauguration of a new mayor, chancellor, or president, there is poetry. At weddings and funerals and graduations—poetry. It is fitting, then, that you consider ending your year with a unit on poetry. "Little Things Are Big: Making Meaning from Poems and Poetic Craft in Literature" helps students see the power of literary devices to impact the reader, whether in the final stanza of a poem or the opening paragraph of a chapter. The instruction begins through shared readings of poems, followed by read-alouds of prose using similar strategies. Given how important it is that children continue reading volumes of text, the flow of the unit accounts for days when readers will have independent or book club books with them in class, checking in with partners and clubs (and you!) about their progress,

and getting some valuable reading time in. These days will be opportunities to show students how to read in search of poetry, even in a novel, and to make the most of the passages where the author has clearly spent time crafting repetition or rhyme or alliteration, developing metaphors, or painting vivid images. The unit begins by focusing on localized craft: analyzing the effects of words and phrases that stand out, then moves in Bend II to considering how parts of a poem or multiple passages fit together to make big ideas or raise questions. Finally, Bend III teaches readers to hold the messages and images from poems in their minds as they read across texts. Your readers will emerge from this study more alert to how poets and novelists work, and to the kinds of messages and questions that cross genres and make a real difference in how we view the world.

If you think your students need more support in nonfiction reading, or if you'd like to ignite their interest in nonfiction and set them up for a summer of nonfiction reading, you might choose "Nonfiction Book Clubs: Author Studies." This engaging unit sets up students to craft nonfiction lives for themselves, by creating their own text sets and studying the techniques that their favorite nonfiction authors use that they most want to emulate.

A Letter to Teachers of Grade 5

Dear Teachers of Fifth Grade,

What a year this promises to be for your kids as readers! One look at the learning progression for fifth grade will probably send your heart into palpitations—but the amazing thing is that your youngsters will be more than game for the challenges.

This letter overviews our thoughts about your yearlong curriculum. I offer those thoughts with tentativeness because local conditions will influence your decisions. Still, my colleagues and I have helped tens of thousands of fifth-grade teachers chart out a yearlong curriculum that does work for their particular setting, and so we have some advice to share with you, in case it is helpful.

Let me say, for starters, that when my colleagues and I devise Units of Study plans, we need to make a decision between making shoes for kids to grow into after they have been in reading workshops for a sequence of years, and shoes that will fit now. We chose shoes that leave plenty of growing space—which means that if your school has just recently adopted Units of Study in Teaching Reading (or Units of Study in Opinion, Information, and Narrative Writing), you are apt to find that the fifth-grade curriculum is a bit of a stretch. It will be vastly easier a year from now, when children come to you who will have grown up within the fourth-grade Units of Study.

In general, our suggestion is for you to feel free to teach some of the fourth-grade units during fifth grade, especially when students have yet to experience the units. The problem, of course, is you can borrow only a fourth-grade Units of Study book that is not currently being taught.

The most important thing I have to suggest is that you and your colleagues make plans that allow you to teach in synchronization with each other. Something really magical happens when curriculum is shared enough that you can support each other. Any one teacher's teaching becomes buttressed by the knowledge and resources that others have to offer. There are few things that matter more than that your school is a place where you and your colleagues plan and teach in collaboration. For that to happen, establishing a shared calendar with dates on which units will be completed is critically important.

Your first unit.

At the start of fifth grade, you will almost surely want to teach *Interpretation Book Clubs: Analyzing Themes*, the unit that begins the fifth-grade year. It was designed to support you in launching all the structures, habits, mindsets, and values that will last across the year. As the teacher of your class, it falls on you to build a culture, and the culture you establish literally creates a world of difference. The first books have a special job to do, and it would be hard to flip a book from later in the year into this spot. This book also builds some essential habits that will be important throughout the year. It rallies kids to care about writing about reading in a new way and helps them work collaboratively in clubs right from the start of the year.

If you are teaching writing units of study alongside your reading units, we strongly recommend you also launch the year with *Narrative Craft*. The two units both do a yeoman's job to launch your workshop.

Your second unit.

You will almost surely want to go right into the second unit in our series, *Tackling Complexity: Moving Up Levels of Nonfiction*. The unit allows for students to read any high-interest nonfiction texts they want and to do so while working on ways to tackle harder and harder nonfiction texts. The final portion of the unit channels students to research topics of interest to them, and therefore that portion of the unit will require some special effort to provision the unit. If necessary, you could divide this unit into parts and simply teach the first part for now, and make the second half, the independent research project, into a self-standing unit for later in the year.

You'll find that this unit is an ambitious one, and yet it gives kids some really high-interest new tools that will set them up well for the year.

Your third unit.

You'll have two choices for this next unit, we think. You could teach a fiction unit, in which case your writing unit could be a literary essay unit, something we recommend you teaching. Otherwise, you'll probably want to devote this unit to teaching students to read and write argument texts. Certainly if you teach *The Research-Based Argument Essay* writing unit now, you will want to also teach *Argument and Advocacy: Researching Debatable Issues* as those two books support each other. Each unit can stand on its own, but your teaching will be much easier because you teach the two in tandem. Both units should be taught before any high-stakes test, especially if it is a CCSS-aligned test.

By this time in the year, your fifth-graders will have studied both fiction and nonfiction. They'll have been inducted into the habits and traditions of your classroom. It is often now that they begin to feel like full-fledged fifth-graders. They are growing up, and with that, students begin to develop a heightened awareness of the injustice and inequity that exist in the world. It is not unusual to hear a fifth-grader exclaim, "That's so wrong!" Because of global standards, youngsters as young as ten years old can read nonfiction in critical and complex ways and analyze multiple accounts of the same event or topic in order to note important similarities and differences. You'll want to tap into your fifth-graders' passions to support reading and writing units that are aligned to each other.

Argument and Advocacy is a unit that continues to support students to read more complex, challenging nonfiction, but this particular unit especially aims to help them to research in order to have an informed viewpoint and to make arguments about provocative, debatable issues. This practice entails reading arguments and informational texts in a more critical and analytic way.

As mentioned earlier, you could, of course, decide to flip the sequence of your units so that you teach now units that are described later. If you were to make that decision, the obvious choice would be to teach fiction now—the next month's write-up describes that choice.

Your fourth unit.

If you taught *Argument and Advocacy* in your third unit, you will *really* want a fiction unit by now, and we think your choices are twofold. You could certainly decide to teach the book—the fourth and last book in your series (*Fantasy Book Clubs: The Magic of Themes and Symbols*)—and it will be a wonderful unit for recruiting students' energy after the winter holidays and ramping up their volume of reading and engagement. But that unit has actually been written with hopes that it comes at the end of the school year and launches a whole summer of fantasy reading. You can decide whether to leave it in that position.

Or, you might channel students to read historical fiction in the lovely unit, "Historical Fiction Book Clubs and Related Informatonal Reading," included in this book. You will probably want to teach the writing unit from the "Literary and Comparative Essays" alongside this. Presumably your students will have experienced that genre last year, but it is such a rush and an important genre that you can easily return to it every year. You can also consider teaching that unit with a different spin. In fourth grade, your students focused on learning to read interpretively and to make connections between fiction and nonfiction. This year, perhaps you want to support a writing unit alongside the reading unit to channel your students to read historical fiction as a writer, bringing that lens to their reading.

Your fifth unit.

We can imagine that at this point you might turn once again to nonfiction, perhaps choosing the unit in this book on westward expansion, "Learning Through Reading: Westward Expansion." The Units of Study in Opinion, Information, and Narrative Writing series contains a very significant book, *The Lens of History: Research Reports*, which could be be taught alongside. Of course, these coordinated units could come any time in the year, but you won't want to miss them.

It is also worth noting that *The Lens of History* is actually about writing about any history topic; although we use westward expansion as a case in point, you could substitute a different historical era and still profit from that writing unit. In the same way, the reading unit on westward expansion could be revised to support another historical era. We are well aware that teachers in Singapore and Brazil aren't apt to teach units that revolve around this particular chapter in American history.

There will be lots of choices open to you as you come to this unit—both in writing and in reading. If you haven't yet taught a unit that aligns reading and writing in social studies, you will probably want to do this. *The Lens of History* is written to be taught alongside "Learning through Reading: West-ward Expansion," and as I mentioned earlier, both those units could have the specific historical era removed and another substituted. Many teachers have devoted not only reading and writing time but also social studies time to this topic and loved taking down the walls between disciplines as a change of pace and a graphic reminder that the skills kids are learning in any one discipline need to be transferred across the curriculum.

Another choice might be to teach a social issues unit "Social Issues Book Clubs: Applying Analytical Lenses across Literature and Informational Texts," another favorite. The power of that unit comes in part because students read across genre—nonfiction and fiction and poetry—and they study the way different authors handle the same issue. Students spend two weeks studying an issue in the company of a club, noticing the perspectives authors take and the important lessons these topics can teach. They develop their own perspectives and questions about issues, and they will talk back to texts, bringing their own stances to the conversation. This is a unit, then, on compare and contrast and on critical reading. As the unit comes to a close, students take on the role of activists. They delve even deeper into current events and think about how they can talk back to these problems, raise awareness, and make differences in the world. Plan to spend a week wrapping up the unit.

Your sixth and seventh units.

If by some slim chance you haven't done so already, then by all means, teach the fantasy unit before the year is over. As you near the end of the year, you will have a nice opportunity to immerse students in the genre of fantasy while, at the same time, inviting students to draw on what they are learning about the elements of fantasy to write fantasies themselves. In fact, you can angle your writing unit to teach readers to read with a special lens, noticing writing craft. Writers will want to try to some of the craft moves they notice in the fantasy novels they love—the description of fantastical worlds, the inclusion of magical objects or characters, the use of symbolism to guide readers toward interpretation, and so on. Students will be able to do this work as writers, especially if they have been reading fantasy novels with an eye toward the decisions that authors have made and the connection between those decisions and the meanings in the stories. Readers can learn to notice moments that provide a strong emotional response and think about why the author might have written those moments in that way and about how those moments connect to the whole text. Then, during the writing unit of study, students can create such moments.

Here's how this unit goes. First you launch the kids into fantasy book clubs or partnerships—the kids are going to want to talk about these books, and you'll want to channel this urge to heighten their intensity and stamina for literary conversations. In the first bend, you'll teach the kids to read with deep comprehension and to synthesize across many pages. Then you'll move in the second bend of the unit to developing their thematic understanding. In the third bend, you'll teach them to learn as they read, including bringing nonfiction to their fantasy reading. Finally in the fourth bend you'll develop their understanding of literary traditions so they begin to see the book they are holding as part of a grander, conceptual text set. Across these parts of the unit and the weeks of the unit, the students will read several books in a series.

To round out your year, you might teach the historical fiction unit, if you haven't done so already. There is one other option for a fiction unit you could teach at this point in the year. If your students are reading easily and quickly but aren't doing the high-level intellectual thinking that you want them to do, if they are too apt to be plot junkies and are not talking and thinking about their books as much as you'd like, another unit that will accomplish similar goals as "Historical Fiction Book Clubs and Related Informational Reading" is "Author Study: Reading Like a Fan." This unit supports students in becoming more skilled at talking about the choices that authors make and the reasons for those choices and at thinking about the relationship between particular parts of a text (places where the author has done something) and the whole text, which is a big part of analytic reading. "Author Study: Reading Like a Fan" also does an excellent job of launching readers into a summer of independent reading. If your students are headed off to middle school next year, we strongly recommend you send them off with this engaging unit.

A Word about Assessment

AS WE DISCUSS in detail in *Reading Pathways*, we strongly encourage you to plan your instruction, and indeed, even to plan the units you'll teach, using your students' work as your guide. Before you begin your overarching plans, we suggest you consider the various assessments that are available and discuss with colleagues which assessments you'll use. It is helpful for children and teachers if some assessments become systemic and if you think about ways to make those assessments as efficient as possible. In *Reading Pathways*, we discuss various ways that this can be done.

The majority of assessments discussed here are formative assessments, which are designed to inform your teaching. We cannot emphasize enough the value of spending some time at the start of each unit to do some informal assessment. The data from such assessment will set you up to plan or tweak the plans for the unit, right from the start. You have options for how to collect this data—and we encourage you to vary the types of assessments you give across the units. As a grade team, you can make an assessment plan for each unit, one that feels manageable to you. To make this plan, consider the major goals for the upcoming unit and how you might assess children on their development toward these goals.

You might, for example, study students' independent jotting about their books, looking to see what they already know about the particular skills that the unit you are about to teach will address. Another option is to embed questions within a read-aloud that address work you want to target in the unit. You will find this sort of assessment for each of the main units in the series and can use these as templates to create assessments for the units in this book. For some units, such as "Historical Fiction Book Clubs and Related Informational Reading," you can use the assessment designed to accompany *Historical Fiction Clubs*, grade 4. Just make sure that you swap in a different text. For other units, such as "Little Things Are Big: Making Meaning from Poems and Poetic Craft in Literature," we suggest you create your own questions that are designed to measure children's understanding of this genre and proficiency with skills you plan to emphasize.

After you have collected your children's responses, we suggest you lay them alongside the appropriate strand of whichever learning progression you are using and assess students' written responses using the progression as a guide. At the end of the unit, you'll likely plan to repeat this same assessment (or a similar one) to measure student growth. Each strand of the progression provides descriptors, showing how the work of a particular skill grows from second-grade levels to middle school levels.

The data you gather will help you assess what skills and lessons students are transferring and applying and how they are making progress toward reaching the reading expectations for their grade. It is important to challenge students to self-reflect and analyze the work they are doing as readers—taking stock of what they are remembering to do but also setting goals for what they might do next to ensure that they challenge themselves to grow. The Narrative Reading Learning Progression and Informational Reading Learning Progression, available in *Reading Pathways*, will help you track your students' growth and can help guide you and your students as you set goals.

Don't fret over finding the perfect level for each student—in fact, you may be able to study only a few of your students' assessments closely, relying on other students' own self-assessments to save you time. The important thing is that you spend time studying at least a representative sampling of your students' work and that you keep in mind the pathway of increased sophistication that your children will be traveling as they progress from less sophisticated to more sophisticated skill levels. Your teaching can become much more responsive based on what you glean from these assessments; that is, you can tailor your teaching to the data you gather.

Once you know where the majority of your class falls along a particular strand of the learning progression, you can meet their needs in your minilessons and read-alouds. It is equally important to know where your outliers stand so that you can plan thoughtfully for the small-group instruction and teaching of individuals you will do throughout a unit. You might gather a few texts at the below-benchmark levels to assess whether the work of the unit is transferable to these texts. For example, some level K books do not lend themselves to deep inferential thinking. This makes the inference work you do during read-aloud and small-group instruction an even more critical component of your instruction.

Keep in mind that all units are intended to teach the *whole reader*. You are apt to find that some students, especially those who are reading far below the benchmark reading levels, will be in need of foundational reading work like monitoring for sense, fluency, synthesizing, and word solving. Meanwhile, students who move up a level likely will need to spend some time applying those foundational skills to this new, more challenging work. The learning progressions have strands you can reference to help students shore up these foundational skills and will help you plan for the teaching you'll do now and across the year.

Of course, you'll continue to track students' progress up the gradient of text difficulty during each unit. In addition to the running record assessments you give at intervals throughout the year, you might assess students periodically using their independent reading books, checking for indications that they are ready to move up. Continue to keep an eye out for approximately how many levels students have progressed through while in your care. If you have any students who have not made much movement, find a time to check in with them or to talk to a literacy coach or colleague and make plans for how to help those students reach toward a new level of complexity. Make use of book introductions, transition baggies (baggies that include books at the student's level, as well as books a level or two higher), and partners or club members who are reading at the new level and can offer support to these readers in tackling more difficult texts.

Once you've assessed your students' work and have a sense of your big goals for the unit (and for individual readers), we strongly recommend you make these expectations clear to students. Just as we suggest you do in the unit books, show your students the learning progression and ask them to rank their own work. Does it look like what a second-grade reader does? A third-grade reader? Fourth-grade? Involve them in revising their work to raise the level by studying exemplars of work at each level. You'll be surprised how many students are able to lift the level of their work right at the start, simply because they *know* what the expectation is. For those who still struggle, you'll know that they will need extra support and teaching.

At the end of each unit, we recommend giving a summative assessment. You might give part of the assessment that you gave at the start of the unit or you might choose to give another, less formal assessment. In either case, it will be important to track your students' progress for yourself and to celebrate their growth as readers as a community.

Learning through Reading
Countries around the World

RATIONALE/INTRODUCTION

The joy of inquiry is ageless. Educator and researcher Deanna Kuhn (2005) asserts that inquiry is an essential component in an education that aims to help children to learn to think deeply and well. In this unit, students see that they can read to learn and undertake inquiry through reading. At its heart, this unit is about helping students read with purposeful intention, grappling with unfamiliar content, deciding what information is most important to grasp and remember, comparing and contrasting information from different texts, and finally, organizing and synthesizing their learning to teach others.

Ideally, students will come to this unit with plenty of previous learning on reading nonfiction texts on which to draw. In the two third-grade nonfiction units *Reading to Learn: Grasping Main Ideas and Text Structures* and *Research Clubs: Elephants, Penguins, and Frogs, Oh My!* students read high-interest nonfiction, built nonfiction reading lives, and strengthened skills in fluency, stamina, and word solving. They also learned that nonfiction takes a special kind of reading and began to pay close attention to the underlying structures of texts in order to determine main ideas and key details. Students worked to synthesize their learning across pages and across books and to grow ideas. In this unit they will build on and extend their prior learning about reading informational texts as they engage in reading nonfiction on a topic (in this case, different countries) to learn all they can about that topic. In addition, if students are also currently engaged in the writing unit *Changing the World: Persuasive Speeches, Petitions, and Editorials*, they will also be building on many of the practices they are learning in that unit (how to categorize information, most importantly). This is a unit rife with cross-curricular connections that will deepen content knowledge and teach students how to read to learn.

A SUMMARY OF THE BENDS IN THE ROAD FOR THIS UNIT

Essential Questions:

- *How can I use all that I know about nonfiction reading and writing in order to launch a research inquiry about the factors that shape life in different countries?*

- *How can I think critically about the reasons that texts offer contrasting information on the same topic?*

- **Bend I: Learning about a Country Using a Variety of Texts and Lenses**

  How can I learn about a country using a variety of different kinds of texts and lenses to fuel my research? How can an understanding of social studies themes help me learn about a community?

- **Bend II: Researching a Different Country**

  How can I research a second country, doing this work with greater independence, and then apply what I learn to help me understand another community?

- **Bend III: Learning and Thinking across Countries: Exploring Similarities and Differences to Grow Ideas**

  How is life in one country similar to and different from life in another country I've studied, and what factors contribute to those similarities and differences?

- **Bend IV: Learning about Countries and Cultures through Literature (Folktales and Fairy Tales)**

  How does literature reflect the characteristics of a culture?

In Bend I (Learning about a Country Using a Variety of Texts and Lenses), students will spend a few days reading different kinds of texts using social studies themes as lenses to learn and grow ideas about a particular country and its culture. This will not be the first time your students have read nonfiction, nor will it be the first time they have worked collaboratively in clubs, so they are well equipped for the road ahead. They already know, for example, how to preview texts, how to listen to and talk with peers, how to identify nonfiction structures and take notes accordingly, and how to remember important information. Today, you will teach students to put that knowledge to use as they tackle collaborative research projects. They will not simply be readers, they will also be researchers.

Across this first part of the unit you will provide many opportunities for students to teach others about what they are learning, culminating with students celebrating their new knowledge, getting to know each other's research, and ultimately making connections and growing larger theories about life in the countries studied.

In Bend II (Researching a Different Country), you will invite students to start the process again, this time drawing on all they have learned. Students are reminded that the skills they learned earlier in the unit can be applied to all the research they do for the rest of their lives. The first two bends are designed to support transference. For now, students will transfer what they learned while studying one country to the study of another country.

By giving children a second opportunity to cycle through a research project, you give them a chance to work with greater independence. What they did with instruction and coaching earlier, they'll now do without you calling all of the shots. For now, you'll teach them to draw upon the anchor chart that captures the strategies they've learned, as well as the work they did during the first inquiry.

You'll still be nearby, coaching them to orient themselves to their text sets and to find a system for collecting and studying the details of their topic. However, you will give students the space to initiate most of this on their own and will step in only as needed. Plan to spend about a week in this bend.

In Bend III (Learning and Thinking across Countries: Exploring Similarities and Differences to Grow Ideas), you'll want to shine a spotlight on the skills of comparing and contrasting to teach third-graders to purposefully look at the new things they're learning in light of what they already know. You'll want to teach them how they can place two "like" features (e.g., two cities, two rivers, or two "ways people dress") side by side and channel them to consider what is the same, what is different, and how these similarities and differences might play out in people's lives. For instance, they may look at a river in China (the Yangtze) compared with a river in Brazil (the Amazon), comparing and contrasting features of these rivers and ways people rely on them. The work of comparing and contrasting will be a key feature of this bend, and we anticipate that it will bolster children's understanding of the world as being composed of far-reaching places that are different but also have much in common. Plan to spend a week in Bend III.

In Bend IV (Learning about Countries and Cultures through Literature [Folktales and Fairy Tales]), you will teach your students to read folktales with the goal of learning more about daily life in their respective countries. You'll also teach them to bring their knowledge to bear on their reading of folktales and fairy tales, for example, by studying setting through the lens of geography and what they know about urban and rural life in different countries. In addition, students will explore the values upheld in a particular culture by thinking about messages or lessons inherent in the texts. As your students read, interpret, and use folktales as a tool to learn about various countries or cultures, you will also teach them to read with nonfiction texts close at hand to deepen their understanding. It should take approximately one week to wrap up this bend and unit.

ASSESSMENT

You'll need to decide the skills you will particularly highlight and, therefore, the skills you will assess in this unit. Presumably, you'll continue to track students' progress through levels of text difficulty, so you will continue to assess students using running records and at times using students' independent reading books, focusing especially on those who are reading below grade level.

If you recently finished the unit *Research Clubs: Elephants, Penguins, and Frogs, Oh My!*, you can likely use the data from that unit's final assessment to plan your teaching in this unit. Pay particular attention to skills that are foundational to this unit such as compare and contrast and cross-text synthesis.

For the final bend, you may decide to embed some questions in a folktale, questions perhaps like those that students could be given on whatever high-stakes exam they take. You could, for example, ask them, "Which of the following summaries best matches this folktale?" You could also model your questions after ones from the performance assessment that accompanies one of our narrative units, such as *Character Studies*.

Another option might be to ask compare-and-contrast questions: "How are these two versions of (titles of folktales) different from each other?" Or take a line regarding the cause and have them talk about which line would represent an effect. Such an assessment would give your students practice tackling the sorts of questions they will encounter on high-stakes tests. Just keep in mind the assessment would not be exactly aligned to the unit.

GETTING READY

Choose your read-aloud(s).

It's crucial that you put together a set of read-aloud texts so you can demonstrate the work your students will be doing. We recommend you choose a few texts to read about China for the first bend and a few texts to read on a second country for the second bend. For the first bend, we suggest Bobbie Kalman's series on China, *The Land*, *The People*, and *The Culture* (with *The People* being a particular favorite). *China: The People* is a guided reading level T. In order to model the kind of work the students are doing, we suggest that you don't read the text cover to cover. Instead you can show students how you purposefully choose sections, depending on the information you need.

We also recommend *The Great Wall of China* by Fisher (600L/Guided Reading Level Q) and parts of *You Wouldn't Want to Build the Great Wall of China* by Morely (980L/Guided Reading W). Keep in mind that your read-aloud texts can be at a level slightly higher than the level of most of your students, but if many of your students are reading below a level N or so, you will likely want to stick with texts mostly at levels P/Q.

During the second bend of the unit, when students will be moving to studying different countries in clubs, we recommend you choose another country to read about. In this curricular plan, we use Greece as an example, but you might choose a different country, depending on your interests or your resources. We recommend reading aloud from *True Books: Greece*, which addresses life in ancient Greece, but the main focus is on life in Greece today.

For the final bend, we suggest you begin by reading stories from the countries you have predominantly studied to demonstrate the work students will do for the bulk of the bend. Then, you might incorporate tales from the United States, China, Brazil, Africa, Greece, India, and other countries in your read-aloud time in order to make use of the wealth of literature available and to bring a truly global perspective to this unit.

Gather resources and organize research teams.

Before the start of the unit, gather leveled text sets on half a dozen different countries and place them in bins. Assign or recruit students into small clubs that will each study a particular country, making sure that readers will be able to read the texts you've collected on their country. You may wish to assign children who need extra support to the China group, so that they get the added model of your demonstrations. You may want to save a few nonfiction texts so that you can introduce them in Bend III for the compare-and-contrast work.

You have several options for helping students form inquiry groups or research clubs. One option is to assign or recruit students to select a premade basket of books about a particular country. This group of books can be sparse at first, and you can recruit kids to add texts to it (maps, photographs, digital texts, texts selected from classroom, school, or public libraries, etc.). After students have chosen a basket for the first bend, have students choose how they want to research.

One option for supporting research is to have students look through the lens of a social studies theme such as education, geography, government, or religion so that as they read different texts from the basket, they are using a particular lens to learn and grow ideas about different aspects of a particular country. Students may be familiar with researching through different lenses (subtopics/categories) if you have previously undertaken the unit *Research Clubs: Elephants, Penguins, and Frogs, Oh My!*

For the final bend, we suggest you organize your fairy tales and folktales according to country or region of origin. Students will need folktales from the countries they studied, as well as access to the nonfiction texts studied in the first two bends. These texts complement the folktales they are reading in this bend, and they can be read side by side, moving between one text and another.

BEND I: LEARNING ABOUT A COUNTRY USING A VARIETY OF TEXTS AND LENSES

Remind students of what they already know about how to plan and begin a research project, as well as effective note-taking strategies.

It's important to remind readers of how to rev themselves up for a research project. If you have previously taught the unit *Research Clubs: Elephants, Penguins, and Frogs, Oh My!*, you can pull out familiar charts from that unit and remind students that they can transfer the skill and process work they learned while studying animals to their study of countries.

Researchers start learning about a topic by doing the following three things:

1. They look over their resources, putting them in order by difficulty.
2. They first read an easy overview book about their topic.
3. They skim the tables of contents and illustrations, to glean the main subtopics, and then read across books in one subtopic after another.

> "Today I want to remind you that readers often read easier texts before moving to harder books about their countries in order to get a quick overview of their country, learn some of the important vocabulary, and understand some of the information that might be found in harder books."

From the start you'll likely need to help students settle into serious reading during independent reading time. If they need some help, get them going through a combination of voiceovers and table compliments. "Rex has a really smart system for planning his reading!" you might voice over to the class or say to a table. "He's marked different pages in different books that he wants to read and numbered the order in which he will read them."

Over the next few days, as students research and take notes, you'll likely see predictable ways that you'll need to support them. For example, you may see students copying large sections of text, seemingly having various note-taking strategies they learned in earlier units. If this is the case for your students, you may want to teach a lesson in which you remind students of all they know about note-taking. In particular, you might focus on how nonfiction text structures should guide note-taking.

> "Today I want to remind you that researchers have a repertoire of note-taking strategies to draw upon when researching. They often use text structures to help guide their note-taking."

You might highlight charts from past units on effective note-taking work. We include some examples next.

Texts that Are Sequentially Organized	Texts that Are Organized by Main Ideas and Supporting Details	Texts that Are Organized by Compare and Contrast	Text that Are Organized by Cause and Effect	Texts that Are Organized by Problem and Solution
First, then, later, next	One way/kind/sort/type . . . another way/kind/sort/type . . .	Similar, similarly	Used to, reasons, because of, also, when, then	The problem is, the question is, trouble
At the beginning, a bit later, before long	Also, in addition, furthermore	Different, differently, another difference, in contrast, on the other hand	So, this led to, if . . . then . . . , since	Help, a solution, one answer is, to solve this
When they are young . . . later . . .	For example, in specific, for instance	Both, although both	As a result, may be due to, consequently, therefore	So, when, then

Researchers Take Notes that Follow
the Structure of Their Texts

BOXES AND BULLETS

Main Idea or Subtopic

- Supporting detail
- Supporting detail
- Add more bullet points if your text includes them

SEQUENTIAL

Main Idea or Subtopic

1. First thing that happens
2. Second thing that happens
3. Add more steps if your text includes them

COMPARE AND CONTRAST

Similarities between two things
- First similarity
- Second similarity
- Add more similarities if your text includes them

Differences between two things
- First difference
- Second difference
- Add more differences if your text includes them

In addition to reminding students all they know about structure of their notes, you may also need to remind them to check the content of their notes. For example, you may need to remind them to check that they have included the names of key people, key places, and key events.

Guide students to choose a focus area or angle for their research.

After students have read and researched for a few days, you might channel them to chooses lenses through which to study their country and thus focus their research. One student might use the lens of education, while another studies employs the lens of geography. You can then channel students to meet with their research teams periodically to compare notes and think about how one aspect affects another. For example, in rural areas in some countries, children might not be able to attend school, while in urban areas schools are well funded.

A note about lenses: Students can take on one lens initially and might move through several texts, reading and researching with this lens. Then, if there is still time left in the week, they can take on an additional lens. All the while, group members can be teaching each other about their individual lenses, comparing and contrasting, accumulating, and synthesizing to contribute to the club's knowledge base.

If you have previously taught your students to section their notebooks into subtopics or work in booklets, you might remind them how to do this and provide stapled-together paper so they can make sections and add to them as needed. Encourage students to revise their notes. One way to do so is to practice grouping sections of notes that seem similar by physically cutting and taping these into their notebooks (or booklets). You might even provide students with index cards, inviting them to take notes on these, so that they can later sort and categorize them.

Teach students to move beyond merely gathering information about their topics to growing ideas.

During this bend, you might also teach students that in addition to listing information and facts in their notes, they would be wise to also spend some time growing ideas. To support this work, you might remind them of the prompts they have used to grow their thinking in other units (*This is important because . . . , For example . . . , This makes me think . . .*). You might model how do this, perhaps going back to a section of your notes and showing students how you might create a new page for thinking. It's also helpful to teach students to leave blank pages in their notebooks every few pages for extended writing and thinking.

You might also notice that some students are taking very few notes. We suggest first checking with these students individually to make sure that the texts they are reading are not too difficult. If this is not the case, we suggest gathering these students in a small group and teaching them that even minor details that may not seem significant at first can help them to grow larger ideas if they pause to think more deeply about them.

You might show how you start with a small detail such as: "Many rural Chinese villagers have packed up and left for the cities for better-paying jobs and more security" (page 20 of *China: The People*). You might model for students how at first this seems like it has nothing to do with what you are researching. But then you might model how you make some connections about how this might relate to what you have already learned. You might look back at your notes to see that you wrote about how Beijing and some other cities are overcrowded. Then you can point out that this new detail might help you understand why some of these cities are so overcrowded. This detail has given you the idea that one cause for the cities being so overcrowded is because people are leaving rural villages to head to the city for better jobs. Then you might push students to consider this same detail and think about how it might relate to what they've learned already.

As students continue to work, you can continue to coach them to make these kinds of key connections for countries they are researching with their clubs. The following prompts might prove helpful in supporting students with this kind of thinking:

Does that remind you of anything you have already learned?

What might be a result of ____?

What might that lead to?

What do you think caused ____?

Encourage them to constantly go back to research further to find the answers to these questions and to jot these questions in their notes.

Give students opportunities to teach others about their topic, thereby synthesizing their learning.

Also during this bend, be sure to provide students with plenty of opportunities to synthesize their learning by teaching the other members of their group what they are learning. You might help groups deepen their conversations by offering them some of the following conversation prompts:

- That fits with what I'm learning because . . .
- That's different from what I read because . . .
- What you just said is making me realize that . . .
- Now I'm starting to have a new idea . . .
- This is helping me to understand why . . .
- This connects to what we learned in social studies because . . .
- Now, I'm wondering . . .

You might also channel students to synthesize their learning by teaching the other members of their group what they are learning. This work can support students' abilities to summarize and can help them to determine importance. As you listen, you'll likely need to coach students into moving away from just reading parts of the text to each other. Include charts from previous units to help students to teach each other well.

Giving students a few minutes to plan their teaching session can help them to decide on the most important information to share with their group members. Students can then offer some key points and a big idea or two they are having about that information. Of course, you can encourage them to include a quote from one of their texts, as long as they also explain why that quote seems important.

At the end of these sessions, allow students some time to reflect and take notes on the new information they learned from their peers.

You will also likely need to help students acquire and use the specific vocabulary they encounter as they teach and take notes. You can help them to see that while the names of people, places, and events matter, other terms matter as well.

One way to know a term is important is if the author repeats it. You might show students that they can raise their writing and speaking to new heights by trying to use more of the words that the author has used often. So if an author has mentioned at least three times that the cities of China are *overcrowded*, students should try to use the word *overcrowded* in their own speaking and writing, taking care to explain what it means.

> **"Today I want to remind you that one way to know if a term is important is if an author repeats it. Researchers raise their writing and speaking to new heights by trying to use more of the words that the authors of research texts have used often."**

BEND II: RESEARCHING A DIFFERENT COUNTRY

Channel students to begin another round of research, this time with more agency and independence.

In this bend, you'll ask students to engage in a second round of research, but this time they will study a new country. In the first session of this bend, you might say to students, "In the first part of the unit, you studied one country and explored it through different lenses. In this second bend, you will have the chance to study another country through those same lenses."

To keep this more complex bend manageable, we suggest that you might use a heavy hand when organizing students into groups and assigning countries. You might allow students to choose their top three countries and aim to give everyone at least one of their top three choices. Doing this will allow students to have a sense of choice while still allowing you plenty of room to orchestrate effective groups and to assign each group a country for which you have reading material at appropriate levels.

Aim to kick off this bend with high energy and enthusiasm. Rally students toward the big work of this bend, which will be repeating a familiar research process while working with greater independence and agency. Your big work in this bend will be coaching students to surmount problems you noticed during the last bend and steering them to consider resources that you know will be helpful.

To support students' work at the start of the bend, you might remind them that when they embark on a new project, researchers make a work plan. If applicable, remind students that they did this when they embarked on a study of a second animal during the unit *Research Clubs: Elephants, Penguins, and Frogs, Oh My!*

Encourage students to think about all that they have learned about reading and research in the first bend of this unit and in earlier units to create their work plans. Be sure to model this for students by creating your own plan. You might channel students to discuss if yours is similar or different to what they were planning.

You might create a work plan that looks something like this:

- Look over the texts, decide what parts to read to get some basic background.
- Read the easier texts first.
- Take notes on what seems most important.
- Make categories of my notes.
- Teach my team what I'm learning so far.
- Start focusing—in this case deciding who I am, where I live, and what I do.

As students work, check in with readers to make sure they are applying previous learning. For example, if you worked with a group of students the previous time to help them to notice repeating vocabulary terms and use these terms in their notes and teaching sessions, you'll want to see them now actively working to acquire and use new vocabulary.

For those students who were only copying the text, you might check that they are reading for a bit of time, then setting the book down and giving themselves a moment to reflect before taking notes. During a share, you might ask students to talk about what resources and charts they think will be most helpful to them in this new part of the unit.

> **"Today I want to remind you that researchers think about tools and resources that were helpful during past projects and then plan to use these as they embark on new projects."**

Teach students strategies for organizing the information they are learning.

You'll also likely need to help students continue to figure out how to organize their learning. So, you might channel students to consider which lenses seem important to research now that they are studying a second country. To do this, you might display the tables of contents of a few books on Greece and guide students to do an inquiry on which lenses seem important to study regarding this country.

Students will likely begin to name the similar (if not the same) lenses that they used when they studied their first countries. They'll likely mention education, geography, history, arts, daily life, government, money, and so on, and you can point out that one thing that makes these lenses so powerful is their universality.

Encourage students to make choices about the lenses they will use to study their countries this time and to organize their notes accordingly. You might suggest that students stay with the same lenses they used during the previous study so as to support the compare-and-contrast work they do in the next bend. *Or,* you might decide to support students' decision-making processes by allowing them to choose new lenses. In either case, encourage them to share what they are learning using their respective lenses in their groups so as to broaden their exposure to a range of lenses.

BEND III: LEARNING AND THINKING ACROSS COUNTRIES: EXPLORING SIMILARITIES AND DIFFERENCES TO GROW IDEAS

Guide students to compare and contrast the countries they are studying.

The purpose of this bend of the unit is to teach students to compare and contrast across cultures. You'll want to shine a spotlight on the skills of comparing and contrasting to teach students to purposefully look at the new things they're learning in light of what they already know. "When you compare and contrast," you might tell them, "it is important not just to name similarities and differences but also to think, talk, and write about why and how these may be significant."

> **"Today I want to teach you that when researchers compare and contrast, they don't just name similarities and differences. They also think, talk, and write about why and how these might be significant."**

Support students with language prompts to help them note similarities and differences between countries studied. Students will also benefit from instruction related to language prompts that will support recognition of similarities and differences.

Some prompts to help steer students toward comparison follow:

- "I think these two _____ (cities, mountain ranges, buildings) might be similar because . . ."
- "These _____ are alike because . . ."
- "Both _____ and _____ are the same. This is important because . . ."

Of course, encourage children to draw upon the lenses they are using to guide their research as they compare and contrast. For example, if students are looking through the lens of statistics, the numbers that reveal China's population, city sizes, quantity of provinces, and languages all acquire new significance if placed next to the corresponding statistics for Greece. Similarly, the maps and images of the two countries will show much that is common, as well as much that is different.

Ask students to develop theories and draw conclusions about the countries they are comparing.

Encourage readers to use their compare-and-contrast observations to develop new theories and conclusions. Remind them that researchers compare and contrast in order to better understand whatever it is they are studying. You might demonstrate this by modeling that it isn't enough to say:

"The Amazon and the Yangtze are different because the Amazon is the second-longest river in the world and the Yangtze is the third longest. But both are similar because they're the longest rivers in their own continents."

Rather, researchers should make more of the similarities and differences that they're noting, for example, by adding a prompt to derive some sort of conclusion.

This suggests something about China (and Brazil), namely . . .

This would mean that . . .

This gives rise to the question . . .

So, to their observation that the Amazon and Yangtze are both the longest rivers in their continents, a researcher might add

"This suggests something about China and Brazil. Both countries probably have many cities on the banks of these rivers."

Or "Both countries probably use this river for transport and to provide water for crops."

Or "Both countries probably have their own kinds of boats."

By this point in the unit, your students' knowledge bases about their countries should have increased enough to support such theorizing. You might, therefore, ask children to revisit their notes from earlier in the unit and use their new understanding of life in their countries to write longer off these prompts, using some of those mentioned above.

Another way to bring the "real world" into your classroom and to encourage reflection with new information is to bring in artifacts that represent aspects of various countries' cultures. For example, you could bring in a Chinese menu and ask children to compare it with a Greek menu. You could have children compare the ingredients used in each type of cuisine and connect those ingredients with local climates, geography, and crops. Artifacts from one country will take on added significance when they are used to compare or contrast with aspects of another country. For example, children will have more to say about a traditional Chinese doll when it is placed next to a traditional Brazilian or American doll or figurine. (You might add that modern dolls such as Barbie® look quite the same in all three countries and that most are made in China!) All of this compare-and-contrast work will lead to new realizations and discoveries about the different countries students are learning about in their groups.

BEND IV: LEARNING ABOUT COUNTRIES AND CULTURES THROUGH LITERATURE (FOLKTALES AND FAIRY TALES)

In the beginning of the bend, you may choose to have your students jot a few notes during a read-aloud as a way to assess their skills and determine the path of this bend. Certainly, if you find that most of your students need significant help determining the lessons or messages of the stories you read aloud, you may choose to focus this bend largely on the skill of interpretation. If this is the case, you may return to the character or series reading units from the beginning of the year as a resource for teaching points. After practicing interpretation skills you could then guide students to use the texts as a means to study culture, as described in greater detail below. Of course, you may choose this path for a small group of students as well.

Launch the final bend with an inquiry into the similarities and differences between folktales, fairy tales, myths, legends, fables, and tall tales.

To launch this bend, you might guide students in an inquiry. While many, if not all, of your students are likely familiar with folktales and fairy tales, you may choose to begin the final bend with an examination of the similarities and differences between folktales, fairy tales, myths, legends, fables, and tall tales. With this goal in mind, you could select a story from each of the various subgenres, read it aloud to your class, and guide students to note the distinguishing features of the text. You might create a chart of these features with your students to serve as a resource throughout the unit. In addition, as you read these texts aloud, model your thinking for students so that they see and hear you thinking about the texts in terms of their defining characteristics, the lessons of the stories, and the ways that one can glean information about a culture from a piece of literature.

Title of Folktale	Defining Characteristics	Life Lessons	Cultural Elements

Of course, it's important to make sure that students continue to hone their nonfiction reading skills during this unit. Demonstrate for students how you move from literature to nonfiction texts as a way to confirm or revise ideas developed from reading literature. For example, when reading *The Five Chinese Brothers* by Claire Huchet Bishop, you may think aloud about the importance of fishing in the story. You might demonstrate how you refer to nonfiction texts to read more about the significance of fishing as an industry and way of life in Chinese culture.

Once you have set up students with foundational work in reading and discussing folktales through your read-aloud, ask students to meet once again in their groups to read stories. We recommend that you provide students with folktales from countries they have studied so that they can draw upon their background knowledge. If you do not have the books you need to do this, some groups may need to read folktales from countries that are less familiar. Providing these groups with video clips or nonfiction books about the country or culture might help them develop and draw upon background knowledge while reading.

Guide your students to read traditional literature through the lens of culture, as a way to learn about a country.

You might teach your students to read folktales with the lens of culture, asking, "How is this story structured?" It is important for children to realize that texts are not all structured the same way. Being able to talk about a text's structure is important. For example, students might notice that texts from one country may all be structured the same way, and they can use what they know about that culture to speculate why this may be so. Youngsters can also look at the cause-and-effect structures in folktales and become accustomed to talking about the portions of the text that convey the causes or the effects.

When you first ask students to read literature and think of it as a way to learn about a country, they may find it challenging. It is not easy to notice or name cultural aspects of the folktales they read. Instead they may focus on the narrative elements to which they are more accustomed, such as plot, character development, or message. Of course, it's important to encourage and compliment students when you see them reading and talking in these ways. But, you will also want to encourage them to extend their reading repertoires to attend to cultural indicators while reading.

You might once again teach students to draw upon lenses to help them to focus their reading. For example, some students might read, paying particular attention to the characters' clothing, wondering how the clothing might reflect their status, occupation, or geographic environment. Other students might pay particular attention to the language that is used, wondering if the names of characters or places or the syntax of the text is indicative of the culture. Students may need to use context clues to figure out the meaning of unknown words or phrases that are left in the native language. You may guide other students to read the text looking for objects or places that repeat, wondering how these items may be significant symbols within the culture. Another group of students could read with the lens of social class, looking for ways characters are depicted as wealthy or poor. The goal is to show students that these stories have a wide range of possibilities for reading to learn and can be reread with different lenses to learn about the culture represented.

You might create a chart such as the following to help guide your students' work of reading folktales with lenses.

Lenses to Use While Reading Folktales to Learn More about Culture

- Examine the characters' clothing. "What can I learn about their way of life by looking at their clothing?" "Do people still dress this way today?" "Are these illustrations accurate?"
- Study the language in the story. "What can I learn about this culture and its values through the use of native language that is incorporated into the story?" "Are there lines or sections that repeat?" "Are similes or metaphors used?"
- Explore power in the story. "How do the people in charge affect the lives of others in the story?"

- Study transportation in the story. *"How do people travel from one place to another?" "Does everyone in the story travel the same way?" "Does this represent the way the people traveled in the past or is this still true today?"*
- Consider the role of money or wealth in the story. *"How do wealth and power show themselves in the story with different groups of people?"*
- Determine possible messages the story teaches readers. *"What values does this story teach/uphold?" "How does this connect with the culture?" "Whose values are these—are they shared by everyone or by certain groups within the country?"*
- Study geography. *"How and where did the author embed information about that place into the story?" "How might the climate and landscapes of the country affect the folktale?"*
- Examine art and architecture. *"How do the illustrations contribute to the story?" "What aspects of art or architecture are present in the illustrations?"*

Encourage your students to take notes as they read one text and then another so that they can compare the texts about one culture or region. To model this, you may choose to read excerpts of folktales closely, annotating them to show your thinking and the sources of the conclusions you are drawing.

You'll set up students to look across the texts, noting similarities and differences. Then, as they move from one set of texts to another set of stories about another culture, they will be able, again, to compare and contrast. "In both cultures there is a wise older grandparent," they might say. "This makes me think that in several cultures folktales teach children to listen to adults."

> **"Today I want to teach you that researchers compare and contrast stories about cultures to learn more about these cultures."**

Ask students to compare and contrast multiple versions of the same tale, from different countries.

To encourage further compare-and-contrast work, you might set up students to read multiple versions of the same tale, set in different parts of the world. As always, encourage and expect students to transfer their learning from earlier parts of the unit to this final bend. That is, students will continue to read the folktales in order to study the culture, moving between fiction and nonfiction, thinking critically, and talking about their findings in their groups.

Through read-aloud, it will be helpful to model for students the way you consider the similarities and differences across texts and the implications of each. For example, in some of the Cinderella stories, the role of the Godmother in the traditional version may be changed to an animal, and students may begin to wonder why this is different in the various tales. Perhaps godmothers are not common in the culture, or perhaps animals hold particular significance within the culture.

While you will get your students started through reading a few versions of the same tale aloud and inviting observation and discussion of similarities and differences, you will want to leave the bulk of this work for your students to discover. You may need to teach them how to look at a single aspect of the story across the versions. For example, when reading across Cinderella tales, you could encourage your students to consider the characters' traits, just as they do in reading workshop, in order to consider what the most valued traits say about different cultures. Is Cinderella hard-working, kind, and resourceful? Are the stepsisters (if they are stepsisters) cruel, selfish, and vengeful? What can students learn about the values of the cultures from which the tales originate based on these traits? It's important to note, here, that while these texts might represent the values of the cultures or countries at the time they were written, these values might not be the same in those cultures or countries today.

As students read and discuss these various tales, be sure that they are carrying forward the different lenses they've learned to read with, such as geography, clothing, family configurations, class, fairness, and power. Encourage them to take notes as a means to compare and contrast and grow ideas about the different cultures represented. Again, it will be important for students to be reminded of the dangers of stereotypes and the need to read the folktales critically.

CELEBRATION

As the unit comes to an end, we recommend you conclude with a celebration that is worthy of the hard work your students have done across the unit. We recommend you honor all of the learning students have done by channeling them to teach others what they know. This teaching not only will highlight all of students' new knowledge but will also cement and refine the learning they've done over the course of the unit. So, give some time to prepare for the final celebration, and coach them as they get ready to teach. For the final celebration, you might hold a fair where each student prepares some visuals and creates a booth, ready to talk with passersby (teachers, parents, other classes) about the country they have studied—about the land, the people, and the cultures.

After the visitors have left, you might gather your students in the meeting area and offer them a moment to share some of the main lessons they will take away from this unit, not just about engaging in research but also about what it means to be a truly global citizen.

BEND I: LEARNING ABOUT A COUNTRY USING A VARIETY OF TEXTS AND LENSES

- "Today I want to teach you that researchers transfer what they know from previous research projects to their work on a new study."

- "Today I want to remind you that readers often read easier texts before moving to harder books about their countries in order to get a quick overview of their country, learn some of the important vocabulary, and understand some of the information that might be found in harder books."

- "Today I want to remind you that researchers have a repertoire of note-taking strategies to draw upon when researching. They often use text structures to help guide their note-taking."

- "Today I want to teach you that one way researchers focus their research is to choose a lens through which to study a topic."

- "Today I want to teach you that researchers don't just spend time gathering facts. They also take the time to reflect upon and grow ideas about the information they are learning."

- "Today I want to remind you that one way researchers synthesize their learning is by teaching others."

- "Today I want to remind you that one way to know a term is important is if an author repeats it. Researchers raise their writing and speaking to new heights by trying to use more of the words that the authors of research texts have used."

BEND II: RESEARCHING A DIFFERENT COUNTRY

- "Today I want to remind you that researchers think about tools and resources that were helpful during past projects and then plan to use these as they embark on new projects."

- "Researchers make choices about how their research will be organized, and they plan their notes accordingly."

- "Researchers share what they are learning in teams, taking notes on information they learn from their group mates just as they would take notes on information they learn from books."

BEND III: LEARNING AND THINKING ACROSS COUNTRIES: EXPLORING SIMILARITIES AND DIFFERENCES TO GROW IDEAS

- "Today I want to teach you that when researchers compare and contrast, they don't just name similarities and differences. They also think, talk, and write about why and how these might be significant."

Use this list as a menu of possibilities, selecting only the teaching points that meet the needs of your students. Use your assessment data (conferring and small-group notes, observations, responses to read-alouds, and other information) to decide on a plan that is tailored to the needs of your class. These teaching points may be used as whole-class minilessons, as mid-workshop teaching, or for conferences and small-group work. You need not use every teaching point. See the unit overview for guidelines on how much time to spend in each bend.

- "Today I want to teach you that researchers use compare-and-contrast observations to develop new theories and conclusions."
- "Today I want to remind you that researchers often revisit their notes after they acquire new knowledge, using their new knowledge to draw conclusions and develop theories about the information."

BEND IV: LEARNING ABOUT COUNTRIES AND CULTURES THROUGH LITERATURE (FOLKTALES AND FAIRY TALES)

- "Today I want to teach you that researchers draw on nonfiction to help them to think more deeply about fiction related to their topics."
- "Today I want to teach you that in addition to studying narrative elements of stories, researchers also read these with the lens of learning more about a culture."
- "Today I want to teach you that researchers compare and contrast stories about cultures to learn more about these cultures."
- "Today I want to teach you that researchers can sometimes learn about the values of a culture by studying the traits of characters in that culture's stories."
- "To celebrate their learning, researchers often teach others all they have learned during a study."

Nonfiction Book Clubs
Author Studies

RATIONALE/INTRODUCTION

By now, your students probably think of themselves as having certain identities as fiction readers. When you ask them what kind of reader they are, they might say they are fantasy readers or mystery readers, or they might say they love Walter Dean Myers's books or books about survival. They know where to find their favorite authors and genres, and they are somewhat expert in them. In this unit of study, you'll help your students develop the same sense of expertise about nonfiction so that they'll be able to answer that question with a "I'm more of a Seymour Simon reader" or "I like Gail Gibbons–type books." Besides developing an identity as a nonfiction reader (necessary if they are ever to choose nonfiction to read outside of school), students will also deepen their skills at comparing and contrasting, analyzing authors' patterns and choices in style and structure, and deepening their familiarity with the literary techniques that are used in high-quality nonfiction.

This unit builds on the work of earlier nonfiction units, in which readers focused on reading to learn and becoming more alert to nonfiction text structures—such as cause and effect, problem and solution, and compare and contrast. Here, you'll teach students to apply their knowledge to texts by particular nonfiction authors while working in clubs. You'll also be able to focus on student engagement and independence as book club members make decisions about which texts they most want to study and in what ways.

A SUMMARY OF THE BENDS IN THE ROAD FOR THIS UNIT

Essential Question: How can I read nonfiction like a fan, getting to know a nonfiction author well enough that I recognize his or her distinctive moves?

- **Bend I: Investigating Nonfiction Identities and Setting Out to Make Those More Powerful**

  How can I author a life as an avid reader of nonfiction, developing tastes and habits?

- **Bend II: Investigating Beloved Authors and Deepening Understanding of Nonfiction Techniques**

  How can I investigate authors I love and deepen my understanding of nonfiction craft moves?

- **Bend III: Expanding Nonfiction Experiences**

  How can I broaden my tastes as a nonfiction reader and try to outgrow myself?

In Bend I (Investigating Nonfiction Identities and Setting Out to Make Those More Powerful), you'll channel readers to gather favorite nonfiction reads and to organize themselves to ratchet up their nonfiction reading by focusing on series and authors they particularly enjoy. They will reflect on their nonfiction reading identities in order to set goals that will shape their work in this unit and empower them to develop habits that will fuel their reading lives in the future. This first bend is short (three to four days) and provides you with multiple opportunities to support transference as you remind students of all they have learned as nonfiction readers this year. Perhaps, most importantly, you will want to teach students to read with new alertness to the parts they really enjoyed, to the parts that make them go, "I'm a fan! Where can I find other books by (insert author's name)?"

In Bend II (Investigating Beloved Authors and Deepening Understanding of Nonfiction Techniques), you'll spend two to three weeks deepening students' understanding of nonfiction techniques. You will set them up to investigate what it is about these particular nonfiction books that they've chosen that makes them so compelling. A major portion of your work will be to teach readers ways to notice and the language to describe techniques they see these favorite nonfiction authors draw on to both entertain and inform their readers. Readers will zoom in on a favorite author or two and investigate the style of those authors, comparing and contrasting, noticing patterns, and analyzing how authors use certain techniques to create particularly compelling nonfiction.

In Bend III (Expanding Nonfiction Experiences), you'll spend a week helping your readers take their reading work up a notch by inspiring them to expand their nonfiction tastes and experiences, leading them to read authors who publish in a variety of styles and media. You will encourage readers to step outside their comfort zone and try out authors or series that they might not have been so quickly drawn to at first. This bend invites readers to spend a few days investigating other kinds of nonfiction that make up a reading identity, including websites, videos, and magazines. To celebrate the work of this unit, students will invent ways to share the great nonfiction they are finding.

ASSESSMENT

As in previous units, you might study data from a nonfiction reading assessment you've given recently, or you might create an assessment tailored to this unit. For example, to get a sense of what students know about author's craft, you might choose to show students two sections of a book by an author such as Bobbie Kalman and ask them some questions about the similarities and differences between the two sections.

- For what purposes has Bobbie Kalman developed the different sections? How are the purposes similar or different?
- What structures has Bobbie Kalman chosen to use in each of the sections? How are they similar or different?
- How do the structures help to show the author's purposes?
- If you were going to say one thing about Bobbie Kalman as an author, what would it be?

You might pay particular attention to the author's craft strand of the Informational Reading Learning Progression to assess students' work. To get a sense of students' growth, you might then repeat this assessment at the end of this unit, perhaps using a different author.

GETTING READY

Gather nonfiction texts for students to read throughout the unit.

To prepare for this unit, gather or be prepared for students to gather nonfiction by authors and series publishers (such as DK Readers). Chances are there are a lot of books from earlier nonfiction units by Gail Gibbons, Seymour Simon, Jean Fritz, Bobbie Kalman, and Melissa Stewart in your room. You may also include the series/sets of DK Readers and National Geographic Kids titles (as these exist at multiple levels and tend to be very similar to each other). If you have multiple copies of texts, you might create more than one club that is studying the same author, or you might also put more than one copy into each club, so that clubs can read the same text at the same time, although this is not essential. Seymour Simon, Gail Gibbons, and National Geographic Kids also have many titles on the same topic.

If you are ordering books, choose parallel topics so your students can compare and contrast more easily (*Hurricanes!* by Gail Gibbons, *Hurricanes* by Seymour Simon). We've chosen *Tornadoes* by Seymour Simon (Lexile 1020), *Planet Earth* by Gail Gibbons (Lexile 800), and *Tornadoes!* by Gail Gibbons (Lexile 970) as anchor texts for this unit, so you will probably want to access those books, perhaps getting multiple copies of them so that small huddles of students will be able to cluster around one copy or another during minilessons.

The most important books, however, will be the single or double copies of books that students will read throughout the unit. Ensure there are enough books to support a high volume of reading. You can find suggested book lists on the Reading and Writing Project website.

A word of advice: Especially if you do not have enough just-right texts for students to maintain their volume of reading during this unit, we strongly suggest that you reserve time every day (at least fifteen to twenty minutes in school and more time at home) for students to continue reading literature at their independent reading levels. And in any case, be sure readers continue to maintain their reading logs so that you can monitor the total volume of reading they do during this unit. The single most important way to accelerate students' progress up the ladder of text complexity is to be sure they are reading a high volume of texts they can read with high levels of comprehension and engagement.

Establish clubs during the first week of the unit.

Generally, in a unit of study that features clubs, we suggest that you organize the clubs at the very start of the unit so that children have maximum time in the clubs. In this unit we suggest you proceed a bit differently.

Before you even launch the unit, we hope you can start recruiting some of your readers to help you sort, organize, and revisit favorite nonfiction authors and series. These activities will then continue throughout the first week of the unit, as children sort out and reimagine their nonfiction reading identities. They'll do this by diving into baskets of books that have already been sorted by author and series. By the end of the first week, children will need to have read enough of the books in their classroom that they are able to sort themselves into clubs that form around authors or series.

To form the clubs, as students voice their interests in the various authors, pay attention to which students will work well together, probably keeping groups small, even if this means that multiple groups are studying the same author. You may also channel some groups toward authors who have more texts at lower levels (National Geographic, Gail Gibbons) and some toward authors who have more texts at higher levels (DK Readers, Seymour Simon, Jean Fritz).

As you approach the specific series/author studies in the second bend, you'll be talking up the upcoming work, inviting students to share their passions, to bring in favorite books, and ultimately to form reading groups based on their preferences, even if you have been doing some behind-the-scenes engineering of these groups.

Choose your read-alouds.

As you are gathering materials for students to read, you'll also need to choose your read-aloud books. For this unit we've chosen: *Tornadoes* by Seymour Simon (Lexile 1020), *Planet Earth* by Gail Gibbons (Lexile 800), and *Tornadoes!* by Gail Gibbons (Lexile 970).

BEND I: INVESTIGATING NONFICTION IDENTITIES AND SETTING OUT TO MAKE THOSE MORE POWERFUL

Launch the unit by encouraging readers to reflect on their nonfiction reading lives.

To launch this unit, you will want to rally readers to reflect on how their nonfiction life is going. You might say something like, "Today I want to teach you that readers often pose predictable questions to push themselves." This provides you with a nice opportunity to support transference, as this is often what we ask students to do when exploring their fiction identities.

> **"Today I want to teach you that readers often pose predictable questions to reflect, set goals, and push themselves."**

If you have such a chart for fiction, you might bring it out and show students how the questions can be shaped to help them reflect on their nonfiction reading lives. You might even show students how you use sticky notes to cover fiction and change it to nonfiction.

- What kind of nonfiction do I tend to read?
- When has nonfiction reading gone particularly well for me?
- How much nonfiction reading am I getting done?
- What could I do to read more or be smarter about my reading?

After students have reflected on their nonfiction reading lives through thinking, talking, and perhaps writing in response to a few of the predictable questions, you can move them toward using their reflections to set goals for themselves. For example, students might set a goal to read more, to make more purposeful and deliberate choices about the texts they read, or to take the initiative to share their nonfiction interests with others.

Set up students to begin creating text sets of nonfiction books they love.

In your next lesson, you might get students going by saying, "Today I want to teach you that readers often think about what they really like about certain books, so that they can find other books like those, and then do more and more reading and become more and more powerful as readers! One way readers begin this work is to sort books into the kind of books they love."

> "Today I want to teach you that readers often think about what they really like about certain books, so they can find other books like those, and then do more and more reading, and become more and more powerful as readers! One way readers begin this work is to sort books into the kinds of books they love."

One way you might organize this exploratory work is to have baskets on tables filled with nonfiction books and ask students to rotate to different baskets, building a collection as they move from one table and basket to the next. Another option could be that students each have a basket at their table and rotate around the table, moving from one basket to the next. You might also build this work into other parts of the day prior to the launch of the unit, where readers either create lists in their reader's notebooks of nonfiction texts they love or assemble book baggies so they hit the ground reading from the very start. You will need to decide how to best organize this work to allow for choice and talk and to provide students with the time to assemble a collection of nonfiction texts they love.

As students sort books, teach them to recognize that when doing this, the purpose is really to think about their reading lives by organizing books in different ways. Encourage students to move from one book to another in their collection and to bring in old and new favorites alike, from home and from the library, that reflect their interests.

Of course, kids shouldn't just be reflecting and sorting books for too long—a day or two at most. They need to be reading to keep volume high. That is, you don't need to wait for students to have perfect piles of authors lined up to start reading. Students will be adding to their collections across the unit. You also will not want students to approach nonfiction as if it is brand-new work. Rather you will want them to bring forward all that they have already learned about reading informational texts to the work of this unit.

Set up students to solidify their learning by teaching their group members all about what they are learning in their nonfiction books.

As your readers read with increased attention to stamina and pace, thinking about which books, authors, and series are making them powerful nonfiction readers, build excitement and encourage them to solidify their learning by setting them up to teach each other all they are learning. Students learned tips for teaching in earlier nonfiction units (an explaining voice, main ideas and supporting details, gestures and pointing to illustrations). It will be helpful to reinstate charts from earlier units or to or create new ones that support their teaching.

You might also coach students to point out what they appreciate about a particular author as they turn and teach.

> **"Today I want to teach you that when nonfiction readers set out to study their nonfiction reading lives, they actively try to improve it while studying it. One way to do this is to get a lot of reading done. Another way to do this is to really synthesize information and teach others."**

By the end of this bend, your readers should have organized their books into some baskets of authors or series they realize they really enjoyed, shared with others by teaching some of the content to partners, and zoomed in on books that helped them get a lot of reading done. They should have an increased awareness of their identities as nonfiction readers, and they should be fired up to make those identities more powerful.

BEND II: INVESTIGATING BELOVED AUTHORS AND DEEPENING UNDERSTANDING OF NONFICTION TECHNIQUES

In Bend II of the unit, you'll deepen students' understanding of nonfiction techniques. Set up your students to investigate what it is about these particular nonfiction books or authors that they've chosen that makes them so compelling.

As they begin, you might phrase your teaching point like this, "Today I want to teach you that like anything else, reading has its own words, its expert vocabulary, so that when you describe a book, you can use this vocabulary to describe the techniques authors use." Suggest that readers will be noticing and discussing many techniques, and as they do so, some expert words will help make their conversations more specific.

To begin, you might remind students of the vocabulary they know for the *structural choices* that authors make to organize information in memorable ways—such as "problem-solution," "compare-contrast," and "cause and effect"—and alert them that these terms can be combined. In your read-aloud, you might read with the lens of these text structures at first, so that students employ the technical vocabulary they have already learned to describe parts of this book that are especially clear and engaging or that explain tricky content well.

Offer nonfiction clubs tips for creating action plans.

Make sure clubs make some plans for how they are going to read. This work should seem familiar as students will have done this in several other units. The following are questions that readers can consider when developing plans for their reading work and considering how to share learning and thinking with those in their club:

- Will they divide up different titles by an author or in a series and read distinct books, then come back to compare what they've noticed?
- Do they have some shared copies they will read in sync?
- Will they bring books home?
- How will they organize their jotted notes to be ready to share?

You may decide to explicitly teach some ways that nonfiction clubs read and talk, or you may choose to observe children as they get started and then tailor your instruction as they show you how successful—and problematic—their choices are.

In any case, make sure that clubs get some plans going and that readers set out to describe to each other what it is that they love about these particular books.

Lead students in an inquiry into techniques that nonfiction authors use to make information interesting and understandable.

The next day, you might guide students in an inquiry and invite them to name some of the other nonfiction techniques that they already know and for which they can use expert vocabulary. They'll most likely know a handful from your information writing units and from their earlier experiences with nonfiction.

With their nonfiction books in hand, you might chart some of these nonfiction techniques. Then you might go back to your read-aloud text and teach students that readers not only use expert vocabulary to describe nonfiction writers' techniques, they also think about *when and how* authors use these techniques—how they make new information really interesting and understandable. After modeling a couple of techniques, send clubs off to investigate their own books. If you use *Tornadoes* or a book like this as your demonstration text, chances are that your chart might end up looking something like this.

Nonfiction Technique/Author's Craft	Possible Purposes of the Technique
Definitions	Teach us expert words
Exciting pictures	Get us interested/explain things
Diagrams	Let us see inside things or see parts or show cause and effect or sequences
True stories	Introduce important people, tell about exciting events
Subheadings	Let us know when something new is introduced

Of course, the important work is not how students notice techniques but how they begin to analyze the books they are reading for author's craft. Part of becoming more expert in anything is being able to talk the talk—to describe and explain and express ideas with language that is detailed and precise. For some students, you might use the words that they would use to talk about baseball, or ballet, or music, as examples of how experts describe things with technical vocabulary.

Channel students to use nonfiction techniques learned from favorite authors to lift the level of their own work.

After exploring different techniques nonfiction authors use, you might teach students that they can use these practices to lift the level of their thinking, writing, and talking.

> **"Today I want to teach you that it's not just nonfiction authors who explain information using effective techniques. Readers use these same techniques when they teach each other about what they've learned."**

The following are just a few different examples of what this could look like when students use these techniques to lift the level of their conversations in clubs. You might see children organizing what they say on their fingers, like subheadings, or jotting a diagram to explain something tricky, or retelling an exciting story to introduce their topic. And they might not only use these techniques when they talk, they might use them when they write, too.

Demonstrate how you look across texts for patterns that highlight a particular author's style.

By now you'll likely be ready to read another book aloud, if you haven't started one already. You might switch to the Gail Gibbons book, *Tornadoes!*, and demonstrate how you take note of the techniques she uses to teach about tornadoes.

Also during read-aloud time, you might teach about style and how writers often have a certain style or signature that helps readers identify the writer behind the words. Seymour Simon tends, for instance, toward the sweeping and the dramatic, with large-scale photographs and big historical and political issues. He uses a lot of staggering comparisons to teach. Jean Fritz tends toward the humorous, making historical events seem funny. She includes detailed anecdotes to make her subjects come alive. You might ask students to bring their own books to the read-aloud, then set them up to talk in clubs to describe their authors' styles.

Teach readers that fans of an author can compare books side by side, looking for patterns.

Over the next few days, continue to teach children strategies for reading closely and figuring out what it is they think is wonderful about the authors they admire. You might teach them that readers often lay books by an author or from a series alongside each other and study patterns to see if they are particularly drawn to certain kinds of writing.

You might create a chart to compare some of the techniques the nonfiction author used in the second text that you read aloud to students with the techniques used by the author of the first text. Your chart might look like this.

Gail Gibbons's *Tornadoes!* teaches with	Seymour Simon's *Tornadoes* teaches with
Drawings and diagrams	Big photos
Maps, charts	Close-up photos
Headings, subheadings, or table of contents	No headings or subheadings or table of contents
Captions, sidebars	Lots of pages of text
Definitions on every page	Glossary

Set up readers to compare and contrast texts in order to deepen their observations about techniques authors use.

Next, you might teach that readers often compare and contrast books by different authors. Looking at two books that are quite different can help them to see more specifically how authors make different moves. You might draw upon the chart comparing your two read-aloud texts or other books on the same topic by different authors.

When coaching your clubs as they work, you might remind them to point to favorite parts of the text, to quote specific parts, to use that expert vocabulary. As they compare how different authors addressed the same topic, assess if they are adding in a little bit of *how* the author taught the subject or *what the author did* to make the information clear or memorable. You might explore other ways to lift the level of engagement around this work by setting up kids in clubs to debate which is the better book on a topic (Simon's or Gibbons's, for example) and why. As students debate, watch for how they use text evidence to support their ideas and defend their favorite authors.

Keep an eye on engagement during this time that students are engaged in close reading. If you start to feel like their work is getting mechanical, set them to reading a lot and stir up their excitement for the content. Ask them to act out important parts, invite them to carry their favorite books into writing workshop, or set them up to mentor themselves by studying their favorite authors.

At the end of this bend, you might invite your readers to nominate nonfiction authors for awards, or they might give book talks or do podcasts that can be shared with family members in which they talk about what's hot in nonfiction.

BEND III: EXPANDING NONFICTION EXPERIENCES

Rally children to the work of the bend by encouraging them to analyze the work they have done so far to set new reading goals.

In this third bend of the unit, you'll remind students that they began by thinking about their nonfiction identities. Then they studied books and authors they loved and analyzed the techniques these authors use that make their writing so wonderful.

To rally students toward the work of this bend, you might say something like, "Today I want to teach you that as readers come to know more about the books they are drawn to, they also know more about themselves as readers, which helps them outgrow themselves and helps them set new goals."

As students set themselves up to create new goals, you might invite them to study their logs and sift through their reading baskets, looking for patterns in their reading habits and interests, asking them to talk about where they are *now* as nonfiction readers and how they might get *even* stronger. Chances are they've now read a lot, and they might be ready to read different authors or more kinds of nonfiction and even more complex nonfiction texts.

Next, you might teach children ways to grow that they may not have considered. You might say, "Today I want to teach you that one way readers grow and expand their reading is by swapping favorite books or by introducing books to each other." As a demonstration or even as a class, you might read some of the blurbs on the backs of books as examples of book introductions, or you might listen to some book talks together, analyzing what makes them compelling. Ideally, all of this book sharing will inspire readers to step outside of their comfort zones to read authors or series to which they weren't initially drawn.

Investigate other kinds of nonfiction that make up a reading identity.

Now that students have a better sense of themselves as nonfiction readers, you might spend a few days investigating other kinds of texts that they might include in their nonfiction diets, including websites, videos, and magazines. Some students might read *Scope* or *Junior Scholastic*, and others might revisit nonfiction magazines such as *Cobblestone*, *Appleseeds*, *Ask*, or *Click*. Channel them to apply the analytical skills they learned during this unit to describe what makes these journals great. Remind them to use their expert vocabulary, and encourage them to talk to each other about the content as well. Clubs might also investigate BBC science videos or clips found at Historychannel.com or the National Geographic website. Your main goals are to stir up your children's interest in consuming nonfiction regularly for pleasure and to build up social energy around that endeavor.

Set up students to solidify their learning by flash-drafting mini-essays as this bend draws to a close.

As this bend draws to a close, you might support students in flash-drafting mini-essays to grow an idea about a topic or text. Encourage them to revisit all of the writing they did previously about their reading, boxing out parts with ideas that they could possibly grow into thesis statements. Encourage them to try on several possible thesis statements before settling on one that feels right. Then, get students going on their writing, fast and furious. Don't worry too much about perfection. What is most important is that they are able to come up with solid ideas that they can support with evidence from their texts.

The following prompts might prove helpful in supporting students with grounding their writing about reading in text-based evidence, analyzing the evidence, and providing further explanation.

To Reference the Text Students Might Say/Write:

For example, the text says, ". . .

For example, according to the text ". . .

For example, in the beginning, we hear that ". . .

(So and so) writes, ". . .

(So and so) describes this, saying, ". . .

The following prompts can help students to connect their evidence with their thesis statements or the ideas they are growing:

This shows that . . .

This illustrates that . . .

This demonstrates that . . .

Readers realize that . . .

This changes everything. Whereas before . . . now . . .

Readers begin to wonder/question/worry/understand . . .

The important thing to notice about this is that . . .

While (such and such) could have (been said/happened), instead this (was said/happened). It is important to notice that . . . (didn't) but instead . . .

CELEBRATION

As the unit heads to its culmination, to celebrate their nonfiction reading journey, children might invent ways to share the great nonfiction they are finding—perhaps creating bookmarks for great sites, recommending videos, or making a handout for parents or for local libraries on what nonfiction is great for kids.

Children who read outside of school do better, and this is true for nonfiction just as much as fiction. It's not just that their reading levels will be higher and their reading rates stronger (though that is true). If students read nonfiction, they'll know more about the world. They'll bring more information and experience to their other reading, to their writing, to all of school, and, really, to all of their relationships and decisions as a human and as a citizen. What could be more important?

POSSIBLE TEACHING POINTS

BEND I: INVESTIGATING NONFICTION IDENTITIES AND SETTING OUT TO MAKE THOSE MORE POWERFUL

- "Today I want to teach you that readers often pose predictable questions to push themselves as readers."

- "Today I want to teach you that readers often think about what they really like about certain books, so that they can find other books like those and then do more and more reading and become more and more powerful as readers. One way readers begin this work is to sort texts into the kind of books they love."

- "Today I want to teach you that readers work a little bit at ways to ratchet up their reading life, and meanwhile, they read a lot, hoping to read more purposefully because of new thinking work but knowing they can carry along with them all the strategies they already know as well."

- "Today I want to teach you that when nonfiction readers set out to study their nonfiction reading lives, they actively try to improve them while studying them. One way to do this is to get a lot of reading done. Another way to do this is to really synthesize information and teach others."

BEND II: INVESTIGATING BELOVED AUTHORS AND DEEPENING UNDERSTANDING OF NONFICTION TECHNIQUES

- "Today I want to teach you that like anything else, reading has its own words, its expert vocabulary, so that when you describe a book, you can use this vocabulary to describe the techniques authors use."

- "The question we will be investigating today is, 'What are some different nonfiction techniques that we already know for which we have expert vocabulary? What are techniques we recognize in nonfiction texts we've read so far?'"

- "Today I want to teach you that readers not only use expert vocabulary to describe what nonfiction writers do, they also think about *when and how* authors use these terms—how they make new information really interesting and understandable."

Use this list as a menu of possibilities, selecting only the teaching points that meet the needs of your students. Use your assessment data (conferring and small-group notes, observations, responses to read-alouds, and other information) to decide on a plan that is tailored to the needs of your class. These teaching points may be used as whole-class minilessons, as mid-workshop teachings, or for conferences and small-group work. You need not use every teaching point. See the unit overview for guidelines on how much time to spend in each bend.

- "Today I want to teach you that it's not just nonfiction authors who explain information using effective techniques. Readers use these same techniques when they write or teach about what they've learned."
- "Readers often lay books by an author or from a series alongside each other and study patterns to see if they are particularly drawn to certain kinds of writing."
- "Today I want to teach you that readers will often compare and contrast books by different authors, because looking at two books that are quite different helps to see more specifically how authors make different moves."
- "Today I want to remind you that when teaching others what you are learning—especially from nonfiction—it helps the audience when you point to favorite parts of the text, quote specific parts, and use expert vocabulary in your conversations."
- "Readers can use an argument/debate protocol to argue which nonfiction author wrote a better book about a topic using text evidence to support a position."
- "Readers celebrate a close study of nonfiction texts by nominating nonfiction authors for awards, offering book talks on nonfiction authors they love, or recording podcasts where they talk about what's *hot* in nonfiction."

BEND III: EXPANDING NONFICTION EXPERIENCES

- "Today I want to teach you that as readers come to know more about the books they are drawn to, they also know more about themselves as readers, which helps them outgrow themselves and set new goals."
- "Today I want to teach you that one way readers grow and expand their reading is by swapping favorite books or by introducing books to each other."
- "Today I want to teach you that readers draw on all that they have learned about what makes for strong nonfiction writing as they investigate other kinds of nonfiction that make up a reading identity, including websites, videos, and magazines."
- "Today I want to remind you that readers can use thought prompts to flash-draft mini-essays where they defend their ideas about authors and texts."
- "Today I want to teach you that readers often celebrate their nonfiction reading journeys, inventing ways to share the great nonfiction they are finding, perhaps by creating bookmarks for great sites, recommending videos, or making a handout for parents or for local libraries on what nonfiction is great for kids."

Solving the Mystery before the Detective

Inference, Close Reading, Synthesis, and Prediction

RATIONALE/INTRODUCTION

The mystery unit is one of our all-time favorite units. Children gravitate toward the excitement of mystery books. They love trying to solve the mystery before the crime solver does. To do this, students need to be able to read closely and attentively, as well as to pull back to make something of the details they are accumulating—to have a hunch or suspicion, to make a prediction. This unit gives students an opportunity, then, to hone several valuable skills: creating a through line in a text, identifying cause-and-effect relationships, predicting outcomes, and reading closely.

Another advantage to this unit is that there are countless books available for readers at a variety of levels, from Nate the Great and Cam Jansen (level K) for earlier readers, to Sammy Keyes (level T) for more advanced readers, and of course the entire range in between. Also, because children will be reading in tandem with their peers, either in partnerships or book clubs, they will have the support of another reader or readers, as well as the benefit of reading the same books. Both of these things support reading with increased volume, stamina, and engagement. Many of the mystery books your students will be reading are also part of a series, and reading from a series positions students to tackle harder and harder books.

The unit also invites instruction in intertextuality, an important aspect of reading that the global standards of today recognize and highlight. In Bend II of this unit, children will read multiple books both within and across series, spotting patterns, and comparing characters, plots, settings, and other story elements.

Finally, the unit includes important interpretation work that builds upon work students will have done in previous units (Unit 1, *Building a Reading Life*, if they are in third grade, or Units 1 and 4, *Interpreting Characters: The Heart of the Story* and *Historical Fiction Clubs*, respectively, if they are in fourth). You'll support your readers in even more sophisticated work as they move to analyzing characters' personalities, motivations, choices, and reactions. As part of this work, you'll teach students to consider life lessons in their mystery books—to read and ask, "Is there a larger message here?" and "What might the author be trying to teach the character/me?" This work will be revisited and extended for third-graders in the *Character Studies* unit.

A SUMMARY OF THE BENDS IN THE ROAD FOR THIS UNIT

Essential Question: How can I read mysteries, collecting and interpreting clues so that I solve the mystery before the crime solver does? How can I not only solve mysteries but also learn life lessons as I do this?

- **Bend I: Mystery Readers Read for Clues**

  How can I use my fiction reading skills (and my knowledge of how fiction stories tend to go) to puzzle over clues and to make smart predictions?

- **Bend II: Reading across Mysteries**

  How can I become knowledgeable enough about the genre of mystery that I can categorize the mysteries I read, seeing some as similar to and different from others?

- **Bend III: Mystery Readers Learn Life Lessons from Books**

  How can I notice and analyze characters' personalities, motivations, choices, and responses to those choices, so that I'm not just breezing through mysteries for plot but am thinking more deeply about the larger messages?

In Bend I (Mystery Readers Read for Clues), children will learn to read closely and attentively in order to notice the details that will help them figure out "who done it." Although you will build up the novelty of reading mysteries, you will meanwhile point out that mysteries are also stories, which means that readers can draw on everything they know to do as readers of fiction when they read mysteries. As part of this, they will make observations about characters' traits and feelings, observations that set students up to grow ideas about characters. Eventually, you will convey that it's not just mystery readers who collect and reference clues to grow theories; in fact, readers of all fiction do this as they notice things about characters and grow theories based on what they see. Plan to spend about a week working in this bend.

In Bend II (Reading across Mysteries), students will learn that there are ways in which any one mystery fits within a set of other, similar mysteries, say, in a series. Students can compare and contrast the actions of characters and the plots and settings of stories within and across series. We recommend two weeks for this bend, longer than the first, and you could even extend it if your class needs additional support with this work. If your students are third-graders, this cross-series work will be new, as it isn't fully explored until the *Character Studies* unit (Unit 3). However, if you are a fourth-grade teacher and teaching this unit as the final unit of the school year, this bend will serve as review. In this bend, you will either raise the level of comparing and contrasting across series or lay the foundation for it, depending on grade level.

In Bend III (Mystery Readers Learn Life Lessons from Books), the focus is on interpretation. Students will learn that readers can take away life lessons by studying characters and plots of books. This work will help them determine central messages, identifying how these are conveyed through key details in a text. In this bend, students will spend about a week comparing and contrasting themes across mysteries.

ASSESSMENT

To assess for goals specific to this unit, you might want to read aloud a short mystery text within the higher end of the 2 to 3 band of text complexity and embed questions to assess these skills. Even reading aloud the first two chapters of a book from a series like *A–Z Mysteries* positions you to ask students to make inferences about the characters, synthesize what they know to predict, and consider what larger lessons the text might offer.

To assess children's ability to infer about characters, you might read a section of the text that reveals information about the character, then stop and ask students to jot the ideas they are starting to have about him or her. Later, as the text unfolds, you'll want to ask a question that assesses students' ability to interpret and support that inference with text details, such as "What theories are you developing? As you write, be sure to include evidence from the text to support your ideas." To assess for synthesis, you might ask, "What are the steps the character takes to solve the mystery? Why did the character take those steps?" To assess for interpretation, you might ask, "What larger meanings or lessons are you starting to see in this story?" At the end of the unit, you'll likely repeat this same assessment (or a similar one) to measure student growth.

You will want to focus your attention on the strands of the Narrative Reading Learning Progression you've just assessed, those that correspond directly to your teaching in this unit: "Orienting," "Retelling/ Summary/Synthesis," "Envisioning/Predicting," "Inferring About Characters and Other Story Elements," and "Determining Themes/Cohesion."

GETTING READY

Increase students' reading volume and stamina.

As the author of the popular Cam Jansen mysteries, David Adler, explains, "Children who are just beginning to read on their own, read slowly. They read every word. But they don't think slowly. To keep their attention it's necessary to keep the story moving." True to Adler's word, most mysteries written for children have a clear, coherent through line in a fast-moving plot, so that even your slow readers will read quickly.

This month, your aim above all else will be to help students increase their reading volume and stamina, knowing that the nature of the books they are reading supports this effort.

You might revisit your start-of-the-year resolution on "reading more," and you'll certainly want to track and celebrate volume surges in reading logs this month. You'll also deliver specific instruction around reading faster and longer. Plan to gather together in a small group any readers who still subvocalize the text or use the telltale finger-under-word crutch for specific instruction on fluency and speed. "Readers don't read one word, another word, and the next word," you might say. "They move their eyes to read groups of words." You might then set up these children to read portions out loud to each other, practicing this. "Are you wondering what happens next? Show that wondering in your voice. Add suspense to your read-aloud." *Building a Reading Life* (grade 3) and *Interpreting Characters: The Heart of the Story* (grade 4) have scores of ideas on how to set the collective class mood for reading with volume and fluency.

Support readers as they handle increasingly complex texts.

You will want all of your readers matched to texts that they can read with at least 96% fluency, accuracy, and comprehension. Meanwhile, you will want to continue supporting their growing abilities to handle increasingly complex texts. By the end of the year, students should be reading and comprehending literature at the high end of 2 to 3 text complexity bands independently and proficiently. This means that they should be reading books that represent their point of opportunity—in other words, books at their instructional level, with your instructional support. Matching readers to books doesn't mean that children will read easy texts. It means they will read books that offer the magical mix of challenge and support that ensures engagement.

To challenge children, tell them that reading their books either with a partner or in clubs will give them the group solidarity that allows each member to make more ambitious goals. One such goal is to tackle texts that are more complex and nuanced. In addition to the support of their peers, you can provide any readers moving into challenging texts with book introductions. Often family volunteers are willing to help out by reading a few chapters aloud to a reader and talking about these pages—this is especially helpful at the start of a book. Or volunteers can read the same book in sync with a reader. If no adults are available to help, you could turn to older students who might enjoy acting as teachers in your classroom.

Series books act as a crucial scaffold for readers moving to new levels, because books within a series have recurring main, and sometimes even secondary characters. Mysteries in a series also tend to follow a distinct problem-solving pattern. After reading one or two Nancy Drew books, a reader will tend to know this "titian-haired sleuth" well enough to be able to predict the things she does to solve a case—her peculiar habits or strategies (that she sometimes goes to Dad when all else fails, for example). This sets up children to describe characters in a story (their traits, motivations, and feelings). Similarly, after reading two or three Encyclopedia Brown books, readers are likely to expect that Encyclopedia will "solve" a case by closing his eyes to think deeply and then asking a single question that will lead directly to the solution. Repetitive characters and plots across a series allow children to predict with ease. If you've already taught the habits needed to read series and to analyze characters in earlier units, expect children to do this work with greater independence and fluency. If this work is new for your class, they may need additional support and teaching around these items. Many popular mysteries such as the Boxcar Children, Jigsaw Jones, or A to Z Mysteries are part of a larger series.

If some of your readers have not progressed as you'd expect so far over the course of the year, now is a good time to intervene. Do these readers need to spend an hour after school, in the building, reading? Do they need to double the amount of reading they are doing at home? Might an older student be employed as a reading mentor?

Gather and choose books for read-aloud, partnerships, and book clubs.

This unit, more than many others, offers a huge collection of books at diverse levels. Before you begin the unit, you may want to round up all the mystery books you can find to set up your classroom library. On the TCRWP website we've included a bibliography of leveled mystery books that you could also refer to as you stock your library. You will note that this collection is, in large part, made up of mystery series in the M, N, and O levels, titles such as the Cam Jansen series, the Jigsaw Jones series or the Boxcar Children series. This list contains many suggestions for lower-level mysteries, too, including series at levels J through L (Young Cam Jansen, Detective Dinosaur, and Nate the Great, to name a few). See http://readingandwritingproject.org/resources/book-lists for book lists (search for "Reading and Writing Project Book Lists").

You will need to have mystery series collections in order for students to do the work of Bend II, Reading across Mysteries. It is helpful to organize your series books so that students have the first two books in the series, at least, and if possible, begin by reading those books. Of course, you will no doubt have some gaps in every series. Colleagues in your school may be willing to combine forces, or you could borrow books from the school library.

You will also, of course, want to choose mysteries for your read-alouds, ideally more than one book inside of a series to mirror the work your students are doing. One such series we suggest is Encyclopedia Brown. Each book in this series contains short, powerful mysteries with strong characters. These mysteries deliberately challenge readers to try to solve the case before they are "told" the solution. The short-text format (each chapter is a new mystery) makes it easy to move across many mysteries quickly and gives students repeated practice reading closely and playing detective. These books are all level P and above 600L.

Create a collection of mystery television shows and games.

Your unit will be especially engaging if you refer to mystery games and television shows in your minilessons. Meanwhile, you'll find that clips of mystery shows allow you to highlight the skills of this unit. If you have several episodes from a series, you can weave snippets of these into some of your minilessons or small-group work, probably returning to the same snippet more than once to highlight new ways of "reading" it.

Consider including older shows in your collection. You can find *MathNet*—a mystery involving math that was always part of episodes of *Square One*—online at YouTube, as well as old episodes of *Ghost Writer*, a mystery series involving a ghost who wrote to the kid detectives. Another option is *Scooby Doo*, whose episodes are short enough that your class can watch these several times, each time with a specific lens in mind. For example, after they are familiar with a particular episode, students can watch that episode a second time, this time intent on watching the criminal closely to note things he or she did or said (or didn't do or say) that gave away that he or she was the "bad guy." In this way, the short clip can help readers see the value of closely attending to characters' behaviors, noting how attributes help or hurt.

You might also consider games to get your students thinking like detectives. The classic board game *Clue* will support students' synthesis and deductive reasoning skills. Another option is the game *Hedbanz* that requires players to ask questions and use deductive reasoning to solve the puzzle of someone's identity. You might also consider having students complete puzzles, perhaps without knowing the whole image they are aiming to create in order to make this work more challenging. You could weave these games or puzzles into choice time, if you have it, to complement the work students will do during reading workshop. You could also make reference to these games and puzzles in some of your minilesson connections so that your students see the broader thinking work they are doing when reading mysteries.

BEND I: MYSTERY READERS READ FOR CLUES

The big goal for this bend is for children to read closely, holding onto and monitoring for meaning by paying attention to details. Just like great detectives are always watchful, not letting anything slip by them, so, too, your children will work to read, intent on spotting key details. These details, then, help them not only solve the crime in their mystery books but also grow theories about characters. In this first bend, students will puzzle over clues, using their fiction reading skills and the predictable narrative structure specific to mysteries in order to make smart predictions as they read. They will make inferences to formulate theories, which they can then continue to revise by evaluating and reevaluating the evidence as they go.

Launch the unit with some drama—a "real-life" mystery—to build enthusiasm, and teach them to approach a mystery, asking, "What is the mystery here?"

You may decide to launch this unit with some drama, staging a mini-mystery in the classroom. Perhaps your glasses or the class's pet hamster "mysteriously" vanished. You might provide a clue or two to help children solve the mystery ("I had my glasses on when I left for the teachers' lounge," or "I saw some tiny footprints near the coat closet"). One fabulous teacher we know introduces this unit each year by coming into the classroom wearing a trench coat and carrying a big magnifying glass. A little drama goes a long way in raising the level of enthusiasm! Once you capture children's attention, you'll tell them that they'll be doing this same kind of detective work in their reading this month. One of the first questions to start off a unit on mysteries is, "What is the mystery here?"

> **"Today I want to teach you that before you start reading a mystery, it is helpful to read the title, the blurb, and the chapter titles and to think: 'What will be the big mystery in this book? Who will solve this mystery?' Then you read, ready to collect clues and suspects."**

You might demonstrate this with your read-aloud and then send your readers off to read the beginning chapters of their independent books, gathering clues and suspects.

On the other hand, if your class is revisiting mysteries for a second or third time, after recruiting children to help you solve a real-life mystery ("Before we start this minilesson, will you help me figure out what I did with my glasses? Let me think, where did I last have them?"), you might then challenge them to name what they did: "You already know a whole lot about solving mysteries. Would you list across your fingers three things we did right now to solve the mystery of my lost glasses—three things that mystery readers do all the time?" Then say, "I heard you say that I first sensed something was wrong. Mystery solvers first figure out what the mystery is! Then you said we became suspicious and slowed down, investigating closely. Yes—mystery solvers became detectives, searching for clues." You could then go on to teach students that whenever they start a book, it helps to think, "What kind of book is this?" and to remember all they already know about how that kind of book tends to go, in order to read it well.

Whether or not your students have experienced a mystery unit prior to now, early on, you will have some big goals. You will want to drum up excitement for this new unit and to rally children to read attentively. And you will want students to use their sense of this genre to channel their attention. A Day 2 teaching point might be around the very active role that mystery readers play in solving the case: "Today I want to teach you that mystery readers read like detectives. They try to see clues, just as the detective does, and to solve the mystery before the detective."

Teach children more about the genre and its specialized language.

As the unit unfolds, you will want to teach children more about the genre, so that they use this new knowledge to pinpoint details that merit attention. For example, you may teach them that detectives are alert to whether a place is a crime scene, and approach that place differently, if so. As detectives collect clues, they also generate lists of suspects and possible culprits. You might teach, "Readers have a list of possible suspects going in their mind, and when they learn new facts, they look back on that list, sometimes eliminating one suspect or another." Through this initial launch work, students will come to see that mystery readers make mental, if not physical, lists of suspects.

You will also want to make it a point to induct students into the specialized language of this genre and encourage them to use this vocabulary in their discussions. After teaching some of these academic vocabulary terms, you might even create a mystery word wall. As new terminology is discovered, the class can add to the word wall. By the end of the first bend, the wall may contain terms such as *evidence, pattern, alibi, suspect, red herring,* and *motive*.

As students begin to read their mysteries, they'll immediately encounter information that they need to hold onto in order to solve the mystery. You may see them overlooking some of the information at the beginning of a book that you know will pay off later. If this is the case, teach students that as they're reading, they need to be on the lookout for information or behavior that seems out of place or unusual, and discrepancies that pose opportunities to ask, "Why would . . . ?" or "How could . . . ?"

> **"Today I want to teach you that mystery readers notice details that are surprising or that seem like they don't fit into the story and ask, 'Could these out-of-place details really be clues?'"**

Your readers could then jot down the possible motivation that each suspect might have for committing a crime. Urge them to ask, "Why would this suspect want to do this? What would she or he get out of it?" of each suspect in their list. They can also ask, "Who had the opportunity to do this?" and "Who was near the scene of the crime or had access to it?" Readers might jot privately as they read and then bring these jots to their club or partnership discussion to collectively brainstorm. If you see students who are not considering multiple suspects, or ignoring certain characters altogether, you may want to teach them that mystery readers consider multiple possibilities and think carefully about *all* of the characters. This type of synthesis work is one of the reasons this unit is so important. In order to tackle increasingly difficult texts, readers need to attend to *all* of the text—the setting, the minor characters, the way characters speak and act—and to make inferences about characters' motivations.

Reinforce children's understanding of narrative structure and the work they do when reading all fiction.

You'll alert readers to the story grammar of mysteries not just to increase their attentiveness to this genre but also to reinforce their understanding of narrative structure in general. Your students should already have a basic awareness of story arc in narrative texts: A problem is revealed, heightened, and eventually resolved. Remind children that mysteries are also *stories*, and so they need to draw on everything they know as readers of fiction when they read mysteries. As they would with any story, readers read to know their characters well enough to describe their traits, motivations, and feelings and to explain how their actions contribute to the sequence of events. To facilitate this work, you might guide readers to ask and answer questions such as:

- How do the character's words and actions help you understand him or her?
- What is the character feeling/thinking? What makes you think the character feels/thinks that?

- What motivates the character/what are the character's motives or possible motives for doing what he or she does (or might have done)?

- What has caused the character to _____?

- What happened because the character _____?

This is a good time to pull out charts from any earlier fiction-based units to remind students of all that they know to do when reading fiction. Most importantly, you will want them to grow ideas about the characters in their mysteries. You'll convey that readers collect clues and use these to grow theories, not just to solve the book's crime but also to grow ideas about its characters. Remind children that just as they read any novel, collecting clues to think about the characters, asking, "What kind of person is this?" they can ask this question of characters in mysteries, too, focusing especially on any special traits or talents that help a character solve the mystery.

Readers of Cam Jansen can identify her gift of a photographic memory early on, to understand that this "camera" memory doesn't just account for her name; it also plays a role in her ability to solve mysteries. Similarly, children will benefit from realizing that Encyclopedia Brown, as his name suggests, relies on his powers of encyclopedic knowledge to crack a case. Understanding a character is a way of understanding a big part of the story—how the problem is tackled and resolved.

> **"Today I want to teach you that mystery readers study their characters—especially the detectives—to know their strengths. Readers know that the detectives (and their sidekicks) will use these traits to solve the mystery."**

Apart from identifying the traits of the protagonist, you might teach students to step inside the main character's shoes in order to understand the detective's mind-set. You might say: "Mystery readers step into the shoes of the detective and search for clues alongside him or her. Put yourself in the detective's shoes. What might you do next to solve this mystery?" In the same way, you'll want readers to discuss secondary characters. You might say: "What role does the sidekick play?" or "How does the sidekick help the main character solve each mystery?" and teach readers to make initial theories about characters that they will add to—or revise—as they read on and gather more clues. Similarly, you can alert children to note what they learn about possible suspects or a villain in the mystery and to note, too, the roles these characters play in creating or complicating the mystery.

Help children problem solve as they read.

If students are reading passively (reading to be told rather than to figure out the mystery), you could conduct a close, shared reading lesson using an Encyclopedia Brown story or another short mystery (*Highlights* magazine has published some nice short mysteries in the past). Read with this group in such a way that you collectively track the mystery, suspects, and clues. It helps if every student has a copy of the text to mark up important clues and to reread, and if you keep the answer or last pages of the mystery a secret. Encyclopedia Brown stories work well for this activity because of the structure of these texts (each chapter being its own short mystery, with each solution written in a section at the end of the entire book). You can simply keep students from reading the solution to the mystery and require that they return to the text to figure it out. In subsequent lessons, you could guide students to transfer this same attentive reading to their chapter books.

Some students may be struggling to figure out the solutions to their mysteries; you can teach more features specific to the mystery genre to strengthen their comprehension. It will benefit readers, for example, to flip back to earlier pages, once they've read to the end and learned the solution of the mystery, to identify the specific red herrings (false clues) that threw them off course. Alert your students to a mystery author's craft by suggesting that they examine these twists in the plot, asking themselves, "What did the author do to trick me? What did this make me think?"

They can follow up this study of the plot's twists to decide, "Now that I know____, I will not fall for this particular kind of red herring in any future mystery I read." Experienced mystery readers can sense the solution to a mystery far better than those new to the genre, simply because they tend to recognize red herrings better as they encounter them. Spotting these, in fact, can contribute to the fun of reading a mystery, once readers come to know this genre well.

Red herrings also play a big role in children's ability to anticipate similar craft moves in other narrative genres that are designed to keep readers guessing. Once children come to expect red herrings in mysteries, it won't be long before they make the connection between red herrings and possible plot twists in other narrative genres such as novels or short stories—that is, they will come to recognize and anticipate this form of author's craft in all narratives.

Spotlight word solving and language work.

Of course, even during a unit of study on mystery you'll want to keep an eye on the bottom lines. Are students attending to meaning? Are they using all they know about word solving, especially when faced with figurative or unfamiliar language? If not, you'll want to remind students that all readers (mystery and otherwise) ensure they have a clear mental movie going as they read. When this movie becomes fuzzy, either because of a difficult part or phrase, they use fix-up strategies to clear up confusion. Some students might benefit from a small group or conference on using the context of a text to determine the meaning of unknown words or phrases. Students reading The Hardy Boys, Encyclopedia Brown, Nancy Drew, or other series that use somewhat antiquated language due to when they were written may stumble upon sentences that are unfamiliar and require a bit of detective work on *their* part.

You might give students such a phrase to practice solving quickly before they turn to their own books for more practice. For example, in *The Case of Merko's Grandson* in *Encyclopedia Brown: Boy Detective* you could read the sentence on page 23, "*But the real blow fell on the Tigers the next day.*" Chances are that most students can read this sentence, but they likely don't encounter or use this expression on a regular basis. Show them how, by reading around this sentence, you can come to an understanding of the phrase.

You could also spotlight figurative language at this point in the bend. Begin by pointing out that the term *red herring* is an idiom, a reference to the practice of burying smelly fish in the ground to train hounds to follow a scent when hunting or to throw them off course. Then explain that mystery writers make use of figurative language, often as a way to add humor to their texts. You might return to *The Case of Merko's Grandson* again, turning to page 24 and the sentence, "*But his voice was weak, and he wore the sick smile of a boy who had taken one ride too many on a roller coaster.*" You might say, "Readers, today you'll continue to use the detective work you have been practicing. I want to teach you that mystery writers use language to entertain us *and* to make us think. Readers have two jobs: They must decipher the mystery, the suspects, and the clues, and they must decipher *how* the mystery was written—the language the author chose."

BEND II: READING ACROSS MYSTERIES

As you enter the second bend of the unit, your students will likely grasp how mysteries tend to go, and if they are already reading mysteries within a series, they'll get a sense for that particular series. The knowledge of how mysteries tend to go helps children exercise their synthesis skills, so they not only read from chapter to chapter but also figure out how one chapter fits with the ones before it. By now, your students are more adept at reading closely, which means they can also read from book to book, synthesizing or noticing common patterns between mystery books. They are ready, then, to take on the intertextual work of reading across mysteries to compare and contrast their themes, settings, plots, and author's craft.

Teach children to take notice of a series' recurring elements to help them solve the mystery.

Since the majority of children's mysteries are part of a series, the major characters and a base setting (e.g., a school yard or a clubhouse) usually make an appearance in each book. While children will find themselves in familiar territory again and again, especially at the beginning of a mystery, the challenge will be for them to pay attention to *other* settings the crime solver visits. These settings are often places the crime solver visits to interview witnesses and, therefore, are full of clues. You will want to teach students that from the start of a story, they need to start collecting clues—the pieces that will later help them complete the jigsaw that solves the mystery. Teach them, too, to pay special attention to setting and to new characters that each book in a series introduces.

Mysteries that are part of a series are easier for young readers to navigate because of the recurring cast of characters and base setting and because they often feature an archetypal role of sidekick. Inspired by Sherlock Holmes's classic "Watson," the sidekick is often a loyal assistant providing many convenient roles: someone to bounce ideas off or patiently explain "elementary" clues to (often for the benefit of the reader). In most mysteries in a series, your students will encounter a sidekick—Encyclopedia Brown has

Sally, Nate the Great has his dog Sludge, Cam Jansen has Eric, and Jigsaw Jones has Mila Yeh. Often, the sidekick unwittingly raises a question or points to a feature that leads the main character to have the big mystery-solving "Eureka!"

Some mysteries, such as Roy's ABC Mysteries or Nancy Drew, have more than one sidekick, each with a distinct personality—Josh has Dink and Ruth Rose, and Nancy has both George and Bess to offer support as well as complicate the solving of the mysteries. Then again, some mysteries, such as The Boxcar Children or Enid Blyton's Famous Five and Secret Seven series, don't feature one main protagonist with a sidekick but rather a group of siblings or friends who serve collectively as a main character. Readers will come to anticipate the predictable patterns, not only of how the mystery tends to be set up and solved but also of the roles that certain recurring characters play in this process.

> **"Today I want to teach you that when people read mysteries that are part of a series, they use their knowledge of how mysteries tend to go, and how other books in the series have tended to go—the characters' traits and roles, the plotlines, the setting—to help them solve the mystery."**

Guide children to read alertly, to vary their pace, to ask questions, and to make inferences.

You will also want to teach children the importance of reading closely, with alertness, noticing details. "Mystery readers read suspiciously," you might teach, or, "Mystery readers find clues in the details that other people may miss." At the beginning of the unit, students noticed that some details are in mysteries to throw readers off track. Now, as they read across a series, they will notice common tricks that particular mystery authors play. "In the *Bald Bandit*, the fact that the character was wearing a wig was important," one club member might notice. "And in the *Absent Author*, someone wearing sunglasses was important. So this author might like to use what people are wearing as clues. We should pay attention to that!" Students are coming to see that the important details, the ones that play a role in the case's solution, are often deliberately disguised. Help them hone their ability to detect details that seem important.

If you are using the Encyclopedia Brown series as your read-aloud, you might point out, as an example, that in the first chapter of *Encyclopedia Brown Cracks the Case*, onions are mentioned a lot. Mrs. Brown keeps sniffing and rubbing her eyes, and Encyclopedia brings up the idea that his dad stinks of onion. Then say, "Adept readers know that this repeated detail is no accident and that onions will likely come into play in a big way later. They know that mystery authors predictably embed clues in details and are alert for those."

You may also want to teach children that mystery readers vary their pace, depending on what is happening in the book. They notice when they come to a part of the story where they should slow down and read carefully. Often this is when the scene of the crime is visited or new characters are introduced. Coach students to read those parts slowly, scouring for clues. Going back to reread and using Post-its to track important parts can be helpful.

If your readers are still overlooking clues, you might point out that when the detective stops to think, that's a time for the reader to pause as well. Advise readers to ask themselves, "What did the detective learn that I should have learned?" and to answer this question by rereading the place the detective realized something that he or she missed. Encourage children to be alert also to the various perspectives witnesses offer. Just like the detective, children will need to sort through all the information and decide whose account—or which clues—they trust. Readers may also benefit from timelining the crime, especially if (as is typical in mysteries) the crime took place before the beginning of the book. This sequencing work will also help them grasp the plot as they talk about the mystery with partners or club members. Because characters in mysteries move between present-day action and reflections on the past (when the crime occurred), children, too, must be able to shift their focus between the current story and the backstory in order to piece together what happened.

If reading is an inferential activity, reading a mystery is doubly so. The work that a detective does in solving a mystery is an apt metaphor for the sort of work readers must do to understand characters and the story. You'll want to teach that skilled mystery readers not only search for clues, they also make something of those clues. They point to particular parts of the mystery to infer and predict, saying, "I think this means . . . ," "I think this could show . . ." and "Because of this, I think . . ."

> **"Today I want to teach you that skilled mystery readers not only search for clues, they also make something of those clues. They point to particular parts of the mystery to infer and predict, saying, 'I think this means . . . ,' 'I think this could show . . .' and 'Because of this, I think . . .'"**

For example, in the second chapter of *Encyclopedia Brown Cracks the Case*, you can point out that because a big deal is made about the fact that the book was signed by the author, we can infer that this fact will play an important role in the outcome of the case. These predictions are based on the inferences that readers accumulate from the text.

Initiate self-assessment work and shared writing about reading.

Now is also an ideal time for students to look at their work against the learning progressions. You might give this teaching point: "Today I want to teach you that when readers are trying to get better at a skill it helps them to use tools that are on hand—checklists or goal sheets—to improve their thinking. They lay their work alongside the tool and study it, thinking about how they can improve their work to lift it to the next level." Students might then work either in partnerships or independently to make quick revisions designed to improve their work. You might set up children with the "Inferring about Characters and Other Story Elements" strand of the learning progression, or with the "Orienting," "Retelling/Summary/Synthesis," or

"Envisioning/Predicting" strands. Just be sure that you give them strands for work you have already taught, either in this unit or in prior ones.

You might also teach children that mysteries teach us to be flexible because we often entertain more than one possible prediction as we read. Readers need to think about multiple possible outcomes no matter the genre, of course, but reading mysteries can hone this skill, as these books are by design meant to pull readers in several possible directions. Mystery readers must therefore hold onto various predictions and come up with rationales for these, often switching gears as they read on and gather more information.

This bend provides a great opportunity to do some shared writing in which children support their hunches with clues from throughout the story. Today's standards call for students to be able to write opinions on texts and support these with reasons. Shared writing work also gives students the benefit of receiving guidance and support from both their peers and their teacher and the opportunity to develop and strengthen their writing by planning and revising. You'll want to do this work with your class read-aloud; stop at a critical point in the story, and ask children to review all of their jottings—including those the class has been compiling together—to think about suspects and to weigh evidence.

You might ask children: "Who might have committed this crime?" The answer to this question then becomes the thesis statement for a mini-essay. Coach kids to write in the air about ways to begin the mini-essay. Once kids have shared a few ideas, the class can pick one for you to record. The essay might begin, "In *Cam Jansen and the Scary Snake*, we figured out that the man stole the purse with the camera in it." Then partners can come up with reasons that support this claim, citing specific evidence from the story. They might quote a part of the text or summarize a scene, then explain how this evidence supports their claim. "One reason we know he did it is because he knew the color of the bag before anyone told him. This proves . . ." You may want to supply prompts for children who need support connecting their idea and reasons with linking words: "One reason is . . . ," "This shows . . . ," "In addition . . . ," "Another example . . . ," "This example shows that . . ." The class could come up with evidence in support of other suspects in the book, or groups could go off and write a mini-essay together. Later, partnerships and clubs will likely do this work on their own.

If you want to extend this writing about reading work, children could make lists of suspects in their independent reading books, with page numbers of parts that show why each one is a suspect. When a child no longer thinks a character is a suspect, he might jot down why to share with his partner or club mates the next day. Children can jot not only the clues but also where and how the clues were found, so that when they read their next mystery, they will carry that knowledge with them. Readers could compile tips for reading mysteries that they add to over time.

Children should also be doing character work as they read their mysteries, jotting traits, observations, and thoughts about the characters in their books. They can reread their jots, drawing on these to solve the mystery or predict how it will unfold. For example: "I know that Josh loves nature and is passionate about protecting it—he hikes, and he owns and uses binoculars to bird watch. Will his keen observation skills and binoculars help him figure out who took the peregrine falcons in *Falcon Feathers?*"

Teach children to think comparatively across the books they are reading.

Another important aspect of character work is comparative thinking. Since many of your children will be reading across a series, they are perfectly set up to do the compare-and-contrast work that today's standards call for. Show them how to lay books in a mystery series side by side and to think and talk about the ways these books go together as well as how they differ. They can ask, "What changes across books, and what remains the same?" and then answer by considering the settings, characters, their actions and reactions, plots, and themes. Once children notice patterns across a series, they can consider these patterns' effects, notice when the patterns are broken, and speculate why. Since characters tend to recur across a series, readers can compare how they behave similarly across the books, or how they react differently in similar situations. You can also teach children to think and speak comparatively about author's craft, writing style, and voice.

> **"Today I want to teach you one way readers push themselves to think *across* books. Readers may ask, 'What changes across books and what remains the same?' They answer this question by paying attention to the setting in these books, the characters, their actions and reactions, plots, and themes."**

You may prompt this kind of thinking work by posing questions about series such as:

- What is similar or different about the characters' choices in each book?
- What is similar or different about the way the characters respond to trouble in each book?
- How is the setting similar or different across the series?
- How are the major events in each book similar or different across the series? Is each story structured the same way, or are there differences?

BEND III: MYSTERY READERS LEARN LIFE LESSONS FROM BOOKS

As the unit progresses, students will likely be growing more confident as they compare and contrast plots and elements that run across various mystery books. Now in Bend III they will have a chance to deepen their interpretation skills. If you find that they are simply breezing through mysteries as "plot junkies," then you will want to teach them to notice and analyze characters' motivations, choices, and emotions. This will set them up to learn life lessons from these texts. In this bend they will learn to read mysteries, following and interpreting the clues and the patterns of the genre in such a way that they not only solve the mystery but also learn valuable life lessons embedded in the text. This might sound surprising, interpretation in mystery. "Isn't mystery reading about solving the mystery?" you might ask. The answer is yes, mystery reading is largely about getting students to read closely, gathering clues, making inferences, and solving mysteries, but with a little nudge, it can also be about thinking interpretively.

Steer children to slow down, paying close attention to characters' actions and the choices they make, and to notice the lessons they learn.

Many mystery readers assume that the only work they must do is follow the fast-moving plot and solve the mystery. However, if they slow down a bit, they will realize that the characters in mysteries are not just on the page to entertain; they also teach valuable lessons that readers can apply to their own lives. It pays off, therefore, to look closely at characters' actions, noticing whether these lead to positive or negative results. The next step, then, is to ask, "What lesson(s) could I learn from the choices this character made?" In *Jigsaw Jones and the Case of Hermie the Missing Hamster*, for example, readers can notice that as soon as Wingnut starts to tear up, Jigsaw has a box of tissues at the ready. And when Wingnut can't afford the $1.00 payment for Jigsaw's services, Jigsaw accepts whatever Wingnut *can* give. Similarly, in *Encyclopedia Brown Cracks the Case*, when Mark Goldberg can't pay for detective services because he used up all of his money buying a fake revolutionary treasure, Encyclopedia does not let this stop him from taking the case.

> **"Today I want to teach you that mystery readers solve mysteries, but they also learn about life. They know it pays off to step back and ask, 'What choices has this character made? What lesson(s) could I learn from these?'"**

If we ask ourselves what lessons we could learn from these two main characters, we might say, "When someone is in trouble, you may have to change the rules to help them." Or, "Sometimes it's important to be flexible." From this, children can begin to learn that even the tiniest actions characters make are choices that reflect beliefs or morals. Each club can write these lessons on large index cards that have an illustrated cover with their club name and display them on a bulletin board space inside the classroom. Clubs can then add to their list of lessons as they read other mysteries. If students are not working in clubs, they can do this work in their partnerships.

Once readers are in the habit of studying characters' actions, paying attention to small choices they make, teach them to also look closely at the big, important decisions characters make throughout the story. When characters follow a lead or keep a secret or confront someone suspicious, readers might stop and again ask themselves, "What lesson am I learning from the character here?" They can consider *why* the character has made this choice and what it teaches readers. Jigsaw doesn't jump to the conclusion that a snake ate Hermie the Hamster even though that is his initial hunch. In fact, when Wingnut gets worried, Jigsaw insists that "he's only a suspect" and that they have to keep an open mind. He then decides to do extensive research about hamsters and their predators. If we asked ourselves what this character's choice has taught us, we might say, "Don't jump to conclusions about someone before you know all of the facts."

Teach children that it pays off to notice when a character has a strong emotional reaction during the story or after the mystery has been solved.

As in many narrative texts, it's important for readers to determine key moments and turning points in a character's journey. Alert students to signals in the text, such as emotional moments for characters. Teach them that expert readers stop and pay close attention when a character is having a very strong emotional reaction and that it often pays to think about what's behind this emotion or what is motivating the character to act this way, and then think about what lesson they could take from it. In *A to Z Mysteries: The Falcon Feathers*, Josh brings Ruth Rose and Dink to the woods to see the nest of baby falcons he had found a couple of weeks ago but discovers they are gone. Josh reacts strongly and wants to report the missing falcons. We might ask readers, "What life lesson can we learn?" Readers might say, "When something means a lot to you, you can't just stand by and do nothing but rather you need to take action."

> **"Today I want to teach you that a helpful time to stop and pay close attention is when a character is having a strong emotional reaction. It often pays to think about what's behind this emotion or what is motivating the character to act this way, and then about what lesson you can take from it."**

You might also teach your readers that another place mysteries offer readers the opportunity to think about life lessons is at the end, when we know "who did it." After we have identified who did it, and after we have figured out why he or she did it, we can think about what we can learn from their motives. Mysteries are moralistic. They are teaching young readers that greed, jealousy, and revenge are wrong. For example at the end of *Falcon Feathers* we might ask, "What can we learn from Kurt, who stole the baby falcons to train them to race so he could make money?" A lesson could be, "When we think only of ourselves instead of others, we might end up making bad decisions that could get us into trouble."

> **"Today I want to teach you that readers can also learn life lessons at the end of a mystery, when they know 'who did it' and why. Readers can learn from the culprit's motives."**

If you'd like to extend your students' interpretive work, you could ask them to return to some of the texts they've read earlier in the year and lay them next to their mystery texts. "What lessons are common among these texts?" you could teach your students to ask. "What do these characters teach us about life?" At first glance, Sammy Keyes and August from *Wonder* might not seem to have much in common, but when students put them next to each other and realize that each character learns that you need to rely on friends in order to solve your problems, they experience a rush of excitement at the new insight they have formed. You can support your students as they reach for these insights through conversation and writing about their reading in quick notebook entries aimed at pushing their thinking.

CELEBRATION

You might end the unit with a fun "Who did it?" celebration in which children dress up as their favorite detective or criminal. Maybe they'll carry or wear special props like a detective's hat or magnifying glass—or any items associated with the character they choose to impersonate or with the crime that's committed. They can then circulate, explaining to one another how they either pulled off a crime or solved one. If your children have read many of the same books, they might even be able to guess one another's roles. You could suggest that they take on the characteristics of the person they are dressing as—that they do a little acting—and that they not identify themselves. You might need to create a few areas of the room in which kids reading at similar levels gather. Part of the discussion could include the life lesson the criminal (or detective) learned.

POSSIBLE TEACHING POINTS

BEND I: MYSTERY READERS READ FOR CLUES

- "Today I want to teach you that before you start reading a mystery, it is helpful to read the title, the blurb, and the chapter titles and to think: 'What will be the big mystery in this book? Who will solve this mystery?' Then you read, ready to collect clues and suspects."

- "Today I want to remind you that whenever you start a book, it helps to think, 'What kind of book is this?' and to remember all you already know about how that kind of book tends to go, to read it well." (*Note: This is an alternate Day 1 teaching point for students who have already had a unit in mystery.*)

- "Today I want to teach you that mystery readers read like detectives. They try to see clues, just as the detective does, and to solve the mystery before the detective."

- "Today I want to teach you that detectives are alert to whether a place is a crime scene, approaching that place differently, if so. As detectives collect clues, they also generate lists of suspects, possible culprits. Readers, too, have a list of possible suspects going in their mind, and when they learn new facts, they look back on that list, sometimes eliminating one suspect or another."

- "Today I want to teach you that mystery books and detectives use specialized language. It's important for readers to incorporate this technical detective language into their discussions."

- "Today I want to teach you that mystery readers notice details that are surprising or that seem like they don't fit into the story and ask, 'Could these out-of-place details really be clues?'"

Use this list as a menu of possibilities, selecting only the teaching points that meet the needs of your students. Use your assessment data (conferring and small-group notes, observations, responses to read-alouds, and other information) to decide on a plan that is tailored to the needs of your class. These teaching points may be used as whole-class minilessons, as mid-workshop teaching, or for conferences and small-group work. You need not use every teaching point. See the unit overview for guidelines on how much time to spend in each bend.

- "Today I want to teach you that mystery readers consider multiple possibilities and think carefully about *all* of the characters. They jot down the possible motivation that each suspect might have for committing a crime, asking themselves, 'Why would this suspect want to do this? What would she or he get out of it?' of each suspect in their list. The can also ask, 'Who had the opportunity to do this?' and 'Who was near the scene of the crime or had access to it?'"

- "Readers, today I want to remind you that mysteries are also *stories*, so you need to draw on everything you know as readers of fiction when you read mysteries."

- "Today I want to teach you that mystery readers collect clues and use these to grow theories, not just to solve the book's crime but also to grow ideas about its characters. Just as you read any novel, collecting clues to think about the characters, asking, 'What kind of person is this?' you can ask this question of characters in mysteries, too, focusing especially on any special traits or talents that help a character solve the mystery."

- "Today I want to teach you that mystery readers study their characters—especially the detectives—to know their strengths. Readers know that the detectives (and their sidekicks) will use these traits to solve the mystery."

- "Today I want to remind you that all readers (mystery and otherwise) ensure they have a clear mental movie going as they read. When this movie becomes fuzzy, either because of a difficult part or phrase, they use fix-up strategies to clear up confusion."

- "Readers, today I want to teach you that mystery writers use language to entertain us *and* to make us think. Readers have two jobs: They must decipher the mystery, the suspects, and the clues, and they must decipher *how* the mystery was written—the language the author chose."

BEND II: READING ACROSS MYSTERIES

- "Today I want to teach you that from the start of a story, mystery readers need to collect clues—the pieces that will later help them complete the jigsaw that solves the mystery. Readers pay special attention to setting and to new characters that each book in a series introduces."

- "Today I want to teach you that when people read mysteries that are part of a series, they use their knowledge of how mysteries tend to go, and how other books in the series have tended to go—the characters' traits and roles, the plotlines, the setting—to help them solve the mystery."

- "Today I want to teach you that mystery readers read closely and suspiciously, alert to details. Mystery readers find clues in the details that other people may miss."

- "Today I want to teach you that mystery readers vary their pace, depending on what is happening in the book. They notice when they come to a part of the story where they should slow down and read carefully. Often this is when the scene of the crime is visited or new characters are introduced."

- "Today I want to teach you that when detectives stop to think, that is also a time for the mystery reader to stop and think. Readers ask themselves, 'What did the detective learn that I should have learned?' They answer this question by rereading the place the detective realized something that they missed."

- "Today I want to teach you that skilled mystery readers not only search for clues, they also make something of those clues. They point to particular parts of the mystery to infer and predict, saying, 'I think this means . . . ,' 'I think this could show . . . ,' and 'Because of this, I think . . . .'"

- "Today I want to teach you that when readers are trying to get better at a skill it helps to use tools that are on hand—checklists or goal sheets—to improve their thinking. They lay their work alongside the tool and study it, thinking about how they can improve their work to lift it to the next level."

- "Today I want to teach you that mystery readers need to be extra flexible, thinking about more than one possible prediction as they read. Readers need to think about multiple possible outcomes no matter the genre, of course, but mysteries are meant to pull readers in several possible directions. Mystery readers must therefore hold onto various predictions and come up with reasons for these, often switching gears as they read on and gather more information."

- "Today I want to teach you one way readers push themselves to think *across* books. Readers may ask, 'What changes across books and what remains the same?' They answer this question by paying attention to the setting in these books, the characters, their actions and reactions, plots, and themes."

BEND III: MYSTERY READERS LEARN LIFE LESSONS FROM BOOKS

- "Today I want to teach you that mystery readers solve mysteries, but they also learn about life. They know it pays off to step back and ask, 'What choices has this character made? What lesson(s) could I learn from these?'"

- "Today I want to teach you that a helpful time to stop and pay close attention is when a character is having a strong emotional reaction. It often pays to think about what's behind this emotion or what is motivating the character to act this way, and then about what lesson you can take from it."

- "Today I want to teach you that readers can also learn life lessons at the end of a mystery, when they know 'who did it' and why. Readers can learn from the culprit's motives."

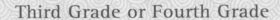

Biography Book Clubs

RATIONALE/INTRODUCTION

A biography unit is an excellent choice for providing practice in reading narrative nonfiction, a chance to develop children's narrative and informational reading skills. Readers will rely on familiar literary elements of story, expecting a character within a particular setting to face and overcome a challenge. Within the "story," however, children will also acquire background knowledge about a specific historical era or setting—what people wore, how they lived, and the societal norms they followed. They'll learn about specific events that occurred during this time period—battles and wars, the passing of historic legislation, the invention of particular technology. And of course they will learn the inspiring details of a notable historic personality, about the trials and tribulations this person faced before achieving fame or greatness.

This genre, then, contains tremendous teaching potential. Global teaching standards call for students to understand a character's traits, motivations, and feelings, and to explain how the character's actions contribute to the events that occur. Readers are required to infer and to grow ideas as well as to back these up with specific evidence from the text. Today's standards also require that students discuss events and their consequences, and that they note the relationships between events using the language of cause and effect and time and sequence. This unit addresses these standards—skills that will support students' work across all narrative texts in the years to come.

In addition, today's standards increasingly emphasize a need for students to be "intertextual," to connect what they are reading with other print and media sources. A reader who is tackling the biography of Martin Luther King Jr., for example, may pair this reading with audio clips of King's historic speeches or with photographs and videos of King leading a civil rights march. Standards also call for children to be able to negotiate multiple perspectives, for example, reading King's biography written by an historian versus reading or hearing his actual speeches. This unit is designed to enable readers to compare, contrast, and ultimately integrate information gleaned from multiple sources, both print and media.

The goal of this unit, then, is not to get kids to remember and memorize every detail of a remarkable person's life. Rather, the aim is for children to grow theories within and across texts, to use their reading of one person's biography as a window into this person's life and times, and to critically analyze what makes this person's story relevant to human history and, ultimately, to their own lives.

A SUMMARY OF THE BENDS IN THE ROAD FOR THIS UNIT

Essential Question: How can I draw on all that I know about reading fiction and nonfiction texts to read biographies (and other forms of narrative nonfiction) well?

- **Bend I: Biography Readers Use All They Know about Reading Stories**

  How can I draw on all that I know about reading narratives and about character development to read biographies well?

- **Bend II: Biography Readers Use All They Know about Informational Texts**

  How can I use everything I know about reading informational texts to learn about the personal story of a subject of a biography, as well as about the time, place, and world in which he or she lived?

- **Bend III: Biography Readers Not Only Follow a Life Story, They Also Grow Ideas**

  How can I develop theories about the subject of a biography that are not unlike the theories I develop about characters in fictional books? Can I think about the person's motivations and struggles, and about what resources the person draws upon in order to overcome difficulties? Can I also think about why this character's achievements matter to the world?

In Bend I (Biography Readers Use All They Know about Reading Stories), you will spend about a week focusing on the narrative, character-driven elements of biography. You will teach students to call on all they know about character (who is this person and what can I learn about him by studying his actions, speech, and interactions?) to get to know this new character, or subject of their chosen biographies. Students will map out the story arc of their subject's life, as well as examine the relationships with secondary characters and influences.

In Bend II (Biography Readers Use All They Know about Reading Informational Texts), you'll shift the focus to the informational aspect of biographies, teaching students to read for information, not just about the subject's personal story but also about the time, place, and world in which he or she lived. Students will not only do this work in their biographies but will also extend this work across texts, reading from sources that are related to the subject or the context in which he or she lived. Plan to spend about two weeks in this bend.

In Bend III (Biography Readers Not Only Follow a Life Story, They Also Grow Ideas), you'll teach students to look for the bigger messages in their biographies, thinking not only about how the subject impacted the world but also the implications for students' own lives. It will take about a week to wrap up this final bend of the unit.

ASSESSMENT

Because biography requires both narrative and expository reading skills, you'll find it helpful to have both the Narrative Reading Learning Progression and the Informational Reading Learning Progression on hand during this unit as you assess children's work.

If you are teaching this unit right after *Research Clubs: Elephants, Penguins, and Frogs, Oh My!* (grade 3) or shortly after *Reading History: The American Revolution* (grade 4), you have likely just—or recently—given a summative assessment in informational reading, and you can now study that data to inform your planning of this unit. If, on the other hand, you are teaching this unit after the test, you will likely have plenty of data on your students' informational reading abilities from the assessment work you did prior to the test. You can then draw on all of that data to inform your planning.

If you do want to gather additional data specific to this unit, you might choose a biography (or part of a biography) to read aloud. As you read aloud the biography, or part of the biography, plan for places where you'll prompt children to stop and jot, and ask questions about what ideas students are having about the subject of the biography or what connections they are seeing between a few historical events. You might also ask students at the end to write about a main idea of the book and what details most support that. In this way, you can assess for both reading literature and reading informational skills.

GETTING READY

Gather biographies at different levels.

You'll want to gather some biographies at different levels for students, of course. On the Reading and Writing Project website is a list of suggested biographies and titles, along with their levels, when available. Go to http://readingandwritingproject.org/resources/book-lists, and click on the folder titled "Archive," then the folder titled "current," and then on the list titled "Biography Booklist." If you choose to teach this unit as a club unit, as we recommend, we suggest gathering multiple copies of at least a few of the texts. Students can work in clubs studying different figures, but they can work more interpretively if they can all look closely at the same text, discussing the content and craft together. They can also hold each other more accountable if they have the same text. If resources are limited, you might begin the unit by making sure that all club members are reading the same text, providing them with more support as they begin this work. As the unit continues, club members can transition to reading different texts (or suggest that half the club read one text while the other half reads another text) as they become more skilled at this work.

Try to choose biographies encompassing a wide range of figures. If you decide to order some new books, you might look through the biographies you already have and decide if there are categories of achievement within which you need more examples. Some possible categories include:

- Figures in American history

- Athletes

- Figures in science and technology (scientists, inventors, doctors, etc.)

- Artists (authors, artists, poets, singers)

- Explorers (astronauts, polar explorers, deep-sea divers, etc.)

- Activists

In addition, you will also want to make sure you have represented people from a wide variety of backgrounds—check for biographies of people of different races, genders, ethnicities, abilities, and nationalities. You may choose to purposefully purchase new texts that highlight achievements of groups of people who run the risk of being underrepresented in your classroom library.

Keep the heroes of your most reluctant readers in mind—is there a sports star or a singer that those students love? You may decide a biography on a figure from the Worldwide Wrestling Entertainment industry (Check out the DK Readers series on the WWE!) would captivate one particular child. Sometimes these famous heroes have their own websites, which include their background history.

In addition to setting up your library with various figures you expect your students will enjoy learning about, consider the multitude of series books that could provide support for your students. For some students it might be helpful to read several books in a series to see how it works and to compare and contrast various figures. Depending on the reading levels of your students, you may choose to add titles from the All Aboard Reading, History Maker, Scholastic, Time for Kids, or the Who Was . . . ? series.

For some teachers, resources will be very limited, and it will be difficult to keep students reading biographies all month. If this is the case, we suggest helping students maintain a steady volume of reading by providing expository texts as the unit progresses. (Remember, though, that your initial lessons will be about helping students read narrative nonfiction differently than expository nonfiction, and you'll want all students to have narrative texts on which to practice this work.) But after these initial lessons, students might alternate between reading narrative and expository texts if biographies are extremely limited.

As always, if your nonfiction is limited, you'll want to support students in continuing a rich fiction life outside of school in order to make sure they are reading a steady volume of books. Reminding readers to fill out and study their logs will be especially important as you look to assess your students' reading volumes and rates.

Organize students into clubs.

If your students are just coming out of another book club unit, you may decide to keep those clubs intact for this unit. On the other hand, after your assessment from the previous unit, you might decide to do some rearranging. As with previous club units, you'll want to do some behind-the-scenes engineering to place students in clubs, while still giving kids the sense that they have participated in their placements. You could, for example, ask students to write a letter before the unit starts, letting you know their self-assessed strengths as a reader, how they have grown throughout the year, and their goals as a reader. Students could also write about their hopes for their club work and what they want their club to help them achieve. They might also suggest the names of a few possible club members, explaining their choices and how the kids they choose will help them become stronger readers. Then, too, you may want to group students according to issues that matter to them. Keep in mind that you'll want all of this work to be settled prior to the launch of the unit so that students can spend their reading time reading!

Choose books for your read-aloud.

While you gather resources for children to read, you will also want to look for texts to read aloud to your class. Just as children will be independently reading multiple biographies to truly get a sense of the genre, you will also want to read several biographies aloud. You should aim to read three to five texts to your children across the month. You might choose to begin with simpler biographies, perhaps picture books or short texts, to quickly immerse children in the genre. A book that we suggest is *The Story of Ruby Bridges*, by Robert Coles, a gorgeous picture book about a child who made a difference. When you are ready to move on to longer texts, one of our suggestions is *Who Was Jackie Robinson?* (Lexile 670L) by Gail Herman (this book is part of the popular Who Was . . . ? series). In addition to this being a story of a famous person in history, we have also chosen it because clips of the movie *42* might be paired with this book.

As in other genre studies, it will be particularly helpful to use your read-aloud time to give students a sense of what it means to read this type of book—to read biographies. Much of the work you do in read-aloud will be mirrored in your teaching points during reading workshop, but read-aloud provides another opportunity to highlight the skill and strategy work in a collaborative and supportive manner. For more about the ways to use your read-aloud time effectively, refer to the *A Guide to the Reading Workshop: Intermediate Grades*.

BEND I: BIOGRAPHY READERS USE ALL THEY KNOW ABOUT READING STORIES

Launch this unit by helping students connect to their subjects, seeing them as real people who lived in real time.

A way to launch this unit on biography is to draw students into the classic questions that all readers ask themselves at the very start of *any* story: "Who is the main character? What kind of person is she or he?" Unlike most fiction stories, however, the main character or subject may be someone children already know something about—George Washington or Albert Einstein, for example. Even though the subject is someone famous and possibly familiar, you'll rally children for the work of this unit by telling them that reading biographies means coming to know this person really well, reading about the unknown secrets of this person's life story. "People think they know about Albert Einstein or Michael Jordan or George Washington," you might say. "But to *truly* know these famous people, they would have to read their *biography*. A biography tells readers who this person really was *much before* they became famous and also what made the person great." Children can begin the work of the unit, armed with the questions: "Who is this person? What are they like?"

Another story element that will figure strongly in this unit is setting. It's important to call readers' attention to the world of their subject. Where specifically in the world does the story take place? What is the time period? How do people talk and dress? For children to develop a full understanding of the historical context of their subject's life and times, it is critical to situate him or her in a particular era and geographical setting. Often, the "character" in a biography lived in an era unfamiliar to the reader. Readers can draw on the details or illustrations—noticing what a character is wearing or the technology or architecture featured—to further develop a sense of time, place, and culture. You might even decide to push children to work harder on developing their concept of this setting through questions such as "How was the world different in Einstein's time than it is today?" or "What was America like at the time when Sacagawea lived here?"

> **"Today I want to teach you that readers ask the same questions at the start of a biography that they do with any other story. They wonder, 'Who is the main character or subject? What kind of place does this subject live in?'"**

It pays to use the class read-aloud to demonstrate this work. For instance, if you decide to use *Who Was Gandhi?* as your read-aloud text, you'll want to model your thinking each time the text helps you answer the questions: "Who is the main character or subject? What kind of place does this subject live in?"

"Mohandas Karamchand Gandhi," you might pause after you've read the subject's full name. "The world just refers to him as Gandhi, but he actually had a first name and a middle name," you might reflect aloud. "His family called him Mohan; he actually had a nickname growing up. I always think of Gandhi as being so important and such a symbol of human rights and hope and peace, but he was a regular person, too, with a family, and he grew up like a lot of kids in India did." As you read on, you'll want to keep pausing to note personal details, reflecting on these details as well, because this helps to humanize the subject in a way that makes him or her approachable to children. The aim of a biography, above all, is to look beyond an icon and see the human being underneath.

"Gandhi had all these older sisters and brothers, but he was the youngest. How many of you are the youngest kid in your families?" Or "Gandhi loved stories and loved to act out the stories he read over and over. How many of you have done this with a movie or book you have loved?"

Just as children connect with main characters in fiction stories, seeing the world through the main character's eyes or identifying with the struggles that this character faced, so too can they identify with the icon they're reading about, no matter how culturally, geographically, or ideologically distant this subject may seem at first. You may even insert a mid-workshop teaching point to highlight this. "I want to teach you that a biography lets the reader see beyond the hero image of a famous person to understand that underneath the fame, he or she was a person just like you and me."

It also helps to prepare children to visualize the setting of the story since they are likely to be reading about people who lived in different times or places from their own. You might say, "These people may live differently than the way we are used to, so we need to look carefully at details, gathering information about their daily lives." You might prompt students to ask themselves, "What am I learning about this person's life? What was their day-to-day existence?" Then, too, you might suggest students compare this daily life to their own, thinking, "What in this book is similar to or different from contemporary society, or my life in particular?" You may point out that though Gandhi lived in India, it was, in many ways, quite different from the India of today. In Bend II, you'll revisit the setting as a cultural and historical entity in greater detail.

Help students bring all of their knowledge about studying characters to bear in this new genre.

Just as they did in fiction, children can be reminded to study all that the character does and says, and use these details to figure out what kind of person the subject is. You'll want to use a demonstration text to model that a reader can pause to take in specific dialogue or actions and use these to articulate a character trait.

> **"Today I want to teach you that as biography readers, it is important to draw on all you know about studying characters. Just as you did in fiction, you can study the daily actions and speech of the subjects of your biographies and ask, 'What does this tell me about him or her as a person?'"**

If you are using *Who Was Gandhi?* as your demonstration text, you might pause at a direct quotation from the subject, such as the one below:

"My books and my lessons were my sole companions."

Encourage children to think aloud with you, nudging them to articulate exactly what this quotation suggests about Gandhi as a boy—that he was studious, maybe that he was lonely, or that he had a serious, bookish upbringing. "Actions speak louder than words," you might add, pushing children to notice how a character's habits and specific behavior give clues to the type of individual this person really was. "What does this tell you about Gandhi?" you could ask children.

This is a good time to remind children that whatever they infer about a subject must be grounded in specific bits of text and should also hold true across the text or be revised. "Be ready to defend your ideas about this subject," you might say. "Note the specific part of the text that helped you decide what this person is like so that you can cite evidence for any idea you have." If your students need support with this work, it can be helpful to provide specific prompts: "The subject is . . . I think this because on page . . . , it says . . ." Challenging readers to return to specific spots in the text and cite evidence for their ideas is a useful practice in any reading unit. Show them how your initial idea about Gandhi is supported as you read on in the text, perhaps by pointing out another bit of evidence that supports and helps you grow that thinking. "I was thinking that Gandhi may have been a bit lonely as a child, but this part is interesting: 'As soon as school ended he would run home. He did not want to have to talk to anyone or risk someone making fun of him.' Maybe he turned to his books and lessons because he was teased and didn't fit in?"

Channel students to work to identify the story arc, including the big challenge or conflict the subject faces and what motivates him or her to struggle to overcome it.

Once you've started children on noticing particular things that the subject says and does, it will become apparent that these dialogues or actions have not been randomly plopped in by the author, that these are emblematic of the "something bigger" that this person had to face—a challenge or conflict. And just as the character in a fiction story faced a conflict and struggled to overcome it, they can bet that the subject in a biography, too, faced a big challenge or a conflict. Teach students that just like in any story, the subject of a biography faces a big challenge that he or she struggles to deal with and overcome. "Just the fact that this person had a biography written in his or her honor means this was an extraordinary life, or this person *achieved* something extraordinary," you might inform readers. "This person's life is not just an everyday story. It is a story of struggle, of facing challenges."

This "challenge" or "conflict" may not be stated outright in the text. You'll probably find that children need to pause, reflect, and find words to describe it, something that may not be immediately easy for struggling readers. As always, modeling this work with the read-aloud will go miles in helping all children. You might demonstrate this work through the very first pages of *Who Was Gandhi?*, reading the description of Gandhi's protest march across India: "Sixty-year-old Gandhi . . . seventy-eight men and women at his side . . . walked 240 miles along dusty, winding roads . . ."

After reading these sentences to the class, you might wonder aloud: "That sounds like a long and uncomfortable walk. I wonder why he is putting himself through this ordeal. What is he struggling for?" Once you've alerted your young audience to listen for the big cause that motivates a subject's struggle, you'll read on, pausing at the parts of the text that answer the question you just posed.

"Unfair Salt Act Laws . . ."

"Started India on a path to freedom from British rule."

Because this work requires some digging and inferring, once you've picked out the part of the text that explains the subject's challenge, you'll want to model paraphrasing it in simple words: "Oh, I see more now . . . Gandhi was walking with all of those people to get people to see how unfair things were. Gandhi faced the challenge of freeing his countrymen from British rule. He was fighting for Indian liberty." To do similar work in their own books, children will benefit from some prompting questions, particularly if they have not yet had much practice unearthing the story mountain in this way before. The following questions will help readers identify the subject's big challenge or conflict:

- Is this person's life easy and simple? If not, what stands in his or her way?

- What is the subject fighting for? What is the subject fighting against?

- Does the subject want to change something about his or her life and world? What?

Now that children are underway in their study of the subject's story arc, you might draw attention to the role that secondary characters play in this struggle. Many biographies chronicle the contribution of other people in enabling a person to achieve greatness: Gandhi's story mentions the role of his mother, Putlibai, in steering his moral compass as a child, just as Anne Sullivan influenced Helen Keller, Steve Wozniak influenced Steve Jobs, and Diego Rivera influenced Frida Kahlo.

> **"Today I want to teach you that biography readers understand a subject's life story better when they note the role that other people have played in their life. They ask, 'Who influenced this subject? What role did this person play in the subject's struggle?'"**

As they progress through the first few chapters of their biography and more of the plot reveals itself, you might help children assimilate the story arc using the predictable "achievement story" structure of "Somebody wanted . . . but . . . so . . ." "The way an 'achievement story' goes is predictable," you might say. "A person shows great promise at a young age or is affected by something in childhood, and then, despite obstacles, the person grows up to do something remarkable!" You may encourage students to approach the book expecting to follow that person's path toward achievement.

As the bend continues, help students maintain volume and stamina.

As you're teaching into the genre, you'll want to keep your eye on reading logs. You might find that some students are slowing down their reading rate. If this is the case, you will want to remind students to heed their reading speed and volume the way they did in previous units. Encourage them to read long and strong, allowing the story of a person's life to create an uninterrupted mental movie in their minds. You might help them set goals for how much to read each day (and night). Students will need directions and reminders to log the total number of pages read each day and to read not two or three but many biographies this month and to log each title.

If the logs still reflect that students are reading too little or too slowly, you will want to research why this is the case. One reason might be that students are encountering many unfamiliar names of people, places, and events. So you might remind students that when we read with speed and momentum, we don't let unfamiliar words throw us off course. Teach them that the most powerful readers don't already know what every single word in a book means, but they instead are able to work hard to figure out what tricky words do mean. Powerful readers create a strong mental picture of what is going on in the story, carrying the meaning of the part of the text they are reading. When readers comes to a word they don't know, they can figure out a synonym that might work as a placeholder for the word and then read on.

Some teachers further support students' work with vocabulary by creating word banks with a repertoire of words associated with biographies: *achievement, obstacle, success, failure, influence, mentor,* and so on.

Once children become engrossed in reading a biography like a story and begin focusing on the subject's personal struggle, you might see that they tend to skip over other details about the larger history, society, or culture in which this character lived. Children can read biographies as stories and forget that they are in fact nonfiction. Just as you tapped into their knowledge of story to get them started in this genre, you'll also feel a need to tap into all they know of informational texts, encouraging readers to look at their book through the lens of history and social culture. This is the work of the next bend in the unit.

BEND II: BIOGRAPHY READERS USE ALL THEY KNOW ABOUT READING INFORMATIONAL TEXTS

Support students in noting and discussing parts of a text that teach information about the subject's world, beyond their personal life.

In the second bend, you will shift your focus from the narrative aspects of biography to the informational ones. A way to start this work is to call students' attention to the fact that like expository nonfiction, biographies are written to teach. That is, these texts will provide lots of information on a topic, and it is the readers' job take in and learn this information as they read.

> **"Today I want to teach you that biographies do not just tell the stories of famous people. They also teach information about the world, including the culture, the time period, and the setting where this person lived or grew up."**

You might decide to demonstrate this work by rereading part of *Who Was Gandhi?*, asking the class to alert you to when a part of the text seems to be about more than just Gandhi's personal life. "Put your hand up when you think there's a part that is about more than just Gandhi's own personal story," you might say. "Let me know when it feels like the author seems to want to teach you something about history or about the rules and culture in the world and place where Gandhi lived."

Read the portion of the text that references Gandhi's engagement at age seven and marriage at age thirteen, asking the students to turn and talk when you notice hands up. These portions of the text provide specific information about Gandhi's world, one where arranged child marriages were common practice, for example. It is useful for children to realize that this wasn't just a quirk in Gandhi's life but a common social practice of the time and place.

As students go off to read today, you might remind them that they will not always find the author teaching information in a big chunk on the page. Sometimes the author will add just a sentence or two or even less to teach some information. It is the reader's job to be alert for that information at the same time as he or she is reading and learning the story of the subject.

This gleaning of information can be tricky for students, and you may decide to give students repeated practice with this work during small-group work and conferring time as well as mid-workshop teaching and shares. During mid-workshop teaching, for example, you might have a student read a part of her text aloud and then explain to the class what information she has learned that is not just about the subject but about the world the subject inhabits. During small-group work, you might sit with a club and ask them to read aloud sections of their book to each other, coaching them to pause and note when information seems to be taught.

You'll want to teach children to pay attention to details such as historical and political references or the descriptions of places and events. Club members might begin making a list (or you can give them a list, if needed) of key events, names, and/or terms that come up in their books. "Each of these events and names has a lot of information behind it," you might tell them. "The author is trying to teach us something about each subtopic." You might ask them to talk about what they have already learned about these key events and names and to be on the lookout for these (and others) as they keep reading. A club reading the biography of Martin Luther King Jr., for example, might create a list containing the Montgomery Bus Boycott, the civil rights movement, and "I Have a Dream" speech. Similarly, a club reading the biography of Marco Polo might begin listing Venice, Constantinople, Kublai Khan, the Silk Road, and so on. You may have a few simple encyclopedic resources ready for children to do quick searches to read up on the items on their list.

Channel kids to read for the main idea(s), chunking the text into predictable sections.

Now that you've called for children to activate their "informational reading muscles," it is a good time to remind them to read for the main idea(s). You'll want children to begin chunking off the text to ask "What is this part mainly about?" or "What is this portion of the text trying to teach?" Teach students that since biography is a kind of informational text, it's important for biography readers to keep an eye open for the main idea(s). As students read, you might have them create little headings or subheadings for various sections of their book or even for separate paragraphs.

Today's reading standards for both fiction and nonfiction place great emphasis on an awareness of text structures. While biographies can be read in a continuous stream much like a fiction story, there are generally predictable sections that biographers tend to use to structure their books. As you teach students about common biography sections, you might count off the five "sections" on your fingers so children follow these points clearly.

> **"Today I want to teach you that all biographies are usually organized in predictable sections. They deal with a person's early life, youth, struggle, achievements, and contribution to history."**

It will be helpful for children to recognize and mark off where each of these sections lies in the books they're reading—ask them to look at chapter titles to sort how the book is organized. You might decide to list these sections as bullet points on a chart to display in the room for readers to refer to as they read and talk about their biographies.

The Structure of Biographies

- Birth and early life
- Youth, life as a student and young adult
- Struggle
- Resolution/achievement
- Contribution to history

Even if the biographer does not follow these sections in a chronological order, children can expect various chapters or sections to fall under one or the other of these headings. By this point in the unit, children will have finished one biography and may be well into their second one. They will benefit greatly from revisiting the book they've just completed through the lens of structure and talking about this within their clubs and also reading their current book with an awareness of structure. As you confer, push children to tell you where they are in the story, whether they are learning about the character's "early life" or reading the section that documents the character's big "struggle."

Teach kids to look across sources to find additional information about both the subject's personality and their world.

In order for children to truly enter the spirit of this genre, you'll need to help them situate the "stories" they're reading within a larger, general culture of nonfiction and research. They will probably have grasped that unlike Poppleton, Ramona, or Harry Potter, the character in their biography was a real person, that this protagonist's roots and influences are not contained within the pages of this one book but in the larger world. One way that children can truly appreciate this is to discover that the events and personalities in their books are referenced in other print and media sources. Just as nonfiction readers learning about a subject reference multiple sources for information about the subject, so too must biography readers realize that the book in their hands is but one source of information about this person.

Clubs can refer to the lists they previously drew up of the key events and people from their biography and research these. You might decide to provide some nonfiction texts to each club—perhaps a few articles about a time period or event that you know will be important to the life of the biography subject for each club. Ask clubs to read this information and discuss what they have learned. "As you read today," you can then tell them, "be on the lookout for information in the biography that reminds you of what you have just read or that adds on to what you have just learned." Clubs can also go back to reread previous portions of their biography after they read some nonfiction on a time period—remind them that their reading will be very different and they will likely pick up on more information they may have missed the first time around, because now, after building more background knowledge with other reading, they will be much more aware of key events, names, dates, and so on and will recognize these when they encounter them. And when they do encounter these historical bits of information now, they will have much more awareness of what lies behind that event. Aided by supplementary information from new sources of nonfiction, club conversations can be guided by questions such as "What might I have misunderstood?" or "What more do I understand about this person's experiences and actions now?"

Photos, songs, articles, news clips, and so on can all help your students to visualize the time period of their books better. An effective way to allow the subject of a biography to come to life is to search for audio or video clips of speeches or documentaries to encourage club discussions. Audio clips of Gandhi's speeches, Steve Jobs's keynote addresses to promote Apple's new inventions, or Martin Luther King Jr.'s "I Have a Dream" speech are examples of audios that will allow clubs a chance to hear the ideas these people stood for. Club members might try jotting the content of these speeches and comparing notes on what they jotted, using one or more of the following questions to guide further discussion:

- What are some of the big ideas of this speech?
- How does this speech connect with what we've learned about this person from their biography?
- Might this speech be considered historic? Why?

You may teach children to pay attention to dates and the age of the person as a way to keep track of time. Timelines can be a very helpful tool to assimilate information, particularly when a book includes flashbacks. Encourage students to keep these out as they read and add on to them, using them to help hold onto where they are in time, if needed.

Help students integrate information from multiple sources and discover connections between the subject's life and historical events.

As students are now reading and talking more about the details of history that they are encountering in their texts, you do not want them to see these as isolated, as something different from the biography. Information and story work together in biographies and you'll want to show students that they need to pay attention to each and also to how they intersect.

> "Today I want to teach you the information that a biography teaches about history usually connects to the life of the person in the biography. One way to figure out this connection is to ask, 'How does what I've just learned connect to the life of this person?'"

You may place a sheet of chart paper on each club table and encourage club members to collaborate to chart a time line of this person's life in one color. Clubs may then refer to supplementary history texts, marking other events that happened within this time frame in another color. Once clubs have a timeline that shows both the events of a person's life and historical events, they may think about the connections between these.

You'll want to demonstrate the construction of such a timeline so students have a clear idea of what to do. Using Gandhi's biography and another text, you might chart the following events:

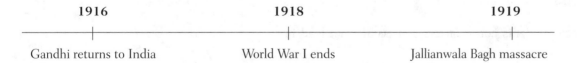

1916	1918	1919
Gandhi returns to India	World War I ends	Jallianwala Bagh massacre

A visual time line such as this provides an ideal springboard for students to talk about how events of the time period impacted the subject's life. "At a time when a young Gandhi returns to India after studying law from England, what does he find happening at home?" You may then point to the historic event (the Jallianwala Bagh massacre of 1919). "This young lawyer sees that British soldiers open fire on his country-men and kill so many. He sees war and violence all around." Allow children to pause and reflect on what this might cause in Gandhi's life. "What might this *cause* a young lawyer think and feel?"

To develop "cause-and-effect" language among club discussions, you might provide prompts like:

- Due to . . .

- Because of . . .

- As a result . . .

- This led to . . .

- One effect of that was . . .

- Following that . . . then . . .

To ensure that such connections are easy for students to make you might have to put in the extra effort to find (or even create) simple informational texts that directly support the biography each club is reading. If children are reading about Marie Curie, for instance, *political events* may not be as relevant as *scientific discoveries* just before and around her lifetime. This investment of extra effort is very rewarding because it allows children to see that a biography is not an isolated story separate from the times but that the life of a person is connected to the world around him.

Often as children study the actions of those they are reading about, they will respond to those actions as children of today. That is, if the subject of their biography lived during a different time period, then her actions are shaped by that time period, but children will think about their responses to events as though these people lived in contemporary society. These are moments for clubs to catch each other, saying "That wouldn't have happened then because . . . ," or "You're thinking about yourself! Step into her shoes and . . ." Book clubs will offer students the opportunity to push their conversations, thinking about a text for longer periods of time and exploring ideas with more depth. Book clubs might explore questions such as

- Would this have happened in today's world?

- If this person had lived in today's times, how might life have turned out differently for him or her?

- What would be your point of view on this issue? Would it be more like _____'s (one person from biography) or _____'s (another person from biography)?

Deepen your earlier teaching about story arc, and help students notice factors and events that lead to important decisions and events.

Now that readers are into their second biography, you can deepen your earlier teaching about the story arcs we find within them. Teach readers to pay special attention to factors and events that trigger a subject's decisions, taking into consideration information they have learned from any additional sources. This synthesis across sources is sophisticated work, and important work, as today's global standards require students of all ages to be able to integrate content presented across sources as well as from various media types. Remind them to ask, "How does whatever is happening now in this story connect with what came before?" Or, "How does this event follow from a previous event or factor in the subject's life?" Students can talk off of their timelines, pointing to events and explaining how one thing has led to another to another.

This is a great time to revisit sections of the learning progression on which students assessed their work earlier in the year. As biographies are somewhat hybrid in nature, following the narrative format but also presenting and teaching information, students can work from several strands of both the Narrative Reading Learning Progression as well as the Informational Reading Learning Progression. Likely, students will have grown in their ability to think deeply about characters and the relationships they have with others, so you'll want to pull out the "Inferring About Characters and Other Story Elements" strand, helping students determine where their current work falls and setting goals for their work within the upcoming bend. You can also pull out sections of the Informational Reading Learning Progression and set students up to self-assess their work in relevant sections. "Cross Text(s) Synthesis" will be particularly helpful as students aim to make meaning while gathering information from various sources.

BEND III: BIOGRAPHY READERS NOT ONLY FOLLOW A LIFE STORY, THEY ALSO GROW IDEAS

This unit so far has helped children read biographies with power by helping them see all the ways they read like narrative stories (Bend I), as well as the many ways in which they read like informational texts (Bend II). By this point, readers ought to understand that the subject's life is not an isolated story but one that was affected by the world around him or her. However, just as the events of the world affected these people, they too affected the world. This bend will help children interpret the lives they're reading about, to see that the biggest message of a biography is that this life *meant something*. "After all," you might say, "There is a reason that this person's life made it to the press. This isn't a story about a person who just went along, thinking only of herself, or a person who was happy to just do okay in life. If somebody decides to write a biography, it is usually because the subject of the story did something big enough for the world to sit up and take notice. The people featured in these biographies are icons. *They changed our world!*"

Teach kids to look for the bigger message in their biographies.

You might pick up a few familiar biographies and hold them high for the class to see their covers, inviting suggestions for how each of these people changed the world. "Harriet Tubman was extraordinary not just because she overcame a terrible situation by escaping slavery but because she then was able to help hundreds of others do the same. Elvis was no ordinary singer—he changed the music scene and still impacts the music industry all these years later. Amelia Earhart was no ordinary woman and no ordinary pilot. She was the first female aviator to fly solo across the Atlantic. She became a role model for women everywhere."

> **"Today I want to teach you that biography readers don't just learn about a person's life story, they see a bigger message in this story."**

Throughout this bend, you'll want to help children interpret this bigger message. Children can be prompted to study the images that occur across the text or study the title picked for the text to figure out a bigger inspirational message.

You might also remind students of the questions they asked themselves in earlier units (Unit 3: *Character Studies* in grade 3 and Unit 1: *Interpreting Characters: The Heart of the Story* in grade 4) to make interpretations: "How does the subject respond to trouble?" or "What difficult choice does the person make during a crucial time?" Many biographies focus on the choices that a leader makes or helps others to make, for example, to raise a voice for the oppressed, to fight for a right, to take a risk by following a dream, or to challenge the government. Students will want to discuss: "Why was this story worth telling? What lesson does it impart? What does it serve as an example of?"

Of course one way to interpret a biography is to look deeper than a subject's story to wonder what this person represents. For instance, Gandhi wasn't merely a lawyer or a politician. He came to personify political concepts such as passive resistance or movements such as the Indian freedom struggle. He became a symbol of tolerance and peace. Within India, he came to be the symbolic champion of local production of consumer goods. Young readers will need to recognize that the subject of the biography they're reading is more than a person; he or she is a symbol of something.

> **"Today I want to teach you that the subject of a biography is an *icon*. He or she actually represents something much bigger. "**

Further, you will guide your students to ask, "Does this person represent a group of people?" (Or more than one group?) If so, we push ourselves to think, "What are we learning about this particular group? What is the life lesson that I am learning from this text?" For example, if a club is reading *The Story of Ruby Bridges* by Robert Coles, teachers might have students pause and discuss how Ruby Bridges is, in some ways, representative of several groups, including African Americans, children, and girls. Students could then use these groups to understand that the fight for equal rights was not just limited to adults. In fact, children just like themselves were (and still are) plagued with injustice. Similarly, students may make comparisons across texts and subjects, perhaps growing ideas about how both Ruby Bridges and Gandhi changed the world.

CELEBRATION

For the celebratory end to the month's work, readers might choose one biography that resonates most for them and write about how the big message from this text has implications for their own life. Teach students that biography readers live differently because of the books they've read. For many readers, reading narrative nonfiction often affects their own personal decisions, that they approach a critical choice, thinking "What would Rosa Parks do?" or "Would Magic Johnson have given up now?" You may want to create a chart of prompts to guide students toward thinking about life lessons:

- I learned from (person) that sometimes people . . . but instead, people should . . .
- I learned from (person) that in life, it is important to . . .
- Even if you . . . , you should . . .
- Don't forget that even if you . . . , you should . . .
- (Person) teaches us not only about . . . , but also about . . . .
- When I first read about (person), I thought . . . but now I realize . . .

Readers might develop these prompts into small literary essays and read these aloud to each other or make quick posters that celebrate the life lessons they have learned from their subjects. You'll celebrate the work your students have done in tackling narrative nonfiction and reading this genre, but you'll also encourage students to recognize that the big lesson of this unit of study is that narrative nonfiction affects the way we live our lives, knowing that these people before us faced life with all its toughness and injustice but came through shining. Their stories are worthy of being told, retold, and carried forward.

POSSIBLE TEACHING POINTS

BEND I: BIOGRAPHY READERS USE ALL THEY KNOW ABOUT READING STORIES

- "People think they know all about famous people, like Einstein or Michael Jordan or George Washington, but to *truly* know these famous people, you would have to read their *biography*. Today I want to teach you that a biography tells readers who this person really was *much before* they became famous and also what made the person great. As they read a biography, readers ask themselves, 'Who is this person? What are they like?'"

- "Today I want to teach you that readers ask the same questions at the start of a biography that they do with any other story. They wonder, 'Who is the main character? What kind of place does this character live in?'"

- "Today I want to teach you that a biography lets the reader see beyond the hero image of a famous person to understand that underneath the fame, he or she was a person just like you and me."

- "Readers, it's important for biography readers to really be able to visualize the setting of the story, since often they are reading about people who lived in very different times or places. Today I want to teach you that biography readers look carefully at details, gathering information about the subject's

Use this list as a menu of possibilities, selecting only the teaching points that meet the needs of your students. Use your assessment data (conferring and small-group notes, observations, responses to read-alouds, and other information) to decide on a plan that is tailored to the needs of your class. These teaching points may be used as whole-class minilessons, as mid-workshop teaching, or for conferences and small-group work. You need not use every teaching point. See the unit overview for guidelines on how much time to spend in each bend.

daily life. Readers can ask themselves, 'What am I learning about this person's life? What was their day-to-day existence?' Readers sometimes compare this daily life to their own, thinking, 'What in this book is similar to or different from contemporary society or my life in particular?'"

- "Today I want to teach you that, as biography readers, it is important to draw on all you know about studying characters. Just as you did in fiction, you can study the daily actions and speech of the subjects of your biographies and ask, 'What does this tell me about him or her as a person?'"

- "Today I want to remind you that whenever readers make inferences about a character, they must be supported by evidence from the text. Readers also know that as they read on, their inferences and ideas should hold true across the text, or be revised."

- "Today I want to teach you that just like in any story, the character in a biography faces a big challenge that he or she struggles to deal with or overcome."

- "Today I want to teach you biography readers understand a character's life story better when they note the role that other people have played in the subject's life. They ask, 'Who influenced this character? What role did this person play in the main character's struggle?'"

- "Today I want to teach you that the most powerful readers don't *already know* what every single word in a book means. The most powerful readers work hard to *figure* out what a tricky word means! One of the ways you can do that is to get a mental picture of what's going on in that part of the story and to think about what makes sense."

BEND II: BIOGRAPHY READERS USE ALL THEY KNOW ABOUT READING INFORMATIONAL TEXTS

- "Today I want to teach you that biographies do not just tell the stories of famous people. They also teach information about the world, including the culture, the time period, and the setting where this person lived or grew up."

- "Today I want to teach you that biography readers pay attention to details such as historical and political references or the descriptions of places and events. Readers sometimes make a list to keep track of key events, names, and terms that come up in their books."

- "Today I want to teach you that biography readers keep an eye open for the main idea. As they read a chunk of text, they think, 'What is this part mainly about?'"

- "Today I want to teach you that all biographies are usually organized in predictable sections. They deal with a person's early life, youth, struggle, achievements, and contribution to history."

- "Today I want to teach you that biography readers know that their book is not the only source of information about this personality and his or her life and times. Biography readers can look to other sources to find out additional information about this person's world."

- "Today I want to teach you the information that a biography shares about history usually connects to the life of the person in the biography. One way to figure out this connection is to ask, 'How does what I've just learned connect to the life of this person?'"

- "Readers, it's important to pay special attention to factors and events that trigger a character's decisions, even taking into consideration information you've learned from additional sources. Today I want to remind you that as they read biographies, readers ask themselves, 'How does whatever is happening now in this story connect with what came before?' or 'How does this event follow from a previous event or factor in this character's life?'"

BEND III: BIOGRAPHY READERS NOT ONLY FOLLOW A LIFE STORY, THEY ALSO GROW IDEAS

- "Today I want to teach you that biography readers don't just learn about a person's life story, they see a bigger message in this story."

- "Today I want to remind you of the questions that readers can ask themselves to help them make interpretations. Readers can ask, 'How does the subject respond to trouble?' or 'What difficult choice does the subject make during a crucial time?'"

- "Today I want to teach you that the subject of a biography is an *icon*. He or she actually represents something much bigger."

Little Things Are Big

Making Meaning from Poems and Poetic Craft in Literature

RATIONALE/INTRODUCTION

A unit on poetry is a chance to reenergize reading workshop. Because they often convey big things in small packages, poems lend themselves to being read, reread, memorized, quoted, recited, sung, treasured, and shared. Poems allow children to notice language and its rhythms and also to notice how a few simple words can evoke strong images or strong feeling. In this unit, you'll help children get started on a love affair with this versatile genre and with language itself. Through strategic read-aloud, you will also model how to notice and interpret poetic moves in prose, then give students time to practice this in their own reading of independent or book club novels.

The children in your room are not new to this genre, even if they've never been formally "taught" poetry in reading or writing workshop. And that is a good place to begin—with the message that poems are all around us. Poems are serenading us in songs and anthems, gracing greeting cards and billboards. Whatever children's prior knowledge of poetry, this unit is about teaching them that a poem is much more than a set of rhyming lines: Poems can touch our very soul. This might well be the transition from singing simplistic "Cat-sat-on-a-mat-eating-a-rat" type of rhymes to a serious consideration of the genre. Or, if your children are already sophisticated readers of poetry, this can be the unit to move them further along with the work of analyzing and interpreting poems. Additionally, this unit will help students find the poetry hiding in the novels they are reading independently, to notice passages that are figurative and pause to consider the effects of the author's careful construction. It's crucial that young readers continue to move through pages and pages of text every day. Finding ways to build bridges between reading poems and appreciating the poetic side of prose will be important.

Traditional ways of teaching poetry have often focused on the poet's own "life" or the poet's "intention" as the lens through which to interpret the poem. In this unit, however, you'll encourage children to create their own meanings, pushing them to ponder a poem's bigger meaning and asking: "What do these lines mean to *me*, in *my* life?" The unit begins on an exploratory note, with children comparing and contrasting several poems to get a sense of the diversity and breadth of the genre. But recognizing that the first reading of the poem is seldom enough, that a poem usually begs a second ("closer") reading, the unit moves onto specific teaching points for meaning making and, ultimately, interpretation.

Notice that each bend also teaches children to transfer the work they've practiced on poems to the context of their independent reading. You'll likely want to reserve a class period per week to check up on this transfer—a day when students will spend workshop time reading only novels, not poems, and your conferring and small-group work will support this.

A SUMMARY OF THE BENDS IN THE ROAD FOR THIS UNIT

Essential Question: How can I read a variety of poems, with attention to mood, sounds, word choice, and images? How can I notice how these elements and the parts of a poem work together to create meaning? How can I read novels with a new appreciation for word choice, figurative language, and imagery?

- **Bend I: Discovering Poetry in Poems and Prose**

  How can I read new poems, examining all the elements that go into creating poetry while also holding on to and making meaning? How can I find poetic lines or passages in my independent reading and pause to think about how these parts connect to something important in the story?

- **Bend II: Reading for Deeper Comprehension**

  How can I challenge myself to look at poems more deeply, noticing how the parts go together to create images and meaning? How can I read a novel and think across powerful parts, noticing how they build to develop deeper meaning?

- **Bend III: Looking at Life and Literature through the Lens of Poetry**

  How can I keep thinking about images and themes from poetry when reading other texts? How can I celebrate the person I've become as a reader of poetry—someone who sees the world in new ways—and how can I share the gift of poetry with other people?

In Bend I (Discovering Poetry in Poems and Prose), you will introduce students to the wide world of poetry, including the use of poetic devices in prose. The unit begins with a class inquiry in which children explore a variety of poems, thinking, "What kind of poem is this?" A poem might tell a story, offer an opinion, raise a question, and so forth. Beyond genre, children will learn to notice various elements of poetry, from form to mood to sound to rhythm to wordplay. They will draw on their exploration of poems to consider how poets play with words, structure, and sound to create meaning. You will also teach readers to notice novelists' use of repetition, of imagery, and of comparisons and to pause to think about the impact of these craft moves. Plan to spend about a week and a half in Bend I.

In Bend II (Reading for Deeper Comprehension), you will challenge students to dig deeper, reading poems with special attention to meaning. Children will learn to notice how the parts of a poem work together to make a whole that conveys an idea. They will learn to notice images in poems, using their imaginations to make meaning of these, as well as learn to think in new ways about the world by posing questions that get at a poem's intended effect. Students will pay particular attention to the endings of poems, gleaning insights from these. You will also give children the opportunity to transfer this work to their reading of novels by considering how multiple well-crafted parts of a book add up to develop important ideas about characters and about life. It should take you about a week and a half to get through this bend.

In Bend III (Looking at Life through the Lens of Poetry), you will draw on the work you began in Bend II, suggesting that your students, as readers of poetry, now see the world with new eyes. Readers of poetry look at things differently from other people and think about things differently, too. You'll then invite students to prepare to share this gift of poetry with an audience through a poetry response, in which they will pose a challenging question or two about a favorite line of poetry and then respond with their insights. You will also teach them to carry themes and images from their favorite poems into their reading of novels. In clubs, they will have the opportunity to co-create artifacts that show the connections they've made across the texts they've read. It will take you a week to wrap up Bend III and the unit.

GETTING READY

Establish clubs prior to the start of the unit.

We recommend that you set up children in groups (of around four) for this unit, using their reading levels in prose as a guide for how to divide them. That is, you will want the members of each group to be roughly at the same reading/comprehension level. Because this genre lends itself to heavy interpretation work, it is essential that group members are positioned with poems that they can comprehend with relative ease. You'll also want to group together readers who can support one another in multiple ways throughout the month's work: to complement each other's strengths, to lift each other's thinking through conversations, and to analyze and recite poems together.

You could decide to arrange for poetry clubs to serve as book clubs as well. This would mean clubs would be able to talk about the same book, share observations about parts that seem poetic, and connect to themes or images from the poetry packet. Of course, book clubs take a bit more management—readers will need to agree on reading assignments, check in regularly, and so on. This arrangement can be a great incentive to read voluminously, but it can also prove frustrating when a group breaks down. You could decide that readers in a poetry club will share only the poetry texts and will bring their independent reading books to the discussions as a way to make connections across multiple texts. This method can help get a buzz going about different titles: Readers in a group may decide to swap books because they've heard about the other members' reads and are now interested in reading those books themselves.

Create packets of poems and poetry compilations for the various groups.

One way to facilitate children's engagement with poems in the company of supportive peers is to create text sets for each group. You might create a separate packet of eight to twelve poems for each group, such that each packet contains poems in various lengths, tones, structures, and themes. This unit calls for children to understand the breadth of this genre, for children to compare and contrast various poems. Variety is, therefore, particularly important.

You'll want to keep the reading level of each group in mind as you pick poems, taking care neither to overwhelm readers with pieces that are too difficult or complex nor to bore them with rhymes that are too simple or ones that don't really provide enough depth for interpretation work. While picking poems, you'll consider the interests and comprehension levels of your students. At the same time, you'll want to push readers into exploring themes or subjects that are new. You may decide to challenge your advanced groups with more complex or lengthier pieces.

There are many poets to consider while compiling these packets. This is a good place to introduce pieces from classic children's favorites such as Ogden Nash, Shel Silverstein, Kenn Nesbitt, and Jack Prelutsky. At the same time, you might include one or two pieces per packet by poets who are not strictly "children's poets" but whose syntax and word choice are simple and straightforward enough for children to grasp. The works of Langston Hughes, Naomi Shihab Nye, Robert Frost, William Wordsworth, and Walt Whitman contain many possibilities, especially poems that are simple yet offer layers of meaning that will invite children to ponder and discuss. Some popular children's authors who are better known for prose than poetry can also populate the packets: Jon Scieszka, Roald Dahl, and Sharon Creech. Contemporary children's poets such Amy Ludwig Vanderwater, Douglas Florian, or poets who offer a glimpse into history such as Joseph Bruchac will enrich the mini-anthologies that you offer each group. Specific poems such as Lewis Carroll's "Jabberwocky" or Laura Richards's "Eletelephony" can be included to teach certain teaching points—for example, the use of invented words. You may decide to have some common poems in each packet, especially poems that you are using as read-alouds or for demonstration purposes.

Choose poems to read aloud from which to demonstrate your teaching.

It is helpful to choose three or four poems that you can revisit throughout the unit to complement your teaching. We recommend that you pick a variety, for example, something short and light such as Ogden Nash's "The Hippopotamus"; a classic, thoughtful piece with vivid imagery such as Robert Frost's "Dust of Snow"; and one or two longer, more challenging pieces such as Naomi Shihab Nye's "The Traveling Onion" or "Valentine for Ernest Mann."

Choose prose read-aloud texts to intersperse with poetry, to demonstrate how attention to specific language and to literary devices can pay off in prose as well.

You will want to decide if you will read aloud several picture books across the unit or if you will read a short novel. If you choose the first option, select picture books that match the level of complexity of what your readers are encountering in their novels. This complexity may come from a density of text on the page or from the thematic sophistication of the story. Some examples include books by Patricia MacLachlan, such as *All the Places to Love*, and *The Other Side* and *Each Kindness* by Jacqueline Woodson. Narrative nonfiction and historical fiction are also options—books like *Paddle-to-the-Sea* by Holling C. Holling, for example. If choosing a chapter book, be sure to pace it reasonably so that you have time to read to the end; endings are so carefully crafted! Given that the point of read-aloud will be to show students how to transfer from analyzing poetry to finding the poetic side of prose, you would probably not choose to read aloud a novel that is crafted in poetry (like *Love That Dog* by Sharon Creech or *Locomotion* by Jacqueline Woodson). These novels-in-poetry would be great options for students as independent or book club reads, however.

Guide students to independent or book club reading that is likely to feature poetic language and imagery.

This is not hard to do, as most great literature for children works on multiple levels and is the product of careful author's craft. But you may want to stock your library with author bins of greats like Roald Dahl, Kate DiCamillo, Beverly Cleary, Jacqueline Woodson, Sharon Creech, Walter Dean Myers, Gary Soto, Pam Muñoz Ryan, and others who are known for the craft of writing for children. If you choose to have students read in club formations, as usual, select options for each club at levels that will not be too far out of range of any of the individual club members' independent reading capabilities.

Set up students to have high expectations for volume of reading plus a new attention to author's craft.

Reading logs will be especially important during this unit, as students will not spend all of class time reading books; some book reading will take place at home because some class time will be spent reading and discussing poems. You will want to save some share time during each bend for students to meet with a partner to reflect on their logs and set goals for reading volume and for what they want to read to notice. You may also decide to have special sticky notes available, so readers can mark the passages they found that were worthy of more analytic reading.

BEND I: DISCOVERING POETRY IN POEMS AND PROSE

Think about how your read-aloud will unfold across the bend.

You will want to stagger your read-aloud work by following up on teaching you've introduced in the context of poetry. This bend begins with inviting students into an inquiry into what they notice in poems. Read-aloud could proceed similarly, with you reading from a picture book or chapter book and pausing to notice any of the craft moves you've charted from poetry. If reading *Each Kindness*, for example, you might pause on page 5, when Woodson repeats the phrase "I didn't smile back." Why might she have written this same phrase twice? What is this helping us see about the narrator? In this way you'll point out some key craft moves that are invitations to stop and think. As you move through the bend and teach into reading for mood, you will echo the teaching points in your read-aloud teaching. In this bend, the focus is mostly on local craft moves—finding and thinking about parts that are figurative, particularly descriptive, repeated, or symbolic. Be sure to mark up your read-aloud with parts to notice, and then decide which you will model noticing and which you will let students notice as you read, by giving you a thumbs up or other such sign.

Set up students to read a variety of poems and invite them to ask, "What kind of poem is this?"

You might begin the unit by immersing students in poems of all kinds and allowing them to explore the breadth of the genre. One way to do this might be to create a packet of poems for partnerships or small groups, such that each packet contains poems that vary in length, structure, style, and mood. As children examine the contents of their packets, invite them to read poems aloud to each other and to notice whether a poem is long or short, whether it is a rhyming poem, whether it is a funny poem or a thoughtful one. This is a valuable opportunity to compare and contrast.

> **"Today I want to teach you that poems come in many shapes and sizes. When readers encounter a poem for the first time, they read it carefully, paying attention to the form, the length, the structure, the style, and the mood. Then they ask themselves, 'What kind of poem is this?'"**

You might choose to read aloud a few of the demonstration poems you selected, to show a variety of different moods and forms. You may also want to have these poems on display so that children have a visual image of their various lengths, structures, stanza divisions, and use of white space.

As you introduce each poem by reading it aloud, you might invite children to wonder and comment on the "kind" of poem this is. The following prompts can be helpful to guide this whole-class inquiry:

- Does it tell a story?
- Does it ask or answer a question?
- Does it give an opinion?
- Does it paint a picture?
- Does it bring up a social issue? A problem in our world?

If your children can handle more complicated observations, you might also prompt them to notice the *structure* of their poems, using prompts such as the following:

- Is the poem short or lengthy?
- Does it have repeating lines?
- Is it divided into couplets or stanzas?
- Does it follow a rhyme scheme? Or is it free verse?

Determine next teaching steps based on your students' experience with poetry. Enhance their knowledge of structure or teach them about mood, with attention to word choice and sound.

As children apply these prompts to the poems in their own packets, comparing and contrasting the various pieces, you might walk around the room assessing ways that they talk about poems, noting the ease (or challenges) they reveal and teaching into these. If, for instance, you realize that students don't seem to have much experience talking about the structure of poems, you might insert mid-workshop teaching points that elaborate what a couplet or a stanza looks like and how free verse differs from poems that rhyme.

On the other hand, if your students reveal little or no problem in comparing poems' structure and are ready for more challenging work, you may decide to extend their understanding of kinds of poems by initiating the conversation about a poem's mood. To introduce the concept of moods, it can be helpful to show a few images (a peaceful lagoon, a smiling baby, a loud carnival, a weeping soldier, etc.) and have a mini-discussion about the feelings or mood that each evokes. Such an analogy will ease learners into noticing that, like images, poems also convey specific moods.

Invite readers to make immediate connections to prose reading.

Either in a share following read-aloud or in a lesson that comes after read-aloud, teach students that they can always be on the lookout for poetic moves. Remind them of the read-aloud work you've already practiced, and prompt them to take the same stance as they turn to their own reading. You may give out special sticky notes for this purpose or have them set up their reader's notebooks with tables that help them track poetic passages and the effect or meaning they interpret these passages convey.

Teach readers to read carefully to find and track the mood of a poem or story.

> **"Today I want to teach you that poetry readers notice the poem's mood. They figure out the mood by paying attention to the setting, the choice of words, and the feelings the poem creates."**

If you're using Robert Frost's "Dust of Snow" as one of your demonstration poems, you might draw attention to the poem's setting (outdoors, near birds and trees, snowy winter) to talk about how the setting alone creates a certain mood that is peaceful or thoughtful. Then, you'll want to contrast that with a poem that has a different mood entirely, for example, Ogden Nash's "The Hippopotamus," which feels lighthearted, even funny. Point out how the word choices help set the mood, words like *laugh* and *delight*.

You might introduce a word bank to help readers talk specifically about mood: *funny, peaceful, wondering, angry, thoughtful, loud, soft, playful, mysterious, haunting, hopeful, lonely*, and so on. Do note that readers do not necessarily have to "solve" each poem's mood with absolute accuracy. It is sufficient to initiate children into noticing and talking about mood at the start of the unit, and particularly if this is the first time children have encountered the concept. As the unit progresses, children's understanding of poems will grow more sophisticated—these early sessions help set the stage for that later work.

As readers ponder word choice and setting, you might remind them to read a poem aloud as yet another way to become attentive to the mood it evokes. Teach students that readers of poetry don't just ask, "What does it mean?" They also pay attention to the sound of the poem, asking themselves, "How does it sound?" You may want to read aloud two or more poems at this point, calling for children to note that your voice, tone, and tempo mirror the poem's mood (and be sure as you are reading aloud, that you are really playing this up). Children will benefit enormously from actually *hearing* that your voice varies as you recite "Dust of Snow" versus "The Hippopotamus."

We readers have an "inner ear" that allows us to "hear" words on the paper, but to actually read a poem aloud can help children with comprehension: a definite case of the ear telling the mind what to think! Encourage readers to notice: "Does it move fast or slow? Does it flow even and smooth, or do certain words stick out?" You might even have groups mark up the poems in their packets with a pencil, circling words that might be whispered and others that ought to be stressed or uttered loudly and forcefully. They might underline words that ought to be said in a questioning voice or a thoughtful voice. They might use the forward slash (/) to mark breaks in the poem's lines for where they might give a short pause while reading. This work will force children to pause and ponder the words and analyze the poem's meaning.

If you decide you want to do more work around using the ear to teach comprehension of poetry, you may have children listen to audio clips of poems being read aloud. Websites such as http://www.poetryfoundation.org and http://www.poetry4kids.com contain audio clips and podcasts that you might decide to play in your classroom. Before playing the poems, you might direct readers to be ready to listen for ways to analyze words that are stressed (and why), points at which the reader chose to pause (and why), whether they would have recited the same poetry differently, and to note whether any background music was played and how that contributed to (or took away from) the effect of the poem itself. Might they have played a different type of music as a backdrop to this poem? Might they have read the poem itself differently? These are all possible conversations, and they will enrich students' appreciation of poetry as a recited genre.

Reinforce students' understanding of reading for mood by giving them opportunities to practice in other genres.

You may want to refer back to the chart you've created with different moods that are possible in poems. Ask students to consider which of these mood words applies to parts of the books they're reading. They might flag different parts with different moods—sad, funny, exciting, and so forth. Then have students work with a partner or their club to reread and figure out what makes a part feel a certain way. You may have them copy particular lines or brief passages onto sticky notes and place them on the chart next to the relevant mood words to create a live, growing wall of examples of how authors can create feelings in readers. For example, you might choose the lines from *Each Kindness*: "I stood there, holding Ms. Albert's rock/in my hand, silent," as an example of an author creating a mood of regret or guilt. Give students time to read on in their novels, with an attention to when the mood in their stories is changing.

Introduce children to poetry's playful, inventive, or archaic use of language.

A unique feature of poetry is its unconventional, often quirky use of language. Children will already have noticed that some of the poems in their packets break a rule of language or punctuation: line breaks without any ending punctuation, or the fact that each new line in a poem begins with a capital letter even though the "sentence" has not ended. "Poets have a license," you might tell children. "They are allowed to use language in ways that breaks the rules. Today I want to teach you that readers of poetry can notice how poets play with language to create rhyme and rhythm."

You may also invite children to talk about ways in which the syntax in poems often differs from the syntax of prose or conventional speech. "In real life, no one would say, 'And yet in moments dank and grim . . . I wonder how we look to him,'" you might point out, referring to Nash's "The Hippopotamus." "If it were normal, everyday talk, the poet would probably say: 'I wonder how we look to him in dank and grim moments.'" You may provide a few more examples to illustrate this point, for example, a simple sentence such as "I gave this flower to her" might be phrased differently in a poem: "To her, this flower I gave . . ."

You might explain that sometimes poets rearrange words because they want to end a line with a word that rhymes with the last word that came in the line before. Or poets arrange words in certain ways to create rhythm in a line. "Poets use their 'poetic license,'" you might teach, "to phrase language in strange new ways." Your mid-workshop teaching might extend children's observations of language play; for instance, you may point out poetic devices such as alliteration and onomatopoeia. "Sometimes, poets actually make use of the 'poetic license' to make words up!" Lewis Carroll's "Jabberwocky" or Laura Richards's "Eletelephony" can be a prime example of poems that are full of invented words.

Children will probably also notice that the language of poems can often be old-fashioned or colloquial. Words such as *ere* instead of *before*, *vale* instead of *valley*, *oft* instead of *often*, or *nay* instead of *no* are remnants from an older way of speaking, and they can make their appearance not just in classic poems but more contemporary pieces as well.

Include word solving in your instruction on poetry.

It pays to scatter the month with big and little teaching points that help children decode complicated words or phrasing in poems. You might suggest that children circle a word or words that don't immediately make sense and try, with the help of a partner, to insert a placeholder or synonym that might work in its place. For instance, in Robert Frost's "Dust of Snow," children might circle the last word, *rued*. In such a case, it can help to remind children to read the words that came before, to figure out what word would make sense in place of this word.

> **"Today I want to teach you that readers of poetry often encounter unfamiliar words. In order to solve these tricky words, readers need to use all their strategies for figuring out the meaning of hard words."**

You'll want children to recall all the strategies they already know about decoding difficult words in prose and apply these to poetry. But when all else fails and the word feels particularly peculiar, children will need to run to the dictionary, so make sure each child has access to one and that children receive support in how to consult it. Once they succeed in looking up a word's meaning, you'll want them to reread the lines to see how their understanding of the poem improves or changes, now that they know what the word means. For instance, in Robert Frost's poem, the word *hemlock* is obviously a type of tree. But if children were to look it up in a dictionary, they'd note that this is actually a *highly poisonous* tree. Word choice is significant in any genre, but never more so than in poetry. You'll want to push children to notice that Robert Frost didn't just pick a cheerful old oak. The fact that poems are short (and hence lend themselves to being reread and dissected) means that readers need to be attentive to each and every word in a way they don't need to in prose; every single word matters. This is why we recommend that dictionaries play a bigger role in this unit than in others.

Confer and coach into small groups to support students' reading of novels with an eye toward making more meaning by noticing author's craft.

You will have dedicated some class periods to students reading their novels. During these times, you will want to use the strands from the learning progression that support students reading analytically as a support for your coaching and small-group instruction. You could teach a small group to begin to connect author's craft to theme. The third-grade descriptor in the learning progression calls for students to be able to think about how an author's choice to repeat an image or to make a comparison connects to something important in the story. The fourth-grade descriptor asks for them to connect these craft moves to what the story is really about or to a deeper interpretation of a character. You might teach a group of students to look across a number of well-crafted passages about a character and ask: What do these passages have in common?

How do they help the reader think more deeply about what this character is really like, or what this story is really about? What exact words did the author use and why?

BEND II: READING FOR DEEPER COMPREHENSION

Think about how your read-aloud will unfold across the bend.

The focus in this bend is on building more complex understandings through considering multiple parts of a text. In the case of poems, you will teach students to think from line to line and from stanza to stanza, not forgetting the title and giving special attention to closing lines. In read-aloud of a picture or chapter book, then, you'll want to model thinking across key scenes—holding an idea or a question that was raised early on and rethinking it in light of a new powerful passage. You might keep a running chart of the well-crafted lines and scenes that you have stopped to consider, and model pausing after charting several of these to think, what can I understand now, thinking about all of these together? How can I use these powerful parts to come up with a big message or question about a character or about an issue? The kinds of passages you are likely to highlight are: parts where the author has used extended figurative language; where the author has introduced an object, setting, or person that seems symbolic of a larger idea; where the author has used description in a pointed or extensive way; where the author's word choice stands out because it rhymes, is alliterative, or feels particularly purposeful; where the narrator or a character speaks in philosophical or persuasive ways—where the text starts to feel speechlike.

Teach children to pay attention to a poem's meaning, noticing how the parts make a whole that conveys an idea.

When children read narrative prose, they often read with momentum, turning pages, moving on, flowing forward on a continuous stream of meaning. But poetry, the genre of the precise word, often asks for each of its words to be savored, weighed and revisited, memorized and quoted. This genre *trains* readers to pause, to reread, to explore channels of deeper comprehension.

In this bend, we suggest that children revisit the poems in their packet, this time around paying closer attention to the layers of meaning hidden within the lines. (You may also want to introduce one or two new poems at this point, specifically poems that invite thoughtful interpretation.) To accomplish this goal, we recommend a series of teaching points that position children to note how parts of a poem fit together, to note specific images in a poem, to ponder the perspective or point of view that the poem offers, and to ask, "Does this poem invite me to feel and think a certain way? What?" Ultimately, we hope children will read more into the words than they initially did, that these sparse words will become springboards for bigger ideas.

To start the bend, you might set up children to notice a poem's meaning, pointing out that despite breaks or fractured lines, the poem is a composite whole that conveys an idea.

> **"Today I want to teach you that readers understand that all the parts of a poem work together to make meaning. Readers push themselves to read new sections and ask, 'How does this part fit with what I read before?'"**

"If one part doesn't seem to fit, readers don't give up; instead they ask, 'How can I use my thinking to fill in what's missing so that there *is* a connection between the parts?'" You may set up readers to use their partners or groups to think across the sections together and talk about possible connections. To mentor this work, you may use a more challenging, multistanza poem such as Naomi Shihab Nye's "Valentine for Ernest Mann," which starts out one way but changes as it goes along. As you read separate parts of the poem aloud, invite children to notice that the stanzas seem to do different things, that they can feel unconnected from each other.

- Stanzas 1 and 2: The poet tells the readers her *ideas* about poetry.
- Stanza 3: Changes into the poet *telling a story* about a husband and a wife.
- Stanza 4: Changes again, to the poet *advising the reader*.

As you guide your class's reading of "Valentine for Ernest Mann," you'll want to reinforce that stanzas 3 and 4 connect to or extend the meaning presented in stanza 1, even though one gives an idea and the others tells a story. "The two parts go together to make meaning," you might tell children, pushing them to notice the connection between the story of the valentine and Nye's idea about poetry.

Lead small groups to support children's comprehension, focusing especially on English language learners (ELLs) and children who are new to poetry.

If children need additional support for comprehension, you'll want to work with them in smaller groups. Some children may be confused by fractured lines or because they don't see text structured in conventional sentences and paragraphs. If you have ELLs or children unfamiliar with reading poems, check to see if you need to teach them that readers read poetry from left to right and down the page. Many children will probably also need to be explicitly taught: "Readers read past line breaks and onto the next line, continuing to read until they get to an ending punctuation mark. This way they are sure that they're reading a whole sentence or a complete thought."

Another way to support small groups is to encourage them to use writing as a comprehension aid. "If a poem is written in a way that is hard to read on the page (words are split up or text is not positioned in expected ways), you can try rewriting it as prose in your notebooks, as a way to make sure you understand the order of the words and how they go together," you might teach.

Teach children to create mental movies from the images in poems.

Poems are often dense in specific images and analogies. You might ask children to return to the poem from their packet that they could picture most vividly in their mind's eye in order to practice creating visual images.

> "Today I want to teach you that readers have to think hard to create mental images. They use the words of the poem and their imaginations to picture these images clearly."

Before children turn to their own poems, it will help, of course, if you read an image-rich poem and model your thinking aloud. For instance, if you use Robert Frost's "Dust of Snow," you might shut your eyes and literally talk aloud about the image you see as a way to enable children to see it too. "I see a blanket of snow on the ground . . . a landscape that is completely white . . . snow-laden branches, everything still and quiet. And then . . ." You might raise your voice slightly to create suspense, "just the hint of a rustle. A scruffy gray wing. A fluffed-up crow seated plumply on the branch, tucking his wings together against the cold. Thumbs up if you can picture it." Invite children to join in your mental movie as you talk, softly, dramatically. "See the way he gives himself a little shake to dry off? Snow dislodges from the branch and plop! Onto the thick wooly coat sleeve of the man below. Nod if you see the man look up and give the crow a small smile that says, 'How do you do, Mr. Crow? You just made my day a little better.'" Children will see that though "Dust of Snow" is a small poem that uses very few words, the image it can evoke is lush. "The poem provides us a few words—we use our imagination to flesh out the rest," you might explain.

Partners might circle the words in their poems that contain vivid imagery, discuss and compare the images they see, and even try a hand at quick-sketching them. You might decide to share artists' depictions of "Dust of Snow" (easily searchable on the Internet) to show that poetry readers are inspired to "see" vivid pictures through their poems.

Encourage children to think in bigger ways about a poem's meaning and about life, seeing especially through poets' eyes.

To further children's efforts to dig deeper into a poem's meaning, you might want to challenge them to ponder the insights that it provides about everyday life. "Poems make us see everyday things in a new and different way," you might say. "They make us stop and smell the roses, or wonder about and rethink the world around us. Today I want to teach you that poems often make the reader stop and consider the unusual. The reader realizes, 'I never thought about it this way before!'"

You might nudge readers' thinking with the following prompts:

- Does the poem give voice to someone or something that usually remains silent?

- Does the poem pose a question that makes us rethink something we took for granted?

- Does the poem make something ordinary look special?

There are many poems that serve as ideal demonstration texts for this teaching. Ogden Nash's "The Hippopotamus" may sound light-hearted and funny, but it pushes readers to consider the hippopotamus's point of view. Robert Frost's "Dust of Snow" converts the ordinary crow into a harbinger of cheer. Naomi Shihab Nye's "The Traveling Onion" makes the reader think twice about an unglamorous vegetable that people take for granted. Invite the class to analyze with you how each of these poems offers an unusual view of the world. Encourage children to write longer about the thinking that the poems in their packets inspire and to share this with partners. It can be especially effective to have a group of children ponder the same poem independently first, and then to come together to share and grow their thinking. The realization that other readers see a poem slightly differently than they did is powerful for children and can be the fodder for important conversation.

Rally students to be on the lookout for new points of view or new ideas about familiar issues in their novels.

You will want to bring students' heightened attention to unusual or unexpected ideas to their reading of literature. A good novel, like a good poem, offers readers original insights into typical settings, characters, and themes. But it takes analytic reading to dig for these insights! Teach students that the same questions they asked of poems will apply to the books they're reading in clubs or independently. How is this novel highlighting a voice that is not always heard from? Readers may have to turn their attention to secondary characters to answer this—a good move for deepening their comprehension of complex texts. How does this novel make us think differently about something ordinary, like a new kid in town, as in Jacqueline Woodson's *Each Kindness*, or a rash, as in *Tiger Rising*? Bringing the kind of attention that poets give to everyday life to the world of novels is sure to open new doors to thoughts and questions they would not have had otherwise. Clubs will be a wonderful place for readers to collect and discuss these thoughts, whether or not they are reading the same novels.

Guide students to focus on the ending of a poem as a way to distill the bigger message or meaning.

Now that children are delving deeper into the meaning of their poems, you might want to talk about the poem's message or bigger meaning. One (of many) way to help readers figure out what a poem is really about is to concentrate on the last few lines.

> "Today I want to teach you that readers pay close attention to the last lines of a poem. They recognize that often the ending of a poem offers new insight into the rest of the text."

Steer children to notice that the last few lines of "Dust of Snow," for instance, help the reader understand why that crow was *worth writing about* for Robert Frost. Children may want to circle and reread the last lines in their poems and ponder how these relate to the ideas and images that came earlier.

If children respond well to this instruction, you might want to continue teaching strategies that will help them with interpretation, for example, by introducing the concept of "theme." In the connection to a minilesson on themes, you might relate the example of a themed party or the decor theme in a store to help children understand. "Do you notice what happens to the city close to Valentine's Day (or Halloween or Thanksgiving)?" you might ask. "Cookie cartons, cereal boxes, and the window displays of all the stores suddenly begin sporting red hearts? Tons of red roses suddenly appear at every flower stand, and every radio channel begins playing love songs? Valentine's Day is everywhere." You'll want to use this example to help children realize that every poem, too, has a theme. "The ideas and images in a poem all go together to convey the poem's main message," you might teach. "That message is everywhere in the words, in the images, in the mood."

Nothing will teach children to understand themes more effectively than watching you model your thinking as you decipher a poem's theme. You might choose to reread Ogden Nash's "The Hippopotamus," for example, and ponder aloud whether its theme is about perspective or tolerance or "looking at yourself through another creature's eyes."

BEND III: LOOKING AT LIFE AND LITERATURE THROUGH THE LENS OF POETRY

Think about how your read-aloud will unfold across the bend.

In your read-aloud of a picture or chapter book during this bend, you will want to engage your class in carrying the messages of poems you've read together into your thinking about the text you're now reading. If you haven't done so already, chart some of the big ideas and questions that the shared poems have inspired. Model pausing during your read-aloud and having an "aha" moment—realizing that something that a poet conveyed is also true or important in the text you're reading. For example, "Dust of Snow" may have inspired the idea that "little events can change how we're feeling in important ways." In the book you're reading, pause at a little moment that is pivotal for a character. Ask students to talk about how this moment is similar to and different from the dusting of snow that the speaker in Frost's poem described. Let your readers experience these "ahas" themselves as well. Sometimes setting up a pause that you know will connect easily to an idea or question that's charted, and letting the class turn and talk to come up with the connection themselves. In these ways, you'll support your readers' understanding that the wisdom of poetry crosses over into other reading experiences.

Teach children to be reflective about the world and the novels they're reading as readers of poetry.

Without poetry, an onion is just an onion, a crow is just a crow, and a hippopotamus is just a zoo animal. But readers of poetry know differently. In this bend, you might invite children to become more reflective and thoughtful under the influence of poetry. "Readers of poetry acquire a special gift: They learn to see life differently than other people," you might say. "They read other texts differently, knowing to expect that small passages can mean a lot, and that surprising truths may be hiding, ready to change a reader's heart and mind."

> **"Today I want to teach you that readers of poetry learn to pay attention to the world around them. Poems teach them to be reflective."**

You might ask children to rifle through all the poems they've read this month and pick one or two lines that were their favorites, or to select lines that affected them the most. "What do these lines make you realize or wonder?" you might ask. This question might serve as the prompt to a sixty-second written reflection that children then share with partners or the whole class. A poetry response might also take the form of discussion, where children pick a favorite line from a poem and use "talk prompts" to extend their thinking.

- This makes me wonder if . . .
- Part of me agrees with this, but another part of me thinks that . . .
- This poem seems to want me to think . . . but other poems (or people) want me to think . . .

Readers might think across two poems or about a poem and another kind of text (novel, story, film, article, etc.) and talk about what they have in common and also how they differ.

The most lasting teaching you can probably deliver in this unit is to enable youngsters to see poetry not just as a genre to study but as words to live their lives by. Poets distill a novel's worth of emotion and wisdom into a handful of lines, which is why they are power-packed with ideas and emotions that can influence the way readers think or live.

> **"Today I want to teach you that once readers connect with specific lines of poetry, they carry these words with them throughout their lives. Poetry can become a lens through which readers live their lives. "**

You may decide to share some well-known or "quotable" snippets of poetry that have influenced you in your own life. How, for instance, you find yourself quoting Milton ("The mind is its own place, and in itself can make a heaven of hell, a hell of heaven.") whenever you're willing yourself to think positively. Or Pope ("To err is human, to forgive divine.") when you're willing yourself to overlook someone's mistake, or even Seuss ("Unless someone like you cares a whole awful lot, nothing is going to get better. It's not.") when you're motivating yourself to make a difference. This is a good time to invite children to pick lines that have the potential to alter the way they live their lives. You may suggest that children reread poems and pick favorite lines or lines that seem to contain a valuable life message. You may even ask each child to rewrite these lines on special paper or recite them to partners or even for the whole class, along with a few words of explanation for why these lines may contain important life messages.

> **"Today I want to teach you that readers of poetry often have a few lines that they know by heart. These lines influence the way they live and contain valuable life messages."**

This is also a good time to teach that readers sometimes commit lines to memory, that they reread and quote their favorite bits of poetry until they know them by heart. It was once customary for students to learn verses of poetry by heart and for good reason. Poetry encompasses the rhythm of language, the friction of certain words against each other, the elusive image and emotion. To learn special verses by heart allows children to internalize the very soul of language. Rather than prescribe specific passages for children to memorize, however, you will probably ask children to choose meaningful lines themselves, lines that speak to them or feel fun. It can be tremendously helpful to have group members help each other with the memorization: Often children will learn a friend's poem by default! You might invite children to wonder why a poem is so much quicker and easier to memorize than prose—how rhyme and rhythm help the brain to retain the words.

Channel clubs to document their collective thinking across poems and novels.

As the unit draws to a close, give students time to take stock of how their conversations, Post-its, and longer writing have helped them to connect poetry with their other reading this month. You might give each club a piece of chart paper and invite them to create a graphic—a table or a map or a chart—that shows the big ideas and questions that the texts they've read have helped them generate. Colored pencils or pens are an excellent resource here, as readers might decide to color coordinate for the common ideas or for the different texts they are referring to. Be sure to challenge them to include quotes from specific texts that connect to the points they're making, and that they in some way graphically show how all the texts connect together through the lens of their club's thinking.

CELEBRATION

To celebrate the end of the unit, you might arrange a poetry recitation or have children come up and paraphrase their favorite verses, explaining why they chose certain pieces to memorize over others. Students may require some coaching and practice before reciting their chosen piece. You might share the following coaching tips:

- Don't recite in a sing-song manner. Practice your expression, making sure to bring out the poem's meaning with your tone of voice.

- Match your mood and tone to the mood and tone of the poem.

- Don't rush nervously through the poem. Pace yourself, and take care to insert pauses where appropriate.

- Establish eye contact with your audience, and don't fidget.

- Make sure that you know how to pronounce tricky words.

If the poem is long enough to allow this, then two or more group members may choose to co-recite one poem, taking turns or dividing the various couplets or stanzas among themselves. You may even invite parents or another class to witness the recital.

POSSIBLE TEACHING POINTS

BEND I: DISCOVERING POETRY IN POEMS AND PROSE

- "Today I want to teach you that poems come in many shapes and sizes. When readers encounter a poem for the first time, they read it carefully, paying attention to the form, the length, the structure, the style, and the mood. Then they ask themselves, 'What kind of poem is this?'"

- "Today I want to teach you that readers look for poetic passages in novels. They notice when an author has used figurative language, intense imagery, or repetition, and they ask, 'How does this help me understand something about what this character or this book is really about?'"

- "Today I want to teach you that poetry readers notice the poem's mood. They figure out the mood by paying attention to the setting, the choice of words, and the feelings the poem creates."

Use this list as a menu of possibilities, selecting only the teaching points that meet the needs of your students. Use your assessment data (conferring and small-group notes, observations, responses to read-alouds, and other information) to decide on a plan that is tailored to the needs of your class. These teaching points may be used as whole-class minilessons, as mid-workshop teaching, or for conferences and small-group work. You need not use every teaching point. See the unit overview for guidelines on how much time to spend in each bend.

- "Today I want to teach you that readers of poetry don't just ask, 'What does it mean?' They also pay attention to the sound of the poem, asking themselves, 'How does it sound?'"

- "Readers, poets have a license. They are allowed to use language in ways that breaks the rules. Today I want to teach you that readers of poetry can notice how poets play with language to create rhyme and rhythm."

- "Today I want to teach you that readers of poetry often encounter unfamiliar words. In order to solve these tricky words, readers need to use all their strategies for figuring out the meaning of hard words."

BEND II: READING FOR DEEPER COMPREHENSION

- "Today I want to teach you that readers understand that all the parts of a poem work together to make meaning. Readers push themselves to read new sections and ask, 'How does this part fit with what I read before?'"

- "Today I want to teach you that readers look back across several powerful passages to think about how those parts go together. They think about what big idea or question they have based on rereading well-crafted parts."

- "Today I want to teach you that readers have to think hard to create mental images. They use the words of the poem and their imaginations to picture these images clearly."

- "Readers, poems make us see everyday things in a new and different way," you might say. "They make us stop and smell the roses, or to wonder about and rethink the world around us. Today I want to teach you that poems often make the reader stop and consider the unusual. The reader realizes, 'I never thought about it this way before!'"

- "Today I want to teach you that readers pay close attention to the last lines of a poem. They recognize that often the ending of a poem offers new insight into the rest of the text."

- "Today I want to teach you that every poem has a theme. The ideas and images in a poem all go together to convey the poem's main message. That message is everywhere in the words, in the images, in the mood."

BEND III: LOOKING AT LIFE AND LITERATURE THROUGH THE LENS OF POETRY

- "Today I want to teach you that readers of poetry learn to pay attention to the world around them. Poems teach them to be reflective."

- "Today I want to teach you that once readers connect with specific lines of poetry, they carry those words with them throughout their lives. Poetry can become a lens through which readers live their lives."

- "Today I want to teach you that readers carry the messages they've learned from poetry into their reading of other texts. They stop at key parts to think about how characters in the book they're reading might learn from the wisdom of a poem or how a novel might offer a similar theme or ask similar questions."

- "Today I want to teach you that readers of poetry often have a few lines that they know by heart. These lines influence the way they live, and contain valuable life messages."

Social Issues Book Clubs
Applying Analytical Lenses across
Literature and Informational Texts

RATIONALE/INTRODUCTION

This unit is unabashed teaching toward social justice. Get ready for it by wearing your own passions on your sleeve. All of us know that sometimes, when we read a wonderful book, we find ourselves welling up with a passionate commitment to everything we believe. Stories remind us that we care very much about justice and injustice and about living meaningful lives. In this unit, you will teach children to take their books and their lives seriously. As you prepare, think about how books have affected you—the choices you make, the kind of person you try to be, the issues you care about—so that you can talk about these particular books and your life with your students.

You may wonder about the term *social issues*. You may ask, "What are these, exactly?" We use the term *social issues* to refer to issues that affect many people, not just one person or one character. A character may worry that she wears torn, ugly, ill-fitting hand-me-down clothes because she does not have access to fine clothing. That is a personal struggle. But we can also think about her individual problem as one that applies to lots of people—that is, as a social issue. Lots of people worry about fitting in and about peer pressure; those are social issues. Poverty is a social issue, and so are homelessness, joblessness, bullying, racism, and bias against older people. Of course, each of these issues is quite serious, and you will want to be sure that you have given careful consideration to the way that you will introduce this unit and these issues to your students. You'll want to consider the way you frame these issues and conversations in your classroom so that you encourage students to be sensitive and critical in their reading and in their conversations.

In this unit, children will learn a very powerful lesson: That by reading, they can watch characters deal with social issues, and through this, they can learn, themselves, how they might deal with such challenging issues (and others). By introducing students to social issues through a reading unit, you set them up to grapple with these first, in a very safe way, through the lens of characters. They can then move on to view these issues through the lens of the world. There are lessons children can take away from their observations of how a social issue is presented in a book, how characters respond to it. The end result is that those lessons trickle out of the books in hand and into the classroom and the world in which students live. That is, students can learn to deal with social issues in the world by studying them in books. This text-to-life connection becomes even more important as the characters in the levels of books most students at this age read play increasingly complex, often ambiguous, roles.

This unit, then, gives students both a way to make sense of their own issues—after all, all of us are touched by some, if not several social issues—and a reason to read. The educator Alfred Tatum says that particularly for disenfranchised or reluctant readers to keep reading, the curriculum has to answer the question, "How can I live my life every day?" This work helps children take more from their books and bring more to them as well.

Stories remind us that we have strong opinions about justice and injustice. This unit gives students the chance to evaluate the issues they see not just in their own lives but in the world. It will give students yet another purpose for reading: to make the world a better place. Students will discover the roots of some social issues through exploring stories, both true and fictional. They will carefully study these and through this will become activists.

This unit builds on many months' worth of reading work and on a repertoire of strategies for thinking, writing, and talking about narrative and informational literature. The work students have done this year building toward deep analysis of texts positions them to do strong work now in this unit. Students have had experience discovering themes in literary texts by drawing on evidence. They've had experience examining how similar themes are developed differently across texts and comparing and contrasting how characters respond to these themes. Likewise, they've learned to discern multiple main ideas in information texts, to develop their understanding of topics through research, and to analyze multiple points of view and perspectives on a topic. Now you will help students combine all these skills and build upon them to become more critical readers and activists.

A SUMMARY OF THE BENDS IN THE ROAD FOR THIS UNIT

Essential Question: How can I apply an analytical lens as I read across both literature and information texts?

- **Bend I: Reading between the Lines to Interpret Issues in Texts**

  How can I read texts—literature, information texts, and texts related to current events—with a lens that lets me see the issues that are hiding in them?

- **Bend II: Analyzing the Way Different Authors Address and Craft Similar Social Issues in Both Literature and Current Events**

  How can I notice how various authors and texts approach an issue differently?

- **Bend III: Bringing Our Reading Lenses to the World—And Making Our Thinking More Complex**

  How can I become more complex in my thinking because I read? How can I become more aware and help others to become more aware too? How can I go through life, seeing more in the texts that I read?

In Bend I (Reading between the Lines to Interpret Issues in Texts), students will learn about some of the issues that exist in the world that authors have woven into their texts. Students will delve into books looking for the problems and injustices that affect not just the character and the reader but entire groups of people in their communities and beyond. They'll spend two weeks learning about these issues by reading stories and articles, noticing the perspectives authors take on to explore these issues, noticing connections between issues, and comparing and contrasting how different characters deal with problems and what important lessons they can learn about these topics. Plan to spend approximately a week and a half in this bend.

Bend II (Analyzing the Way Different Authors Address and Craft Similar Social Issues in Both Literature and Current Events) builds on this foundation. Students will spend a week exploring particular social issues by reading literature and current event articles side by side, with specific lenses. Students will also develop their own perspectives and questions about issues, and they will talk back to texts, bringing their own stances to the conversation. Students will explore the imbalances of power in the stories they read and in current events and will question why these problems exist in the world. At the end of this bend (which may last a little over a week), students will read and reread their novels and nonfiction texts closely for authorial perspective and craft, studying and analyzing how different authors approach similar social issues.

In Bend III (Bringing Our Reading Lenses to the World—And Making Our Thinking More Complex), students will approach all texts they encounter with a critical lens. Now that they've developed an awareness of the issues, they'll begin to notice those issues everywhere, even when not explicitly addressed. As the unit comes to a close, students will take on the role of activists. They'll delve even deeper into current events and think about how they can talk back to these problems, raise awareness, and make differences in the world. Plan to spend a week wrapping up the unit.

ASSESSMENT

This unit places a strong emphasis on inference and interpretation work and on making connections across texts. Before the unit begins, you might plan a short read-aloud in which you ask children to stop and jot in several places. "What issues are you starting to notice?" you might begin. "Write a bit about what you're noticing the text seems to be saying about the issue, and don't forget to give evidence from the text to support it."

Once children are done, assess their responses, noticing what level they are on the "Inferring About Characters and Other Story Elements" strand. Notice, too, their ability to interpret. On the second day, you might read aloud a second text (perhaps in a different genre) and ask children to do cross-text work. "Stop and jot about how this similar issue is treated by this author compared to how it was treated by the author whose writing I read aloud yesterday. Do the two authors have the same things to say about it? Do they say it in similar ways, with similar writing moves? Remember to use evidence from the text," you might say.

If the majority of your students still struggle to develop theories about characters' personalities, you might consider returning to some of the work you did in earlier character units you've taught this year: *Interpreting Characters: The Heart of the Story* or *Historical Fiction Clubs* (if you teach grade 4) and *Interpretation Book Clubs: Analyzing Themes* or *Fantasy Book Clubs: The Magic of Themes and Symbols* (if you teach grade 5) instead of charging ahead with this unit. Plan to repeat this assessment at the end of the unit, and expect to see dramatic growth.

GETTING READY

Gather books and other materials around various social issues.

We recommend that in addition to a large supply of novels, picture books, and short stories, students have access to a wide range of nonfiction texts (including both informational books and articles) related to current events. The integration of nonfiction will serve several purposes. First, it supports intertextual work across genres, teaching children to integrate information from two texts and helping them write or speak about the subject knowledgeably. Also, students will receive extra practice reading informational texts, thus helping them comprehend at higher and higher levels. It will be important to show students that when they read a collection of texts on a topic, they gain background knowledge, learn domain-specific vocabulary, and develop a context from which to better understand the social issues in their fiction texts. Of course, you'll want to make sure that you use instructional methods such as shared reading and read-aloud to support readers in tackling more challenging texts.

Since this unit is focused not only on a deep analysis of social issues in novels but also on current events, you will want to choose a range of nonfiction texts, such as articles from magazines, editorials, first-person accounts, speeches, and other short texts. You can also incorporate excerpts from biographies, historical accounts, anthologies, and expository texts. Additionally, you'll want to decide how important it is to you that every person in a club is reading the same text; perhaps this is not necessary if the topic or social issue is shared. It is also helpful to set up your room so children can be resourceful readers, seeking out information when needed. Consider using your classroom computers to bookmark sites of interest, choosing sites that are written for kids and provide general information regarding social issues and current events. Some current event websites we have found helpful are: timeforkids.com, dogonews.com, kids.nationalgeographic.com, sciencenewsforkids.org, and indykids.net.

Before you organize your novels and nonfiction articles, consider this: Part of the thrill for young readers is to discover and name the issue, or multiple issues, that surface in their reading. Consider this, too: When books are labeled with the name of an issue, students may respond by going on a sort of scavenger hunt ("Oh, here's bullying!") for issues rather than looking at a book as a whole. They may miss that, in fact, more than one issue exists in most books, and that what a book is about is open to many possible interpretations. So, while it is highly likely that you already have in mind a list of books categorized by issue, we suggest you leave most, if not all, of the discovering to your students. If you have emergent readers, you may want to rally them around an issue for which you have within-reach books and give them a basket of mixed-genre leveled texts that make an issue visible. Or you could give them a basket of texts that will naturally point them to an issue that they are passionate about, perhaps even one that has been the talk of the class for a while.

We suggest you deliberately make all of your collections very small—no more than three books and a handful of short texts—so there's room for children to add to the collections. If you don't classify the books your children know best, this is something they can do, and they'll see how books and other texts can spotlight many issues. You will also want to create one basket (and one issue) for the whole class to study together during your read-alouds and minilessons. You may choose to nudge readers needing extra support to the class topic, providing needed scaffolding for those students.

For suggestions of books organized by level and theme to include in your unit of study, please see the Book Lists on the Resources section of our website (http://readingandwritingproject.org/resources/booklists; search for "Reading and Writing Project book lists"). For possible nonfiction texts, we suggest that in addition to looking for updates on our website, you begin to collect current event articles that deal with issues you know will likely be discussed in your room (knowing what fiction books you have available). These articles can be found in children's magazines such as *Time for Kids*, *Scholastic News*, *WR News*, *Highlights*, and *New Moon*, as well as online.

Choose your read-aloud(s).

To mirror the work that your students will be doing, you'll want to choose a few texts that you know will likely create rich conversations when read together. There are many short novels you might read aloud that would provide this. One recommendation we have is *Locomotion* by Jacqueline Woodson. This poetic novel grapples with a range of social issues that have deep connections to current events happening in the United States that are relevant in young people's lives today. Some social issue topics that run throughout *Locomotion* are: power, race, family structure, death/loss, inequity of education, black boys/men in America, foster care/adoption, arts education, poverty, and genetics/illness. As you mine this text for social issues, it will be easy to make connections to many current events covered in the news today as well, and you can begin collecting nonfiction articles related to the social issues you are discovering. For example, when thinking about family structures in *Locomotion*, you might collect statistics and demographics on children in foster care. Please note, this read-aloud is really most appropriate for fifth-graders. If you teach fourth grade or below, we suggest you choose another book.

Establish clubs prior to kicking off the unit.

If your students are just coming out of another book club unit, you may decide to keep those clubs the same for this unit. On the other hand, after your assessment from the previous unit, you might decide to do some rearranging. As with previous club units, you'll want to do some behind-the-scenes engineering to place students in clubs, while still giving kids the sense that they have participated in their placements. You could, for example, ask students to write a letter before the unit starts, letting you know their self-assessed strengths as a reader, how they have grown throughout the year, and their goals as a reader. Students could also write about their hopes for their club work and what they want their club to help them achieve. They might also suggest the names of a few possible club members, explaining their choices and how the kids they choose will help them become a stronger reader. Then, too, you may want to group students according to issues that matter to them. Keep in mind that you'll want all of this work to be settled prior to the launch of the unit so that students can spend their reading time reading!

Study academic and professional literature on critical literacy.

Because this unit teaches toward social justice, you might consider reading some literature on critical literacy. Paulo Freire's ideas and his notion that "when you read the word, you read the world" are foundational to critical literacy. Barbara Comber, Rebecca Rogers, Marissa Mosely, Stephanie Jones, Randy and Katherine Bomer, Vivian Vasquez, Anne Haas Dyson, Peter Freebody, Allan Luke, Hilary Janks, Carole Edelsky, and many others have written extensively about helping students read texts more critically, about issues of power, and about the importance of engaging in social action. Familiarizing yourself with their ideas may be helpful as you prepare to teach this unit.

BEND I: READING BETWEEN THE LINES TO INTERPRET ISSUES IN TEXTS

Teach students to identify and read with various lenses.

This unit begins with an exploration of the issues hiding within the books students know well. Return to favorite read-alouds and recruit the class to join you in finding social issues that exist within them. You may also choose to kick off the unit with a picture book rife with social issues, like *Fly Away Home* and ask students to dig deep to name these.

This discussion could lead you to create a chart—or even a wall—full of social issues and some texts that address these. You will want to spotlight that some of these books address many of the issues so that students do not get stuck on the idea that each book is about just one thing. You might point out that *Home of the Brave*, for example, isn't just about immigration; it is also about discrimination. "The Marble Champ" (from *Baseball in April and Other Stories*) isn't just about wanting to win and pushing oneself until a goal is reached; it's also about testing limits and moving beyond one's comfort zone into uncharted territory. Your goal is that throughout the unit, students look up at this chart or wall and say, "Wait a minute, 'absent parents' is an issue in *this* book, too! Let me show you." Another goal is that these categories become lenses that students use to view both the texts they read and the world.

> "Today I want to teach you that critical readers choose the lenses through which they view texts—and life. When you decide to read critically, you put on lenses that allow you to see social issues that thread through books. Reading for social issues can help you better understand and empathize with people in books, movies, and the world."

Students may soon recognize that the issues they see in the books they read also thread through their own writing. Some teachers have found that when students bring their writer's notebooks with them to reading workshop, they have greater success making this connection. Students can then reread their own entries for issues they've experienced. These issues may weave through personal narrative or fiction writing, or they may have been explored in expository work like persuasive writing. Not only will students come to see that they have their own issues, but they may also find themselves empathizing more with characters. This is a good time for students to pull out their reader's notebooks and do some writing about these connections. They might use prompts such as

- The social issue I'm seeing here is . . .
- This connects to . . . in the news.
- I've also seen this situation in life when . . .

Teach kids to consider multiple ideas and multiple issues in any one book.

One predictable problem you may see is that students are quick to identify "the" theme of the text. You don't want them to go on a scavenger hunt looking for a correct answer. That's not what readers do. Instead, readers consider multiple ideas; they know that texts often have multiple, larger meanings and that what a reader sees in a text also depends on the reader. So, you'll want to quickly counter the notion that there is just one way to see a text and just one issue that is central to a text. Teach students that there are multiple issues in any one book. *Locomotion* is not just about one boy's struggle to cope with the death of his parents, the loss of his family. Layered within this novel is also Lonnie's struggle with fitting in, with a new family, with his peers who don't care about poetry or writing the way he does or even really understand who he is. There might be one or two main issues, and a few smaller ones, but no book is about only one issue. Readers know that issues travel in packs—much like wolves.

Now might be a good time to turn to the "Determining Themes/Cohesion" strand of the Narrative Reading Learning Progression. If students have been writing about their club books or the class read-aloud, they can compare their writing to the criteria in the progression and set goals that will push their inferences and interpretations further, perhaps looking to the next section up in these strands and setting a goal to trace issues as they develop across a text.

Channel students to reread with different lenses, zooming in on crucial scenes that evoke a strong reaction to learn more about the issue.

This work guides children away from sequential retelling toward developing one lens for determining importance in a story. You might also teach your young readers that when people intend to read a book with a particular lens, often first, they read for the story, for what happens, and then they read asking, "What does this story teach about _____?" (homelessness, bullying, losing someone, etc.). You'll likely need to teach into this work again and again as it is not easy. You might also challenge students to see particular scenes—scenes where the reader has a strong emotion in response to the text—as windows into larger meanings.

These scenes, you'll explain to students, are sometimes located in parts of the text that bother us, that we feel are unfair, or that seem implausible. Children can read these crucial scenes closely and try to mine them for what the character is going through, how he or she is reacting, and what we might learn about the issue or group that scene seems to be about. Say to students, "Today I want to teach you that when readers want to learn about social issues in a book, they pay close attention to scenes that bring out a strong reaction in them—ones that present an unfair situation. They notice how characters react to this situation and then think, 'What am I learning about this issue from this scene?'"

For example, you may want to bring students' attention in the read-aloud to the chapter of *Locomotion* where Lonnie describes The Throwaway Boys, "Group Home Before Miss Edna's House." You might ask your class, "How does Lonnie feel about these boys, the ones that look like regular boys but are really 'The monsters that come at night snatch the covers off your bed, take your pillow and in the morning steal your bacon when the cook's back is turned'? How is this experience a stark contrast to the life Lonnie knew when his Mama and Daddy were alive? What is Jacqueline Woodson saying about this issue? And how do you, as a reader, feel when Lonnie comes to the realization that he, too, is a Throwaway Boy?"

Guide students to view the social issues in their books through the lens of character.

You might also set up students to identify the struggles characters face and how those struggles may be named as social issues; that is, students will see those troubles as windows into the deeper issues of the book.

> **"Today I want to teach you that critical readers know how important it is to study when and how a character struggles and to ask, 'What do this character's troubles suggest about the social issues in this book? What do they suggest the author wants to convey about those?'"**

Students might compare and contrast characters from previous read-alouds and independent reading books to those in their current books. You could then chart past characters' troubles and the social issues surrounding these, asking readers to consider how different authors address the same—or similar—issues and what each author is conveying about those issues. As books become more complex, their larger meanings can be statements about social and political issues. Students should begin to see the need to ask not only, "What issues seem to lie within this text?" but also, "What does the author seem to be saying about these issues?"

Children might also consider the different perspectives of the various characters in a book. Readers might ask, "What are the different characters' reactions to these issues? How do they deal with these issues in similar or different ways? What perspective on these issues does each character have? If the perspective is different, what explains the difference?" For example, how is Lonnie's perception of his separation from his sister and of Lili's new mama different from Lili's take on things? What do we learn about Lili and her perspective when she says to Lonnie, "You find God, Lonnie . . . then maybe me and you can be together again." Students can prepare for book club conversations by putting Post-its on moments when they see characters first facing the issue, then struggling with it, then overcoming or not overcoming it. Students can then analyze how other characters act during this moment or how they view it, and they can examine whether what the other characters do reveals something new about the issue at hand. This work will take students past a surface read of the story to a much deeper one.

For instance, a student reading *There's a Boy in the Girls' Bathroom* by Louis Sachar (level Q) might read it on a surface level, simply as a school story. If that student reads or rereads it with the lens of "acting out because you feel different," he may notice a lot of moments he missed the first time. If he then asks himself to consider the role that the character Carla plays in developing the story's meanings, or how she fits into the issues that the text explores, the reader might now also notice *several* issues, wording them as statements about life:

- This story shows that one adult can make a huge difference in a child's life.

- This story shows the importance of having people believe in you.

- This story shows that when people act out, they may need to be listened to more closely.

Of course, reading a book through the lens of the problems a character faces is a very different task when the books one reads are more complex. Often books like these offer solutions for the more obvious, concrete problems but not for the ongoing, situational ones—the problems that are often classified as social issues. In order to read and make sense of more complicated texts, students need to grasp that not all problems a character faces will be neatly resolved. A community hit by war or some other disaster won't easily recover; a family living in poverty won't suddenly be financially secure; a deceased parent won't magically regain life; a boy separated from his sister in a different foster home won't suddenly be reunited with her and live happily ever after. This means that students who read through the lens of a character's struggles (and, ultimately, through the lens of a social issue) must be ready to identify the ways in which a character does change, does heal, even when her situation remains largely the same. That is, children must develop the ability to detect more complicated character development.

Even in lower-level texts, in which problems and solutions and character development tend to be more straightforward, more black and white, reading with a lens can be an introduction to realizing that books can be about more than one thing at a time, and readers can read for more than plot. Readers of lower-level texts will also benefit from noticing that underneath even a seemingly straightforward story often lie several issues, that these are worth noticing, mulling over, and analyzing. These readers will do well to realize that paying close attention to the details in a story and talking about those details with others can lead to a richer understanding.

Encourage students to locate and analyze critical scenes in their texts.

Once students have some experience locating issues in their books, they can use this lens to extend their reading and conversation. They can return to particular scenes where the issues they've identified are glaring. Scenes such as this often live in parts of the text that bother us, that feel unfair, or seem implausible. You might say, "Today I want to teach you that in addition to studying characters' struggles, another way to think deeply about social issues in books is to pay attention to crucial scenes. You can mark those pages and consider how and issue is shown there. You can notice how characters react to the situations in these scenes and determine what that teaches us about the issues."

These scenes, you'll explain to students, are sometimes located in parts of the text that bother us, that we feel are unfair, or that seem implausible. In your minilesson, model how you read these crucial scenes closely, and try to mine them for what the character is going through, how he or she is reacting, and what we might learn about the issue or group that scene seems to be about. You could bring students back to the scene in the chapter "December 9th" where Lonnie wakes up sick, with stomach pains, no appetite, and throwing up: "Nothing but bitter stuff [comes up]. And tears." We read on to realize that this sick day is a regular occurrence, falling every year for Lonnie, on the anniversary of his parents' death. Throughout the book we've noticed Lonnie coping with their death through his poetry, being strong for his sister, making the best of his life with Miss Edna. But then we come to see that even though Lonnie puts on a brave face, his body knows better. His body carries the burden of his parents' death. Turn to the class, and work through this scene. "This scene," you might say, "is crucial. We can look at it as a window to what the book is *really* about. What does this important scene tell us about what this book is *really* about?"

Clubs can then go on to read any "crucial scenes" they identify in their book closely to notice how the author presents the issue at hand, how different characters experience it, whether they react in the same or different ways, and what readers might learn about the issue. You'll want to teach into this close reading of complex scenes so that children see the many ways they might return to parts of a story, linger, and uncover new understandings. In this way, you'll support children's analytical skills—in particular, their understanding of how parts of a text relate to the book as a whole—which today's global standards emphasize as important to students' development as readers.

If your students are struggling to determine which issues their books hold, or what is worth bringing to club discussions, suggest that they consider how fairness/unfairness plays out in their book. This topic is at the root of many social issues.

> **"Today I want to teach you that one way to approach a conversation about social issues in a book is to examine the book through the lens of fairness and unfairness. Readers can say, 'I think this is fair because . . .' or 'I think this is unfair because . . .' and 'This matters because . . .'"**

You will want to support students in continuing to think more critically about abstract social issues. By now, students have learned that one way to approach the subject of social issues is to think, "What is the struggle this character is facing?" Now you might teach them that that is only a starting point. When they are trying to get at more complexity, they might then ask, "What is the more universal issue this book is addressing?" For example, in *Locomotion*, students might first identify that Lonnie is having trouble dealing with being in foster care and feeling lonely. Once students have talked at some length about Lonnie's life, the issues of foster care, and the struggles surrounding it, they may reach for a more universal thought: "Being in foster care can make children feel alone in the world."

If you taught any historical fiction units, you might find it helpful at this point to revisit any work your class did around themes of power, struggle, and adversity, as these themes will likely arise in this unit, too. Students may connect some of the lessons they took from their historical fiction reading to the modern world in which their characters—and they themselves—live. These connections will be rich resources to which students can turn as they identify themes around modern social issues. Some students may question why these issues still exist, even after so much time has passed—an interesting topic they could then explore further during club conversations.

The tools that students used during the historical fiction unit to hold onto and deepen their thinking can also be helpful now. For example, students can chart power just as they did when reading historical fiction, by creating power timelines. Students might also make webs showing different characters' relationships with specific issues of power. You could remind them of this during a mid-workshop teaching. "I want to remind you that readers don't use a reading tool once and then retire it. Readers remind themselves of tools they've used in the past that might help them now. One way they do this is by touring their reader's notebook, recalling when and how they used a tool in the past. They ask, 'Would this tool help me now? How might I make use of it in this new work?'"

Incorporating nonfiction into this bend is crucial. You will want to make sure that the nonfiction texts you provide come from a variety of sources and cover different sides to an issue—as well as explore an array of societal groups. By having access to these texts, students will have an easier time identifying the issues that live in any one text. You can then teach students that when readers have a healthy diet of fiction and nonfiction, one kind of reading ends up informing the other. You might gather some current events articles and say, "Today I want to encourage you to look outside your chapter book to nonfiction resources to deepen your understanding of the social issues you are reading about." By having access to nonfiction texts, students will be more likely to spot the myriad issues living in any one text. You can then encourage students to select nonfiction texts that "go with" their fiction. For example, a student may choose to read an article about the possible connections between food dyes and ADHD, because she is reading *Joey Pigza Swallowed a Key*. After reading this article, the student will know to read forward with focus on which factors are out of Joey's control and which are in his control. Similarly, the student's interpretation of the article will be affected by the impressions left from Joey and the struggles that he is facing.

As students read nonfiction texts, you might consider having them write quick informational entries in their notebooks. For example, once they have read across several texts, they might jot about the ways in which people can stand up to bullies, drawing on their Post-its and other quick jots in order to gather text-based evidence. If you see students grappling to understand and write about the issues that lie within their texts, remind them of thought prompts they have used in the past to write long and think on the page. It is crucial for students to give themselves time to think about these issues, to determine what they themselves feel about these. Thinking on the page is an important way to reflect on this work.

BEND II: ANALYZING THE WAY DIFFERENT AUTHORS ADDRESS AND CRAFT SIMILAR SOCIAL ISSUES IN BOTH LITERATURE AND CURRENT EVENTS

In the first bend of this unit, students learned to read through issues they identified in their books: bullying, divorce, and so on. In the second bend, you'll introduce students to the fact that there are often yet more complex issues that underlie these (e.g., power and invisibility), and you'll steer them to read through the lens of these issues.

> **"Today I want to teach you that there are some issues that hide in texts that are a lot harder to analyze. To consider these issues, readers usually ask some tough questions of their texts. They use those questions as a lens, reading and growing new ideas with them in mind."**

Guide students to explore these deeper issues in texts and their own lived experiences, recognizing membership in multiple groups.

You could introduce a list of questions that might act as a lens for students to consider for both the read-aloud text and their own books, for example, questions about power and voice.

- Who has power? Who is powerless? Why?
- How is power maintained? Who maintains it?
- Whose voice is heard? Whose is missing?

You might then model how to think about your read-aloud through the lens of these questions. Sit with your copy of *Locomotion* open in front of you, as you ponder the first question. "So who has the power in this book? Who is powerless? Hmm, . . . I think that the adults in this novel—Ms. Marcus, Miss Edna, Lili's new mama, even the social worker (who Lonnie refers to as "the tall lady")—all seem to have power, while Lonnie and Lili appear to be somewhat powerless. Yes, Lonnie can use his poetry to express himself and come to terms with his situation, but does he have the power to change it? Probably not. It's not his decision to live with Miss Edna, to only see his sister every so often, and only for an hour at a time. He can cope with the hand he's been dealt, carry himself in a way that he thinks will be favorable to Lili's new mama, but I think deep down, Lonnie knows that he and Lili will not be together the way they used to be, that they won't live as a family. The power lies with the adults in charge." Then, in the active engagement portion of the minilesson, you might have students think about the read-aloud in terms of the other two questions.

When students move to their club books, you may find that they can successfully find places in the text that fit with bullying or divorce but struggle when asked to read with the lenses of power, class, invisibility, and so on. These are complex issues, not always lodged in something concrete. Bullying and divorce, on the other hand, are visible events. One way to help children begin to grasp how these issues play out in a story is through writing or conversing about them, in relation to their own lives. You might ask your kids: "When have *you* felt powerless? Excluded? Powerful? Why? Do these times relate to any of the issues our class is considering—class or race or poverty? How do your lives relate to what you are reading?"

You could also point out that each of us is a member of many groups—groups that are determined by our gender, race, religion, and class and also by our interests, values, and hobbies. We can talk about how a group identity shapes us. How does your position as, say, a Latina woman or a third-grade teacher affect your response to today's headlines in the newspaper? Ask students to think about what groups they belong to and how those groups shape who they are and how they think. Once children have a firmer grasp of the notion of group and identity, you can ask them to consider the groups that the characters in the class read-aloud and in their own books belong to, using this information to think about their various perspectives.

As children move forward in the unit, reading more, they'll now read with a raised awareness of certain key issues, and, perhaps, with a growing investment in these. It will be important for students to talk back to the texts they have read together in their clubs. Talking about social issues can be hard. You'll want to encourage students to keep an open mind and to collect information. Questions can serve as an entrance point to difficult conversations. Students might ask each other: Are we okay with how this group is being represented? Does this fit with what we have seen in the world? Is there something the author seems to want us to know about being a member of that group? Does this fit with our lives? What kind of community is this? What causes people to act this way? What would happen if the character's group were "flipped," that is, if a girl character were a boy or a poor character were rich? Would that change their choices or reactions? What does this say about what we believe?

In their book, *For a Better World: Reading and Writing for Social Action*, Randy and Katherine Bomer suggest that teachers ask readers to make webs, lists, or Venn diagrams or invent their own ways of depicting the various groups to which they belong. This examination of their own group identifications—and with any related issues—positions students to identify and empathize with the characters in their books.

A student might, for instance, belong to the following kinds of groups: male, female; Indian, Korean, African American, Irish American, Haitian; piano player; tennis player; pet owner; and so on. Some groups are fixed, such as race and ethnicity. Others, meanwhile, are fluid: artists, "extreme sports" fans, soda drinkers, Harry Potter fans. Students will realize that not only are the characters in their books members of different groups that contend with particular issues but they are, too.

Students can bring all of this knowledge—of the groups they and their club mates belong to and the groups that exist in the world—to the texts they are reading. You might begin this work by saying to students, "Today I want to teach you that once readers learn more about the social issues they see in fiction, they can examine their own lives—and the social issues that affect their lives—and bring any insights to their book conversations." Then say, "For example, say I jot down a few groups I belong to: female, Latina, teacher, sister, vegetarian. Then I could write or talk about what it means to be a member of those groups: the challenges and rewards, any misunderstandings people have about a group, the obligations that come from being a member, issues that this group deals with. I can then consider how the groups I belong to are (or are not) represented in my book, and what new thoughts occur to me now about the book's representation of similar groups/issues."

You could go on to think aloud, commenting on how your role as a member of the "teacher" group impacts the way you view Ms. Marcus, how in general you found her to be a sympathetic character, but then on occasion you were struck by some of her seeming insensitivity—to Lonnie's lot in life, such as the day she asked him to write about his family, or to Eric's illness, and her technicality when she stands in front of the class and explains his absence. But then you pause and reflect on what it means to be a teacher, to be part of this shared group with Ms. Marcus, and you are able to empathize a bit, to have a better understanding of why she handles these situations as she does.

You may decide to add on to your list of questions of power and voice, now including

- Who has power? Who is powerless? Why?

- How is power maintained? Who maintains it?

- Whose voice is heard? Whose is missing?

- Whose values are included? Whose values seem excluded?

Invite students to turn to nonfiction as a way to deepen their understanding of the social issues they are studying.

Students might also read nonfiction about the issues they see in their books in order to think about what is said about them in the world. In this second bend of the unit, then, students will begin to explicitly make connections between the social issues they are exploring in all their novels to nonfiction texts. Students will look to current nonfiction texts (if they have not already) as a means of learning about the issues they are unpacking in their books—and as a way to back the opinions they are beginning to develop in their talk with other club members. We can model this ourselves with our read-aloud work. When we have finished reading *Locomotion*, we can then follow up saying, "You know, reading this book gets me thinking so much about what is happening in our country around the issue of foster care and the well-being of children and teens involved in foster care. So I thought I would read this article to help me get a stronger understanding of what is happening in our country now regarding this issue."

"Today I want to teach you that critical readers read multiple sources of nonfiction on the same topic to get an even deeper understanding of the topic."

Invite students to bring in nonfiction texts that complement the work they are doing within their clubs. Explain that they can share these different sources and then come together to share what they've learned, as well as discuss whether, based on their growing knowledge of an issue, they agree or disagree with the nonfiction texts they are reading.

Students will read nonfiction texts with a lens. What issues are they seeing depicted? Do they agree with the way these issues are being portrayed in the text? How does belonging to one group or another change the way one reads a nonfiction text? For example, as a teacher, you likely read every newspaper article on education differently than your friend who is a chef. You might consider showing this to students if you want to highlight the role of critical reading in all genres.

Support clubs in lifting the level of their work together by drawing conclusions and studying craft.

At this point in the unit, you should notice students' conversations are growing stronger, richer. You should see them coming with critical scenes marked—with writing long in their notebooks about those scenes or with time lines they have created, tracking power in their text. As they meet with their clubs, you should see them hashing out the different perspectives involved in a scene and multiple issues that can be seen lying within a moment. You should see them reaching back to bring other characters and stories into their conversations and drawing on quotes from texts to help them to do so. You may also see some ways that you will need to work to help extend the club's work together. So at this point, you might decide that you need to do some lessons on how clubs can do even stronger work together.

One thing you will certainly want to teach your clubs to do, if needed, is to draw conclusions from their conversations. That is, you want to help your students see that it is not only the books they read that should lead them to think and read differently; it is also their club's conversations that should influence their thinking.

"Today I want to teach you that just as you let the texts you read change the way you think about the world and new texts, your club conversations should also influence your thinking. One way to let the conversations you have lead you to new insights is to ask yourselves, 'What do we now think about the book after our conversation? What do we now think about the social issues we have been discussing? How will our future reading be different?'"

You will want to coach students to let their conversations help them to raise new questions that they will then keep in mind as they read forward or develop new theories that they can track and revise. You might ask your students to set new plans for themselves that are based on the work that the club did that day, pushing them to think, "How does our club conversation today influence the new reading work we need to do until we meet again?" You might also push clubs in new conversations to reach back, not only to mention and discuss previous texts read, but previous *conversations*. And of course, students will see here that to do this, it helps to take notes as conversations are happening so that future discussions can be richer.

In addition, during this second half of Bend II, you will want to ask students to identify the craft moves authors use in their books to present a stance on social issues. That is, they will closely read and reread sections of their novels and nonfiction texts asking: "Why did the author most likely include flashback (or quotes or dialogue or another writing technique) here? Why did the author choose this setting as opposed to another? Why did the author use these words in particular to describe . . . ? Why did the author present two characters who think and feel so differently?"

Students have thought about craft and structure in the majority of the reading units up to this point, and rather than reteach those lessons, you want to push students to consider and draw on what they already know and then watch them to see what you will need to review and extend. So you might involve them in an inquiry, asking them to use all they know about reading and analyzing craft and structure as they go off to read and talk today. You might say, "Today I want to remind you that authors shape texts to convey meanings and to say something about life. You have been studying the ways in which authors shape texts this whole year. I am going to ask you to draw on all you know about reading to analyze craft and structure and spend time today pushing yourself to do some of that work. When you meet with your clubs, I am going to be listening especially to hear how you discuss the ways in which you see the author shaping the text you are reading. I'll be listening to hear all that you have learned this year about reading to analyze craft and structure."

You can involve students in discussing a scene from the read-aloud, asking them to draw on all they know about analyzing craft and structure to discuss the scene with their clubs. Focus in on several critical chapters from *Locomotion* ("First," "Commercial Break," "Parents Poem," "Describe Somebody," "Eric Poem," and "Birth" to name a few), perhaps assigning one to each club for analysis. You can coach them to keep drawing on past learning as you listen in. And then you can send students off to prepare, reminding them that today you would like their preparation to be especially focused on craft and structure and that you'll be listening in to hear them talk about how the author has shaped the text they are reading. And as you listen in, you will hear what students are taking up and what you will need to strengthen and support.

This is a great time to remind students of the "Analyzing Author's Craft" and "Analyzing Perspective" strands of the Narrative Reading Learning Progression and involve them in assessing their own writing and conversations. You may find that you need to return to close reading work for a few sessions, involving the class in again studying sections of a text closely and asking them to notice patterns in word choice or to consider the choice of a structure or perspective and how that helps to shape and convey larger meanings. You can also push students to do more of this type of close reading work in their clubs. That is, they can discuss swaths of the book, or they can focus their conversation on one critical scene, analyzing together the specific moves the author has made to craft this scene and then discussing how this scene fits into the overall text and helps to convey meanings.

Once students are feeling successful at studying author's craft, set them up to compare and contrast the treatment of the same issue across multiple texts in literature and nonfiction. They might do this by paying close attention to the tone of different texts; how two different authors address the same problem or issue; the use of language, structure, and literary devices (including word choice, metaphors, cause and effect, pros and cons); the varying points of view that have been presented; the information that is given and left out; the ways in which the texts differ from each other; and the different effect the texts have on the reader.

BEND III: BRINGING OUR READING LENSES TO THE WORLD—AND MAKING OUR THINKING MORE COMPLEX

Support students in stretching their thinking to encompass viewing the world through the lenses of various social issues.

Once readers have some understandings about critical concepts, you can ask them to turn to any texts—not just the ones readily available in the classroom baskets—with those same lenses. This is more difficult and perhaps not yet possible for many children, because their understanding of how the world operates is naturally naive and yet to be developed. You can help by practicing looking at anything you read and wondering about how hidden and subtle sources of power, race, class, and gender operate in our culture, more specifically in current events.

Readers who are deeply engaged in their reading and thinking about a particular issue will become fired up and begin to see that issue everywhere in their lives, in fiction reading, and in current events reading. This provides more teaching opportunities; you can help students see their own lives laid alongside their books and articles. Ultimately, you want readers to be able to seek out the roots of these issues, understanding their complexities and why they are not so simple to solve.

Reading across texts and genres and looking at their own lives as backdrops to their reading work will help young readers see that the issues their characters face can be seen from multiple perspectives and have multiple causes, some of which are not what they seem.

> **"Today I want to teach you that readers can examine their own lives as well as texts in other genres to deepen their understanding of an issue they find in fiction. They can discover new perspectives and learn more about the various causes for this issue."**

This is a perfect opportunity for students to return to their reader's notebooks and to use their writing to think through new ideas and concerns about the issues they've been studying across their books. Students might also look at the front page of some newspapers. Taking on whatever lens they've chosen, they can look to see where their issue is played out even in articles that don't even explicitly address the issue.

They'll be sure to see multiple issues, in fact—power, gender, race, and class, to name just some—in these texts. Students might revisit thought prompts to stretch their thinking and to write long: "This makes me think . . ." "On the other hand . . ." "This connects with . . ." "I used to think . . . but now I think . . ." or "Some people think . . . but I think . . . ." Students can use their writing both to start new conversations with their clubs and to angle the way they read new texts.

And here is when you'll likely want to continue the work you started in Bend II of challenging students to consider how their conversations have influenced their thinking. You might teach them, for example, that just as they can write long to prepare for conversations, they can write long in response to these talks, letting themselves analyze the conversation, grow new insights, and wonder.

> **"Today I want to teach you that growing as a book club member means pushing yourself to take the club's conversations and make something of them. Just as you can write in *preparation* for your conversations, you can also write in *response* to those conversations. You can think on paper about how the club's conversations have shaped and influenced your own thinking and given it greater complexity."**

Remind students to bring all they know about reading to bear on their work in this unit.

As students develop and begin to hold more firmly to lenses for these issues, they should continue to use everything they know about reading in service of developing a stronger understanding of the issues they are reading about. We have seen that often, when students become involved in an issue, they forget to do much of the good thinking work they have been studying all year. If you haven't already done so, this is a perfect time to bring back charts with various reading strategies from earlier in the year such as ways to think more deeply about character, tips for synthesizing within and across nonfiction, strategies for understanding what a text is really about, and, of course, reminders for how to keep one's reading volume up even when you stop more often to talk and write about your reading. If you did not previously have these charts hanging in your classrooms, these might be charts you develop or present during teaching shares and read-aloud time.

CELEBRATION

A final and vital component of any critical reading practice is action. Action is often what gives students hope when the issues under study have weighed them down. By taking action, students will gain a sense of ownership and power in the world. You can well imagine how seeing issues playing out around them will inspire students to want to learn more and to do something to help. In addition to inspirational articles and biographies, you might lead students to texts such as *Change the World for Ten Bucks*, or *101 Ways You Can Save the Planet Before You're 12* to show them that they have the power to effect change in their lives and the lives of others. Students might investigate how others have tried to solve some of the problems associated with the social issues and current events they are studying. They might even critically read about these attempts, analyzing if they were successful, and why or why not. Students might assess whether the efforts deal with the roots of the issues they've studied or just the surface.

If possible, use a day or two at the end of the unit to give clubs time to create mini–social action projects as spin-offs to their work they have done together throughout the unit. These can be quick emails or letters, presentations to the class, poster campaigns, the creation of text sets for others to study their issues, or scripted and videotaped public service announcements. Remind students to draw on all they know about writing to make a real-world difference.

You might, in fact, choose to direct any desire for activism into students' independent lives. Encourage students to think about the issues that have touched them over the course of this unit, and to then narrow this list down to one that they want to commit to learn more about, understand more deeply, and perhaps take action around. Students can collect a list of resources—books to check out of the library, websites they can learn from, and so on—which will serve as their go-to materials when they are away from school. You might consider having students create social action proposals, in which they record their future reading plans, as well as any action plans they might take.

POSSIBLE TEACHING POINTS

BEND I: READING BETWEEN THE LINES TO INTERPRET ISSUES IN TEXTS

- "Today I want to teach you that critical readers choose the lenses through which they view texts—and life. When you decide to read critically, you put on lenses that allow you to see social issues that thread through books. Reading for social issues can help you better understand and empathize with people in books, movies, and the world."

- "Today I want to teach you that there are multiple issues in any one book. Critical readers consider multiple ideas; they know that texts often have multiple larger meanings and could have one or two main issues as well as a few smaller ones."

- "Today I want to teach you that when readers intend to read a book with a particular lens (like social issues), often first, they read for the story, for what happens, and then they read asking, 'What does this story teach about _____?' (homelessness, or bullying, or losing someone, etc.)."

- "Today I want to teach you that when readers want to learn about social issues in a book, they pay close attention to scenes that bring out a strong reaction in them—ones that present an unfair situation. They notice how characters react to this situation and then think, 'What am I learning about this issue from this scene?'"

Use this list as a menu of possibilities, selecting only the teaching points that meet the needs of your students. Use your assessment data (conferring and small-group notes, observations, responses to read-alouds, and other information) to decide on a plan that is tailored to the needs of your class. These teaching points may be used as whole-class minilessons, as mid-workshop teaching, or for conferences and small-group work. You need not use every teaching point. See the unit overview for guidelines on how much time to spend in each bend.

- "Today I want to teach you that critical readers know how important it is to study when and how a character struggles and to ask, 'What do this character's troubles suggest about the social issues in this book? What do they suggest the author wants to convey about those?'"

- "Readers, oftentimes the same issues are addressed in many books. Today I want to teach you that readers consider how different authors address the same—or similar—issues and what each author is conveying about those issues."

- "Today I want to teach you that readers consider the different perspectives of the various characters in a book. Readers might ask, 'What are the different characters' reactions to these issues? How do they deal with these issues in similar or different ways? What perspective on these issues does each character have? If the perspective is different, what explains the difference?'"

- "Today I want to teach you that in addition to studying characters' struggles, another way to think deeply about social issues in books is to pay attention to crucial scenes. You can mark those pages and consider how an issue is shown there. You can notice how characters react to the situations in these scenes and determine what that teaches us about the issues."

- "Today I want to teach you that one way to approach a conversation about social issues in a book is to examine the book through the lens of fairness and unfairness. Readers can say, 'I think this is fair because . . .' or 'I think this is unfair because . . .' and 'This matters because . . .'"

- "Critical readers know that one way to approach the subject of social issues is to think, 'What is the struggle this character is facing?' Today I want to teach you that that is only a starting point. Readers also need to ask themselves, 'What is the more universal issue this book is addressing?'"

- "Today I want to teach you that when readers have a healthy diet of fiction and nonfiction, one kind of reading ends up informing the other. Critical readers look outside their fiction reading to nonfiction resources to deepen their understanding of the social issues they are reading about."

BEND II: ANALYZING THE WAY DIFFERENT AUTHORS ADDRESS AND CRAFT SIMILAR SOCIAL ISSUES IN BOTH LITERATURE AND CURRENT EVENTS

- "Today I want to teach you that there are some issues that hide in texts that are a lot harder to analyze. To consider these issues, readers usually ask some tough questions of their texts. They use those questions as a lens, reading and growing new ideas with them in mind."

- "Readers, each of us is a member of many groups—groups that are determined by our gender, race, religion, class, and also by our interests, values, and hobbies. This group identity shapes us. Today I want to teach you that these groups shape who we are and how we think. Readers consider the groups that the characters in their books belong to and use this information to think about their various perspectives."

- "Today I want to teach you that once readers learn more about the social issues they see in fiction, they can examine their own lives—and the social issues that affect their lives—and bring any insights to their book conversations."

- "Today I want to teach you that critical readers read multiple sources of nonfiction on the same topic to get an even deeper understanding of the topic."

- "Today I want to teach you that just as you let the texts you read change the way you think about the world and new texts, your club conversations should also influence your thinking. One way to let the conversations you have lead you to new insights is to ask yourselves, 'What do we now think about the book after our conversation? What do we now think about the social issues we have been discussing? How will our future reading be different?'"

- "Today I want to remind you that authors shape texts to convey meanings and to say something about life. You have been studying the ways in which authors shape texts this whole year. Thoughtful readers closely read and reread sections of their novels and nonfiction texts to analyze craft and structure, asking themselves: 'Why did the author most likely include flashback (or quotes or dialogue or another writing technique) here? Why did the author choose this setting as opposed to another? Why did the author use these words in particular to describe . . . ? Why did the author present two characters who think and feel so differently?'"

- "Today I want to teach you that readers compare and contrast the treatment of the same issue across multiple texts in literature and nonfiction. They might do this by paying close attention to the tone of different texts; how two different authors address the same problem or issue; the use of language, structure, and literary devices (including word choice, metaphors, cause and effect, pros and cons); the varying points of view that have been presented; the information that is given and left out; the ways in which the texts differ from each other; and the different effect the texts have on the reader."

BEND III: BRINGING OUR READING LENSES TO THE WORLD—AND MAKING OUR THINKING MORE COMPLEX

- "Today I want to teach you that readers can examine their own lives as well as texts in other genres to deepen their understanding of an issue they find in fiction. They can discover new perspectives and learn more about the various causes for this issue."

- "Today I want to teach you that readers can use writing to stretch their thinking about what they are reading. Some helpful prompts include: 'This makes me think . . .' 'On the other hand . . .' 'This connects with . . .' 'I used to think . . . but now I think . . .' or 'Some people think . . . but I think. . . .'"

- "Today I want to teach you that growing as a book club member means pushing yourself to take the club's conversations and make something of them. Just as you can write in *preparation* for your conversations, you can also write in *response* to those conversations. You can think on paper about how the club's conversations have shaped and influenced your own thinking and given it greater complexity.

- "Today I want to remind you that readers are always building on what they already know. Readers use strategies they've already learned in order to develop a stronger understanding of the issues they are reading about."

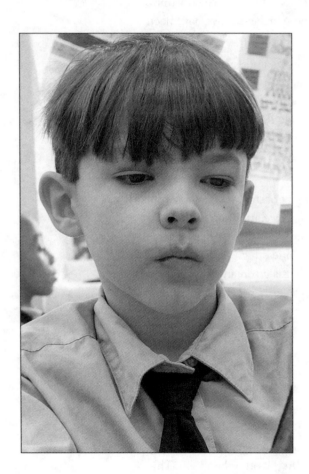

Author Study
Reading Like a Fan

RATIONALE/INTRODUCTION

Every teacher recognizes the children who have become lifelong readers. They may have come to you this way, or they may have turned a wondrous corner in your class. These avid readers are recognizable because they carry books around. They talk about genres and authors. They try to get other people—adults and children—to read the books they love. They are fans. The goal of this unit is to turn *all* your students into fans of books, of authors, and of reading.

You'll already have accomplished this work for a lot of your readers, and this unit will serve to deepen their commitment and expertise. Reading workshop, at its heart, aims to set young people on the path to becoming lifelong readers. But what about the youngsters who come into your room preconditioned to believe that they aren't "great readers"? Every teacher worries about those students who are slower to grasp the habits of "real" readers: They can't really remember the books they read recently, they have no "next must-read" books lined up in their minds, and they often leave books unfinished. Of course, these are probably the same students who need help decoding and synthesizing, who might even need help with phonics still, and who likely have not found enough books to engage them at their within-reach level. But far deeper than all the mechanics, these kids may not even think of themselves as readers. They may be hovering on the periphery of your inner circle, never quite identifying with the things that make *other* students passionate, nose-in-book, lost-to-the-world readers. At this point in the year, you likely have these students first and foremost on your mind. "There's not much time left," you might be thinking, "Is there another way I might be able to reach them?"

In this unit of study, you'll stretch your arms wide and gather *all* of your students into the inner circle. Whatever their level and previous success with reading, in this unit, your students will articulate their identities as readers. Specifically, they will identify one book, one author, who speaks to them—and then become experts and insiders on everything this author has written and everything this author stands for. It is a powerful thing for a child to be able to say, "Oh my favorite author is so-and-so." Name-dropping alone is a way to hitch himself to the literary world. It is even more powerful for this child to be able to tell you precisely *why* his favorite author is special, to list titles by the author, and to comment on how the author has changed this student's way of living in and seeing the world.

This unit of study taps into the power of studying an author's work closely, of eagerly anticipating reading another book by this author, and of becoming enriched by the craft and life lessons this author's books provide. This work will pull students firmly into forging a unique personal literary identity by attaching their own name to that of an author who speaks to them. With your help, this is work that *all* students—not just the strongest ones in the room—can do.

Although you could teach this unit earlier, we suggest you save it for close to the end of the year. By setting up students to become fans of particular authors, you set the stage eventually for voracious summer reading. Students can't possibly read all of the books by one author in the final weeks of the school year. They can, however, whet their appetites and practice coming up with the kinds of focused game plans for independent reading that will lead to growth later over summer vacation. That reading will be crucial to their ongoing reading growth.

Another important goal to bear in mind is that this is a crucial opportunity to provide readers with support in moving up levels of text difficulty. Now is the perfect time to help students who are ready to break into another level to do so. You know how to do this—put them in collections of texts that transition to the next level or band of text complexity, provide text introductions and same-book partnerships, and support some of the new vocabulary that readers will encounter. The real job, however, is providing motivation. With a final push, your students will enter a new grade reading at a whole different level. Just think about the texts that will become accessible to them as a result! So do the book talks/book buzzes that create excitement around the newly accessible books, pulling in any kids who've loved these books to help sell them. The social energy of the kids who've loved these books will help energize this final push.

A SUMMARY OF THE BENDS IN THE ROAD FOR THIS UNIT

Essential Question: How can I connect to an author and his or her body of work in a way that inspires me to become enriched by the craft as well as themes that this author embraces in their writing?

- **Bend I: When Readers Read More Than One Book by the Same Author, They Come to Know That Author**

  How can I follow an author like a fan, learning not only about the distinctive craft moves the author tends to make but also about the topics and themes that the author tends to address? How can I notice the similar and different ways that an author approaches the same themes throughout his or her writing?

- **Bend II: Reading Many Books by a Beloved Author Means Apprenticing Oneself to That Author's Craft**

  How can I come to know an author well so that I am aware of that author's distinctive craft moves? How can I study the way an author uses craft techniques to develop his or her theme? How can I apprentice myself to an author's craft so that I read, aware that I could try some of what an author has done in my own writing?

- **Bend III: Becoming an Author Expert**

  How can I become an author expert, becoming so knowledgeable about an author that I can talk about and reference that author's works almost automatically, as if I were a literary critic?

- **Bend IV: Readers Explore the Deeper Connections That an Author Inspires in Them**

  How can I learn life lessons from the authors that I love? How can live my life differently because of what I read?

In Bend I (When Readers Read More Than One Book by the Same Author, They Come to Know That Author), students will spend a little over a week working in clubs to get to know an author, by reading or rereading one or two books by this author. Students will study particular aspects of the content in the book they are currently reading and think about how these aspects might in fact be hallmarks of this author's body of work.

In Bend II (Reading Many Books by a Beloved Author Means Apprenticing Oneself to That Author's Craft), clubs will draw on all the work they have done across the year around authorial intent to note and name specific craft moves that this author makes, apprenticing themselves to the author's craft and use of language. Bend II should take about a week.

By Bend III (Becoming an Author Expert), your readers will have read many books by this author and perhaps texts about the author; they will then be in a better position to compare and contrast across texts. At this stage, clubs can begin to analyze themes that recur in the author's books and also evaluate the bigger life messages that the author seems to forward in every book. Plan to spend about a week in Bend III.

In Bend IV (Readers Explore the Deeper Connections That an Author Inspires in Them), students will end on an introspective note, with each individual reader exploring why he or she gravitates to one particular author over another and noting ways in which a favorite author's work moves and shapes his or her own thinking about a particular subject. With that author's work firmly in the reader's grasp, the student will then make plans to use everything he or she has learned over the unit to prepare for a summer filled with passionate reading. You should be able to wrap up the unit in just a few days.

GETTING READY

Select an author that you are a fan of, to use for demonstration purposes throughout the unit.

The first thing you'll want to consider is: What author and book are you a fan of? You'll want to demonstrate the enthusiasm and knowledge that you want your children to show for books. So ask yourself: Will you go back to a childhood favorite? Will it be Nancy Drew, or *Misty of Chincoteague?* Will you show kids how you are a fan right now of certain books and authors? Will it be *The Hunt for Red October?* You'll also talk about television series you've been a fan of, so think of those. Are you more of a fan of *Breaking Bad* or *Downton Abbey?* Your children will pick up on the genuine enjoyment you feel. You may also want to be strategic and choose a series that you'll talk about, as you know it will do your students so much good to fall in love with a series that they might continue over the summer. So maybe you'll bring out The Babysitters' Club, or The Boxcar Mysteries. When you know what you'll have on hand to demonstrate your own "fan" status, then think about what books you want to have on hand for children.

Engage students in helping you to gather and create text and author sets.

Next, you want to make it easy for your students to dive into author studies. Children can help you with this work—in the days before the unit, gather some of your readers and ask them to help create text sets, thinking about the authors they've loved, roaming the school gathering books, asking families to loan books, or going to the library.

You'll want to pick the strongest, the best-selling, and the most popular authors to anchor this unit, authors like Gary Paulsen, Jacqueline Woodson, James Howe, Kate DiCamillo, Sarah Weeks, Pam Muñoz Ryan, Gary Soto, Patricia MacLachlan, Wendy Mass, Patricia Reilly Giff, Clyde Robert Bulla, Walter Dean Myers, Laurence Yep, Judy Blume, Tom Angleberger—this could be a very long and varied list. The determining factors are the students in your room. Mine your library for the titles that have proven most popular in the preceding months, and invite feedback from your kids. Distribute slips of paper for them to write the title of the one or two books they've loved the most, or the authors they'd love to read more of, and factor this in when you make text sets.

Remember that you want your children reading a lot in this unit, so think about what kinds of books they might most like to read. As you consider reading interests, ask yourself whether some of your students crave Gary Paulsen-esque adventure stories and sulk through slower-paced relationship-oriented stories. Might others love to come together to talk formally about Judy Blume's plotlines? Do you have a few philosophers who can unpeel several interpretive layers off a Patricia MacLachlan novel? Keep your students' faces in mind while handpicking the authors around which you create a text set of books. Keep in mind your students' reading levels, too. One advantage is that some authors, like Gary Paulsen, have written books at a variety of levels that can support a range of readers. Paulsen titles include *Worksong* (J), *Dogteam* (P), *Hatchet* (R), *The Winter Room* (U), and *Sarny* (W).

You will notice that in addition to writing at many levels, Paulsen also has a variety of books at each level. You might choose to have two separate text sets for this author, to cater to two clubs reading at separate levels—or even make the bold move of putting different-leveled readers in the same Paulsen club. The latter would require enough books to hold everyone's interest across the month. This uneven pairing of different levels might pull some students up to a higher level, since they'll have more proficient peers with whom to discuss and interpret a shared author. Or it may backfire and frustrate readers who are used to reading and interpreting at disparate levels! These are calculated risks that only you, with your knowledge of your particular students, can make. Monitor club progress closely to offset such problems before they bloom full-fledged.

Set up clubs prior to launching the unit.

Create reading clubs with no more than four students per club, if possible. If half the class opts fervently for the same favorite author, you might create two different clubs for this one author, guiding the clubs to swap books after they have read and discussed them and perhaps later asking these clubs to come together to compare notes. As much as possible, match readers to their first author choice. You'll want to make informed, carefully weighed decisions about which readers are placed in which particular club, putting readers' taste preference at the forefront of this decision. You'll also want to group together readers who can support one another in multiple ways throughout the month's work. Encourage clubs to get their own books as well—do they want to actually bring books in, so they can write in the books? Can they bypass that bag of chips and soda to get a favorite book? Do you want to have a class bake sale and buy used books? Teaching children to seek books is teaching them to be lifelong readers.

Choose your read-aloud(s).

As you consider what texts you'll use for your read-aloud, you'll want to base this choice on a few factors. A primary concern, as in your choices for your club texts, will be students' interests. Choose an author that you know will grab your their attention. Make sure that the author you select has at least a few short texts that you can get through relatively quickly, as this unit addresses cross-text work. You might, therefore, choose an author, like Sandra Cisneros or Patricia Polacco, with a variety of high-level shorter texts. You might also choose to focus on an author who has a combination of shorter and longer texts such as Cynthia Rylant, James Howe, Kevin Henkes, or Sarah Weeks, or a collection of stories in an author's anthology, such as Avi's *What Do Fish Have to Do with Anything?*

ASSESSMENT

Chances are that you have available both performance assessment data and reading levels for your students. You'll want to study those reading levels and think about which students need to really focus on moving up levels in this unit of study. You might want to channel those students into some series reading, so that their volume of reading is high. You might also plan some guided reading groups that introduce them to their next instructional reading level and set them up to continue at that level with some assistance from you. When you study your performance assessments, which are probably reading responses, think about the reader's notebook work students might do in this unit.

As with all units, we encourage you to tailor your teaching to the data you gather. If the majority of students still struggle to develop more interpretive ideas about the lessons in stories, you might consider returning to some of the work you did in the character, historical fiction, or social issues unit. Plan to repeat this assessment at the end of the unit, and consider if there are ways that you might pass these assessments onto the next grade's teachers.

The importance of reviewing your data gathered throughout the year is critical as we approach this last unit. You'll start by guiding students as they continue to move through and up reading levels. Toward the end of the unit, you will want to help students set up reading plans for themselves so that this work continues independently through the summer. This is a chance to keep pushing for growth and end the year on a strong point, helping students to feel confident in their reading levels as they embark into summer and prepare for middle school.

BEND I: WHEN READERS READ MORE THAN ONE BOOK BY THE SAME AUTHOR, THEY COME TO KNOW THAT AUTHOR

You'll launch this study by having students read or reread books by their chosen author, marveling at the craft and the story, allowing themselves to be swept away by the author's writing. They'll read a bit about the author, and compare what they've read before, and then students will get down to the work of reading (and rereading) a lot of texts.

As the study launches, guide clubs to read or reread a book by their chosen author, studying it deeply to begin to notice the hallmarks of the author's craft and story.

This will mean different things for different readers. To readers who begin this study having only read a single book by their chosen author, you might suggest that they start off by *rereading* that one book. Other clubs might decide that because they all know different books by their author, they will start the unit by choosing a new one together, perhaps with familiar characters (if the book is part of a series). Either way, readers will study this first book closely, looking for the author's fingerprints.

How does one really get to know an author? Flocks of tourists throng to see Hans Christian Andersen's Copenhagen house, tourists seek out the bronze sculpture of Lewis Carroll's Alice sitting on a mushroom in Central Park, and, now, crowds rush to drink butterbeer at the Harry Potter theme park in Orlando. This, however, is not the stuff an author study is truly made of. Nor does one really get to know an author by mining biographical trivia. To become an expert on an author, we don't need to visit their shrine or hometown or interview them. To become an expert on an author, readers devour as many books by that author as they can lay their hands on. We read and reread favorite parts and underline the lines that make us laugh aloud or stop to think again. This is the message you'll want to begin this unit on author studies with, teaching clubs to simply read and reread books that their chosen author has written.

To be a true fan of an author, one of the first steps readers will take, whether this is their first book by the author or their twenty-first, is to marvel at the craft *and* the story. Students will learn to stop and take notice when they find themselves laughing out loud, gasping with excitement, tearing up, or in other ways impressed by their author. You want students to fall in love with their authors—to come to club meetings with favorite moments, sentences, even just words marked and ready to linger over and share.

On this first day you might gather your students and say something like, "You know how when you're a fan of a musician, you listen to that singer's songs over and over and memorize every word? And when you're a fan of a sports team, you try to see every game? You might even buy your favorite player's jersey to wear, right? Well you can be a fan of an author in the same way!" Then launch into your teaching point.

> **"Today I want to teach you that when you're a fan of an author, you try to read every book that author has written—sometimes more than once—poring over and marking favorite parts to reread and share—parts where you laughed, cried, or were surprised."**

Guide students to think about story elements as they are analyzing their author's style and getting to know him or her as a craftsman.

Once readers are immersed in their stories and enamored with their authors, you'll expect to see them remembering lessons learned across the year on the importance of particular story elements, perhaps turning their attention to the kinds of settings the author describes, the themes she explores, and, of course, to the characters she creates. About the setting, readers might ask, "What is the world of the story?" and "Does this author always create this same world or similar worlds?" Or they might turn their attention to the main character and ask, "Who is the hero of this story? Is this hero like the hero or heroine in another book by this author?" In their club conversations, each child might report on the setting and the characters in his or her book, and together, the club can then begin to compare these.

The Patricia MacLachlan Club might note, "The stories *Journey* and *Sarah, Plain and Tall* both take place on a farm." Then they might inquire, "How is the setting for *Edward's Eyes* different from these? How is it alike?" The students reading these books will each be in a position to comment on whatever their book reveals about this common author. Similarly, the Barbara Parks Club might ask, "Is Alex from *Skinny Bones* at all similar to Howard from *The Kid in the Red Jacket*?" and "How are Alex and Howard similar to or different from Maxie?" You'll want to remind students that studying characters' struggles can reveal things about them as people and any themes that the author might be approaching in his or her work.

> "Today I want to teach you that readers can move past studying characters in just *one* book by an author to compare and contrast the characters in *several* books by that author. Readers can then ask themselves: What does this character want? What are his or her struggles? How are these things similar to or different than those of the characters in other books I've read by this author?"

Do not expect that all clubs will come up with "correct" answers as a result of these conversations. Just asking these questions, however, is important to forging a literary awareness of the author as a "craftsman," one who molds characters and settings in specific ways. If, for example, students are simply noticing settings but not doing any more analytical work when thinking about the author's choices or settings across books, you might say, "Readers, it's not enough to just notice the settings in the books your authors write. I also want to think about what these settings tell me about the author and what his books are really about. So I won't just say, 'Most of the books I've read by Gary Soto take place in schools and homes in California.' I need to push further. Since I already know that most of Gary Soto's characters are recent immigrants from Mexico, it makes sense that California is where the stories take place; Mexico is very close to California, and lots of people from Mexico choose to live or work there. But also, many of Gary Soto's characters live in places where people are struggling, so I know that factor can have an effect on how the characters act, the choices they make, and so on."

You might also coach clubs to note whether the setting feels like their hometown or like another kind of place, whether it feels like modern times or historical times. You might ask whether the characters seem like familiar kinds of people or people that feel different from the people in readers' own world and then to compare across books and see if this is true for everything the author writes. Of course, setting and characters are only two such lenses that will help direct students' gazes.

Remind students of work they have done throughout the year and how they can bring that prior learning into their author study.

You might return to other lenses your students have read through, and been captivated by this year (the ones they explored during the *Interpretation Book Clubs* unit, for example, or *Historical Fiction Clubs* or *Fantasy Book Clubs*, depending on which grade you teach and which units you have selected). You might also pull out old charts during your mid-workshop teaching and shares, to encourage students to note particular things about the work an author is doing in his or her books. Remind students of the elements they can analyze to consider how authors can approach themes: characters' choices, what perspective an author has chosen to present the story, the role that minor characters play, and so on.

As students read more, they should continue to collect favorite and admired parts of the books they are reading, just as they did in the first days of the unit. Students could return to their Post-its about specific parts that evoked a strong response—ones that made them laugh out loud or feel sad or suspect that something was about to happen that would twist the story in an unexpected direction. In clubs, they may consider, "Do all these books by this author have parts that make us laugh? Is this author funny in every story?" Or "Three readers in this club have noted that all seems well at the start, and then the story begins to change and everything goes wrong all at once. Does this seem to be something the author does in all of her books? Is there a predictable structure to her writing?" You might push the class further and frame a teaching point about studying the patterns or structure of an author's work.

> "Today I want to teach you that another way to study an author's body of work is to consider what patterns in structure exist across those texts. One author might favor flashbacks, another might tell stories through multiple perspectives, and another might tend to include twist endings. Studying the plot structures of many books written by the same author can reveal patterns—and breaks in patterns—giving readers extra insight into how that author writes."

For clubs to come up with such observations, they will likely need coaching from you. As club members talk, listen in and note patterns in their conversations. It is likely that many will merely be retelling the story—or sharing parts they love but not using those as a jumping point to do deeper work. Nudge club members to ask analytic questions. Remember that one of the main goals of this unit is to get students to think deeply about an author's work in order to become more passionate and informed readers. Retelling will certainly not reach that goal. Students should grow to have the kinds of conversations that book lovers have on a regular basis. It might help you to think of the last book you read and were eager to discuss with other people. What did you want to talk about? How did that talk change when the person had read the book too? Did you discuss themes? Exciting moments? Deeper interpretations of the text?

If you can, now is a good time to grab a colleague, a literacy coach or administrator, or even a student whom you've prepped, and model an intense book talk about the read-aloud author's books your class has heard. Then quickly turn it into a class conversation and involve all your students in discussing the author. Or give each club a different read-aloud from the same author and then read aloud a new (short) book, stopping to do cross-text work and challenging all of the clubs to compare and contrast the new read with the book in front of them. "Here, I notice that the author sets up the character to make a pivotal choice. What pivotal choice has the author had the character in the book in front of you make? What is similar about those choices? What is different? What does that tell you about this author as a writer?"

Readers might look deeper than the literal plotlines of their books when nudged to notice the decisions that went into developing them. For example, students may begin to note and compare the pacing of stories: "Is there a lot of action in this story? Does this story begin with action? Is there a lot of dialogue? Do things happen quickly or is the story slow-paced and full of description? Do I have questions about this story right from the start?" Challenge them to consider whether the author tends to make them grip the edge of their seat with worry or if she builds atmosphere by richly describing the setting—and if this is true of every book club members have read by that author or if this and other structural decisions vary from book to book. These sorts of questions will likely prompt others that get children to think meaningfully about their particular author and author study.

BEND II: READING MANY BOOKS BY A BELOVED AUTHOR MEANS APPRENTICING ONESELF TO THAT AUTHOR'S CRAFT

Without even knowing that we're doing this, humans tend to mimic whatever we love. This is especially true for kids. They'll talk like their parents, dress like their best friends, and even copy moves from us, their teachers—mimicking expressions or actions they find the most effective or enticing. However, it isn't as easy for a child to mimic a beloved author while writing, or we'd have millions of Roald Dahls. With explicit instruction, however, students can certainly note and name the specific craft moves that favorite authors make and internalize these when they're thinking, talking, or writing. With practice, they can develop the habit of reading like writers, learning not merely to be wowed by but also to pay attention to the science behind the magic trick, so that they can create similar magic of their own.

Since this is the reading workshop, you'll want to keep the focus on reading rather than writing, but readers can certainly read with a writer's eye even if they don't immediately pen long pages using the techniques they've observed. Certainly the effects of this bend's work will spill over into the writing students do, but our specific focus here is to create a lifelong habit for students to look at texts the way a mechanic looks at cars—pulling all the pieces apart, then putting them back together to develop a deeper understanding and appreciation for how and why the book was written. Students will experience this through periodic close reading that you'll conduct in your read-aloud text.

Teach students to notice author's craft as they are reading as a way to get to know their authors better and develop a deeper appreciation for their work.

You will want readers to notice how authors use repetition or symbolism, how they have chosen specific words in their books, and how they might start or end their books or chapters in similar or different ways. You will want to challenge students to consider their own past works as writers and maybe even bring some of their narrative writing to their reading clubs, comparing and contrasting their own craft moves with those of the author under study.

> "Today I want to teach you another way readers get to know a particular author's books better and become even stronger readers. They do this not just by studying the books from the outside in, as readers, but also by studying those books with their clubs, as writers. Readers think about how they've structured their own stories in the past and then look at the structures of the books they have read by the author to see if patterns emerge."

One way students can conduct a deeper study of an author's craft moves is to examine different aspects of one text in isolation and then use these as a lens to compare the first book with other works by the same author. Students might copy a short section of text that they love from each of the books they've read so far into their reader's notebook and study it for its sentence variation, for example, or for its punctuation or word choice, mimicking the close reading you've done as a whole class. Clubs could choose a passage together that you can photocopy. Then, club members can annotate these passages for craft moves. Often, students find our "Techniques and Goals" visual charts from Units of Study for Teaching Argument, Information, and Narrative Writing helpful when analyzing and comparing and contrasting author's craft.

Invite students into the world of fan fiction.

One way that a lot of passionate fans pay homage to the writers they admire is they write fan fiction—they write scenes from their favorite books, sometimes filling in gaps in the story, sometimes writing from another perspective, sometimes subverting the gender roles or plot! You might invite students to write into the gaps of a story, imagining what happens in scenes that are not included. They might first think, "What scene is missing that I wish the author had included?" or "What part of the story was left unwritten that would have given readers a clearer sense of this event/character/relationship?"

"Today I want to teach you that readers who really love an author's work will sometimes write alongside that author—writing fan fiction by drafting scenes that could be inserted into existing stories. To do this work, readers study the characters, setting, plot, and style of the author."

Once they have chosen a missing scene to write, children might ask themselves, "What do the characters sound like? What do they say? What do they do?" This kind of quick exercise will look different depending on the author in question. The club studying Jon Scieszka might try their hand at writing wicked humor, whereas the one studying Kate DiCamillo might attempt to weave a little magical realism or raw emotion into their added scenes.

You can also teach students that a way they can apprentice themselves to an author is to pore over sections that stick with them, ones that make them respond in a strong way or pause in admiration. They can then look to see if there is evidence of this or other craft moves the author tends to make across texts.

Students might copy the short section that they admire into their reader's notebooks and then spend a little time studying what the author has done in that part that is affecting them so much. Is it the situation the character is in? The way two characters interact in a pivotal scene? Is it the words an author uses to bring something—a setting, an action, a person—to life? Maybe it's the sentence variation or punctuation an author uses, or her way of making readers laugh out loud.

Finally, it is worth mentioning that if your students are working on independent writing projects in writing workshop at this time, these authors they are studying could very well serve as mentor authors for their writing pieces. Students can try their hand, even if just experimentally in their notebooks, at writing dialogue or descriptions in the style and cadence of their author.

> **"Today I want to teach you that just as a close eye for an author's craft helps you become stronger readers, it can also help you as writers. You may find yourself marking places in a book not just because it moves you as a reader but because you want to try what the author is doing in your own writing."**

You might then suggest that students copy sections of an author's writing they admire on an index card and then look for a section of their own writing that they can revise based on what they have noticed in that author's writing. They might play around with varying sentence lengths—writing some very long ones and then some short. Or they could try adding more realistic or humorous or heartfelt dialogue to their writing. Some kids may want to weave more action or setting into their writing. There are many, many ways to emulate an author one admires. Encourage your children to take risks as they try this exercise . . . and to have fun!

BEND III: BECOMING AN AUTHOR EXPERT

If J. K. Rowling were to release a new book tomorrow, it would be read one way by a Rowling newbie (who has never cracked open a Potter book) and completely differently by a Rowling fan (one who's devoured every Potter book ever written, several times). While the newbie might read with casual interest, a true fan's reading would buzz with cross-text references, with memories of previous Rowling characters and plotlines, with satisfied recognition of familiar craft moves and syntax patterns. This second way of reading is powerful—it is the reading of an expert, a critic. The reader who truly knows an author can recognize that author's voice and style immediately, much as one recognizes the footfall of a family member in the dark. In this bend, readers will seek to become this kind of expert on their authors.

Challenge readers to discover themes across texts, noticing which of these the author comes back to time and again.

By this time in the unit, your readers ought to have finished at least two books by their favorite author. They will be in a position to say what the author tends to do, connecting patterns across the two (or more) books and coming up with a theory about the themes that this author typically addresses. Clubs will of course support individual efforts to do this. Now, clubs will be ready to look at their books interpretively, noting the deeper undercurrents of what their books are *really* about. Students may recall some of the common literary themes that they explored in previous units of study and ask which of these the author tends to revisit.

Does the author write about relationships between friends and family members or about isolation? Does the main character lose one thing but find something else of deeper value—and if so, what is this newfound thing? Is every book about a battle between good and evil? About growing up? About finding the courage within? Or about being resilient and fighting challenges? What is the main character's journey of growth? Once readers unearth the theme in one novel, they can ask, "Does the author address the same theme in another book?" They can list all the themes that they see in books by this author and notice whether any common ones emerge. Readers may notice, for example, that Gary Paulsen's stories are usually about a boy who suddenly has to become an adult, or that Patricia MacLachlan's books often feature children who've lost birth mothers who then seek motherly comfort in someone or something else. You might point out that many authors have a few themes they tend to revisit again and again in their books.

> **"Today I want to teach you that once readers are experts on an author, they can lay out the books they have read and note what issues and themes come up, and whether some of these run through several of the books."**

Readers might falter at the start, especially if they can't seem to find a common theme. In *Bridge to Terabithia*, one of the big lessons Katherine Paterson touches on is that we can take lessons we have learned from the people in our lives, even if we lose those people. But in *Lyddie*, Paterson deals mostly with the power one gets from becoming educated and how education can help people escape from bad situations. There might appear to be no common denominator. Students might look at a third, fourth, and possibly even fifth Paterson book. As a result, they may just come away with the realization that Paterson is diverse; she can write about an angry foster child who causes havoc for her latest, loving foster home, and she can also write about the Bread and Roses labor strike in 1912. This is fine. But they might discover an idea the books have in common: that kids can gain strength from outside of themselves—whether from books or from people—that can help them to become happy and independent.

Either way, this club ought to be able to tell you that as diverse as she is, Paterson is immediately recognizable by her style and voice. Kids might ask themselves and each other, "If you had to recognize this author's work from among a pile of many coverless, nameless books, how might you be able to tell his or her voice apart from the rest?" Eventually, readers will be able to piece together a sense of who this author is and also the kind of things this author stands for. For example, the club will tell you that Katherine Paterson might write about a very serious and grown-up theme, but she will always do it in a way that sounds exactly how real kids would act in those situations, and that she doesn't shy away from issues and topics (death, poverty, social services, labor) that most people think only adults can handle reading about.

Imagine the literary critic who knows an author so well that her review of the author's latest book drips with knowledge of everything the author has ever attempted in the past. Such a critical review might tell you: "This work is typical Joyce Carol Oates," "With this book, Oates has grown as an author. She touches new, previously unexplored themes such as . . . ," or "This is Oates at her most eloquent, surpassing even the vivid imagery she achieved in ____." Only the critic who has immersed herself in a thorough study of Oates's work would be able to make claims such as these. By this point in the unit, your students will be able to do no less. As their clubs grow to form a clear picture of a particular author's literary identity, young readers will be in a position to tell you if their book is "typical Dahl" or "Dahl at his funniest" or "Dahl being more disgusting than ever."

Teach readers that as they get to know a particular author, they are able to build a sense of what the author is known for, comparing everything new they read by the author to what they already know.

You might return to the analogy you made earlier in the unit about music fans and sports fans being like author fans, only this time put the spotlight on the musicians and athletes and authors. Point out that just as some musicians are known for their outrageous costumes or some athletes for their daring plays, authors are often known for touching on certain topics or themes or for writing in a particular style.

> **"Today I want to teach you that as readers begin to understand the themes and topics that an author tends to return to, they start to build a sense of what the author is 'known for.' Readers can use that knowledge to anticipate how the next book they plan to read by an author will fulfill or be different from their expectations about this author's work."**

You might teach students that as readers go forward in books, reading an author they know well, they compare everything new they're reading with older works by this author. They ask themselves, "What is this author doing that is new? In what way is this part like a part in another book by him?" Everything about the author's craft, choice of theme, setting, and characterization should feel vaguely familiar to your readers by now, like listening to the voice of someone they know well.

> **"Today I want to teach you that readers can use their knowledge of an author's body of work—the topic choice, themes, craft moves, plots, settings, and characters—to compare and contrast the author's books."**

"*Baby* is classic Patricia MacLachlan," you can then say. Or, "This book is a return to the settings MacLachlan made famous." Or even, "*Edward's Eyes* is different than the usual books you've come to expect from MacLachlan." Then invite students to make these comparisons across the books they've been reading by their authors.

Sometimes it can even be challenging and fun to test your students by copying a page each by various authors and see if they can match up the pages to the authors—a true assessment of their expertise!

BEND IV: READERS EXPLORE THE DEEPER CONNECTIONS THAT AN AUTHOR INSPIRES WITHIN US

Just as students will have seen in *Interpretation Book Clubs* unit, they will again see that reading changes the way we look at the world. Reading Gerald Durrell, the naturalist, might make one forever look at a wall gecko differently; reading William Zinsser might mean that one never again writes a sentence in quite the same careless way. As an example of the impact that an author can have, Seymour Simon dedicates his new book *Extreme Oceans* to another writer. He writes, "In thankful memory of Rachel Carson and her wonderful book *The Sea Around Us*, which made me realize that I wanted to become a writer."

For young readers, a favorite author has the potential to do far more than just entertain. From favorite authors, readers learn important distinctions between courage and cowardice, callousness and empathy, honor and disgrace. For this last bend of work, you might invite readers to pick up pencil and paper and explore the ways in which their favorite author offers valuable ways of looking at or coping with the world.

Encourage students to connect to their author or particular books, exploring the personal connections readers make.

Even though this is largely personal, introspective work, club members might still assist one another in exploring the lessons that the author teaches in one book or again and again across several books. Urge students to connect these lessons with the issues that they themselves see or face in everyday life.

This work requires students to grow an idea and is therefore quite well-suited to being a writing task. You might decide to have students pen a quick literary essay explaining their connection to a particular book or particular author. The thinking for this work can start as students jot quick notes as they read and as they talk in clubs. They might mark the parts of their book that resonate for them and quickly jot about why that particular part of the story spoke to their own life or experience. During club time, they may share these jottings with peers to expand upon these ideas. You may also choose to replace some club time with quiet writing time so that students can flesh out the personal responses that reading evokes in them.

> "Today I want to teach you that readers look to the places that resonate for them most and then ask themselves, 'What is it about me that this part of this text is speaking to?'"

> "You may not know the answer right away, so it can help to write long about that part, or to talk to other people about it. These moments help you realize you care more about some things than you might have even known."

By this point in the unit, not only will your readers know their authors well, they will have also learned about themselves and what it is that connects them to certain authors and books. This is the perfect point for students to think about how they might move forward in their reading lives. If you've chosen to end the school year with this unit, this is the perfect segue into summer reading plans. For many students, this will mean continuing the work of following their author. They should be aware of a variety of ways to access books—visits to the public library, book orders, book swaps, or even loans from the class library—so that they can independently fuel their reading lives. Depending on your students, you might even find that students want to set up follow-up book club meetings at a club member's home, at a local library, or a restaurant or café. Or, particularly if you chose to give this unit toward the end of the school year, you might decide to set up a special reading across the spring and into the summer reading book collection, complete with sticky notes and a bookmark, that students can crack open on the last day of school.

> "Today I want to teach you that your love of authors doesn't have to stop just because the author study is over. You can continue to live with your author, gathering books that you haven't yet read. You can find new titles by asking your club mates or the librarian, or by going online and visiting your favorite author's website. Or you could find another author to study, to become an expert on!"

BEND I: WHEN READERS READ MORE THAN ONE BOOK BY THE SAME AUTHOR, THEY COME TO KNOW THAT AUTHOR

- "Today I want to teach you that when you're a fan of an author, you try to read every book that author has written—sometimes more than once—poring over and marking favorite parts to reread and share—parts where you laughed, cried, or were surprised."

- "Today I want to teach you that when getting to know an author deeply, readers can pay attention to the kinds of settings the author describes, the themes she explores, and, of course, the characters she creates."

- "Today I want to teach you that readers can move past studying characters in just *one* book by an author to compare and contrast the characters in *several* books by that author. Readers can then ask themselves: What does this character want? What are his or her struggles? How are these things similar to or different than those of the characters in other books I've read by this author?"

- "Readers, it's not enough to just notice the settings in the books your authors write. It's also important to think about what these settings tell you about the author and what his books are really about."

- "Today I want to teach you that readers pay careful attention to specific parts in their text that evoked a strong response—ones that made them laugh out loud or feel sad or suspect that something was about to happen that would twist the story in an unexpected direction. Readers then consider whether multiple books by this author have similar parts."

- "Today I want to teach you that another way to study an author's body of work is to consider what structural patterns exist across those texts. One author might favor flashbacks, another might tell stories through multiple perspectives, and another might tend to include twist endings. Studying the plot structures of many books written by the same author can reveal patterns—and breaks in patterns—giving readers extra insight into how that author writes."

BEND II: READING MANY BOOKS BY A BELOVED AUTHOR MEANS APPRENTICING ONESELF TO THAT AUTHOR'S CRAFT

- "Today I want to teach you another way readers get to know a particular author's books better, and become even stronger readers. They do this not just by studying the books from the outside in, as readers, but also by studying those books with their clubs, as writers. Readers think about how they've structured their own stories in the past and then look at the structures of the books they have read by the author to see if patterns emerge."

Use this list as a menu of possibilities, selecting only the teaching points that meet the needs of your students. Use your assessment data (conferring and small-group notes, observations, responses to read-alouds, and other information) to decide on a plan that is tailored to the needs of your class. These teaching points may be used as whole-class minilessons, as mid-workshop teaching, or for conferences and small-group work. You need not use every teaching point. See the unit overview for guidelines on how much time to spend in each bend.

- "Today I want to teach you that readers who really love an author's work will sometimes write alongside that author—writing fan fiction by drafting scenes that could be inserted into existing stories. To do this work, readers study the characters, setting, plot, and style of the author."

- "Today I want to teach you that one way that readers apprentice themselves to an author is to pore over sections that stick with them, make them respond in a strong way, or pause in admiration. They then look to see if there is evidence of this or other craft moves the author tends to make across texts."

- "Today I want to teach you that just as a close eye for an author's craft helps you become stronger readers, it can also help you as writers. You may find yourself marking places in a book not just because it moves you as a reader but because you want to try what the author is doing in your own writing."

BEND III: BECOMING AN AUTHOR EXPERT

- "Today I want to teach you that once readers are experts on an author, they can lay out the books they have read and note what issues and themes come up and whether some of these run through several of the books."

- "Today I want to teach you that as readers begin to understand the themes and topics that an author tends to return to, they start to build a sense of what that author is 'known for.' Readers can use that knowledge to anticipate how the next book they plan to read by an author will fulfill or be different from their expectations about this author's work."

- "Today I want to teach you that as readers go forward in books, reading an author they know well, they compare everything new they're reading with older works by this author. They ask themselves, 'What is this author doing that is new? In what way is this part like a part in another book by him?'"

- "Today I want to teach you that readers can use their knowledge of an author's body of work—the topic choice, themes, craft moves, plots, settings, and characters—to compare and contrast the author's books."

BEND IV: READERS EXPLORE THE DEEPER CONNECTIONS THAT AN AUTHOR INSPIRES WITHIN US

- "Today I want to teach you that readers look to the places that resonate for them most and then ask themselves, 'What is it about me that this part of this text is speaking to?' You may not know the answer right away, so it can help to write long about that part or to talk to other people about it. These moments can help you realize you care more about some things than you might have even known."

- "Today I want to teach you that your love of authors doesn't have to stop just because the author study is over. You can continue to live with your author, gathering books that you haven't yet read. You can find new titles by asking your club mates or the librarian, or by going online and visiting your favorite author's website. Or you could find another author to study to become an expert on!"

Historical Fiction Book Clubs and Related Informational Reading

Tackling Complex Texts

RATIONALE/INTRODUCTION

Every year Hollywood seems to split its time making blockbuster films and television shows around two genres: action and historical fiction. (Mega-blockbusters, like *Indiana Jones*, often combine the two.) It's clear why action draws audiences—the drama, the heart-pounding edge-of-the-seat excitement. And yet, audiences are just as drawn to historical fiction. Why? Historical fiction lifts us out of ordinary lives into lives of great adventure and heroism, into the challenge of survival under duress—extreme weather conditions, epidemic disease, political and social unrest, war. Historical fiction stories written for children invite a younger audience to live vicariously through the eyes of kids their age who have had to grow up much more quickly, to assume enormous responsibility (and freedom, or lack thereof), to often play important roles during their lives, with key consequences. Historical fiction is alluring; it stirs children's imaginations and their desire to read—and read a lot.

This unit offers you the perfect opportunity to rev up students' reading lives again: rebuilding volume and engagement and giving you a chance to ramp up the work your students did in *Historical Fiction Clubs* in fourth grade. Last year was students' first crack at tackling the complex texts that come with a study of historical fiction, both through close reading and in the company of friends.

Historical fiction is inherently complicated—it happens in a time and a place the reader has never inhabited, the characters are entangled in historical and social issues of great significance, and the events of the story are intimately related to real historical events. And historical fiction lends itself to pushing students to read across fiction and nonfiction. You'll teach children to turn to their nonfiction books and articles when seeking to understand more about a time period or when trying to understand a historical backdrop. Your goal is for your kids to emerge from this unit of study as knowledgeable readers who have new confidence in tackling complicated literature.

In prior units, students learned to bring agency and intellectual independence to their reading, and they strengthened their ability to study, interpret, and analyze literature. Students developed more nuanced ideas about characters and other story elements and began to compare characters and themes across texts. You will support students in building on and extending this work and the work of prior years' teaching during this unit. While your students have likely studied historical fiction before, chances are their books were not as complex as they are apt to be now. You'll find that the books themselves, much like the books students worked with in *Interpretation Book Clubs: Analyzing Themes* (Unit 1) and *Fantasy Book Clubs: The Magic of Themes and Symbols* (Unit 4), bring a new level of complexity to the strategies you teach.

If you have already taught *Interpretation Book Clubs* and *Fantasy Book Clubs*, you may find that your students need less support with this portion of the unit. You can simply bring back the charts, sentence starters, writing about reading strategies, and any other tools that will help students transfer what they learned in prior book club units to this one. Students might revisit goals they set for themselves and re-create book club folders or other systems for tracking their self-assessment, talk, thinking, and writing about reading.

A SUMMARY OF THE BENDS IN THE ROAD FOR THIS UNIT

Essential Question: How can I draw on all I know about reading literature to rise to the challenge of reading even more complex historical fiction texts? How can I read in a way that lets me trace themes in and across stories and think about the author's craft?

- **Bend I: Deep Comprehension and Synthesis of Complex Story Elements**

  How can I get lost in the grand drama of historical fiction while also attending to the challenging work of tracing setting, plot, and characters across a text? How can I develop a deeper understanding of the characters and the setting by learning about that period in time?

- **Bend II: Interpreting Complex Texts**

  How can I draft and revise my interpretations based on my growing understanding of both the story and the interpretation itself?

- **Bend III: Becoming More Complex Because We Read**

  How can I almost write the story of my own reading—noticing things in the text that perhaps no one else notices, thinking and questioning what I see, and letting nonfiction texts spark new ideas and connections?

In Bend I (Deep Comprehension and Synthesis of Complex Story Elements), you will launch book clubs with high levels of engagement and independence. Your instruction will focus on deep comprehension and synthesis of complex story elements. With support from a book club, readers will reuse strategies from the past and learn new ones in order to keep track of (often multiple) plotlines, unfamiliar characters, and shifts in time and place. Like synthesis, envisioning, too, will hold new challenges, in part because students are reading higher-level books. Because the time, place, and political circumstances referenced in their historic novels may be unfamiliar, because the setting contributes actively to the plot, and because the expectation of many books at higher middle-grade levels is that students will learn about a time period, readers will need help, from the very start, to navigate the worlds of their stories. You may need to spend up to two weeks in this bend.

In Bend II (Interpreting Complex Texts), you will build on the work you did earlier this year, focusing on interpretation. If you choose to follow the scope and sequence outlined in this unit, you'll focus especially on paying attention to perspective and point of view and on carrying ideas across a text. As called for by global standards for fifth-graders, there is also a renewed focus on authors' use of craft and structure as vessels for meaning. As the unit progresses, you'll want to teach children to compare and contrast, across books, the approaches to similar themes and topics as well. Plan to spend about a week in this bend of the unit.

In Bend III (Becoming More Complex Because We Read), you will help readers move across texts, both fiction and nonfiction, developing their thematic understanding and potential as social activists. You'll teach children to turn to their nonfiction books and articles when seeking to understand more about a time period or when trying to understand a historical backdrop. Then, too, you'll teach them that after reading nonfiction we take a fresh look at the theories we've developed about our stories and see implications for living our present lives from what we have learned about the past. There is little doubt you will see direct correlations (and opportunities for connection) with the work you and your students did in *Argument and Advocacy: Researching Debatable Issues*. If you are choosing to teach that unit *after* this one, fear not—this last bend will prime students for the work of reading, deconstructing, and talking back to texts. It will take you about a week to wrap up the unit.

ASSESSMENT

You might assess children at the start of the unit by embedding questions within a read-aloud that addresses work you will teach. For example, you might read aloud a part of a historical fiction book that falls within the higher end of the four-to-five text complexity band, perhaps at a level T or U. As you read the selected section aloud, plan for places where you'll prompt children to stop and jot.

"Why did the author include this setting/quote/description/etc.?" you might ask. "Write a bit about your ideas. Give evidence from the text to support it." And later, "What might the theme or lesson of this story be? How did the author show this?" Collect these prompted responses and assess them using the Narrative Reading Learning Progression, noting where your students fall on the "Determining Themes/Cohesion" strand. You may decide, also, to use the "Analyzing Author's Craft" strand to assess students' understanding of author's choice. These strands will help you place children at a specific level and provide ideas for what students must do to move to higher levels.

After you have collected your children's responses, lay them alongside the progression to assess them. At the end of the unit, you'll likely repeat this same assessment (or a similar one) to measure student growth. You will find the "Inferring About Characters and Other Story Elements," "Critical Reading," "Determining Themes/Cohesion" and "Analyzing Author's Craft" strands helpful.

You may also decide to ask students to write an interpretive literary essay about that historical fiction text, in which they write about and develop a big idea. If you need to be more directive, prompt them to write about what the text is really about, about life lessons the text is teaching, making sure to support their ideas with clear evidence from the text. You'll have a great "before teaching" story to contrast with your "after teaching" story. These data will then help you think about how to take your students from where they are to where they need to be.

This assessment will be particularly useful because there are several ways that this unit can and does overlap with the fourth-grade historical fiction unit. You will want to know what areas to reinforce with additional teaching to shore up places they still need to work on from last year and other areas where you can build off of their strong foundation and move more quickly into more challenging and complex fifth-grade (perhaps even higher!) skills and concepts.

GETTING READY

As you get ready to teach this unit, you will want to make sure that your students have lots of historical fiction books at their independent reading levels. You will also want to make sure that there are enough nonfiction articles to support cross-genre reading for deeper comprehension of various historical eras, and you'll want to do some prep work to make sure clubs are established before beginning the unit.

Gather historical fiction books at different levels, with a special eye on your lowest-level readers.

Before beginning this unit of study, the most important question is: Do you have enough historical fiction books so that students can read books at the appropriate level and make choices about what they read? All our studies, and those of Richard Allington, show that students need to be reading with high volume and high interest all of the time—and we know that interest and choice go hand in hand. This means that within the unit, you'll need enough books at your children's within-reach levels so that they can still choose books they want to read. Don't put a reader in books that he or she cannot read or doesn't want to read just so that the reader can "be in the unit."

Be particularly thoughtful about the needs of your struggling readers. Even more than others, these students need to be reading a lot, and they need to read books that they find fascinating. So first, look at your book options, and do everything possible to gather many titles at various levels. You will also need to do some good book talks about the titles you have available, so you can lure your children to them. We included some "time travel" books, such as Magic Tree House, so as to make available more lower-level books for students. The American Girl historical fiction novels, with their accompanying nonfiction texts, are also good choices.

Especially with the lower-level choices, you'll want to practice and master the art of "book buzzes." Even if a book is not new, your students don't need to know that. Anticipate problems students might have with books and tackle them head on. You might say: "I saw this book at the bookstore the other day and thought, 'American Girl, how exciting can that really be?' But I decided to check it out, so I sat down on the floor and started to read this one about Kirsten, and before I knew it, I was filling my basket with the whole series!" Open the book and show students the cool text features, pictures, as well as the "companion" nonfiction text that comes with it. "I don't have enough copies for lots of you to read these at the same time, but if we share, I think you'll all get a chance."

If possible, you'll want to create text sets focused on a time period, which also include some lower-level texts so that readers can develop background understanding and vocabulary of the time period before tackling more complex novels. Easier texts can introduce an era and scaffold the understanding of the harder texts set during the same era. Of course, you'll also fall back on your previous assessment notes on individual readers to ascertain that books in each club's text sets conform to the reading levels of the children within that club. Typically, you'd want to have at least one book in the set that is decidedly lower in level than the reading levels of the kids in that club, to help the group understand the historical details referenced in the harder texts, especially if the time period is one you have not yet studied in the content areas. For example, if you have a group reading about World War II, in addition to books like *The Upstairs Room*, *The Devil's Arithmetic*, *Daniel's Story*, and *Snow Treasure*, you might also include a few picture books like *The Butterfly*, *A Cello for Mr. O*, and *Rose Blanche*. We encourage you to make use of the historical fiction book lists on our website, which include some of our favorite titles, organized by time period and reading level (http://readingandwritingproject.org/resources/book-lists; search for "Reading and Writing Project book lists").

You might consider shaking up your library a bit. Find out which books were popular last year, or used for read-alouds, if the fourth-grade team taught a historical fiction unit (the final unit book in grade 4 is *Historical Fiction Clubs*, so this is unlikely to be a new genre for your fifth-graders). Place those books in a special section in your library, calling students' attention to the old favorites. Some students won't have been able to read them independently last year but will be able to now and might be thrilled to test their new muscles with these familiar texts. You might consider putting in a book order—whether books for purchase or through the library system—to bring in titles that are new (or at least new to students). You may also consider swapping books with another classroom—or perhaps even a colleague at another school—if fresh books are what your students need most.

Another trick is to keep the main, essential books for each unit in a bin or closet in your classroom. By taking them out of general circulation for the school year, you ensure that they will feel new when this unit comes along. If you have a shortage of book club books, an option is to compile books with your colleagues and create a "historical fiction book club cart." This can work for any book club unit and is a great way to pool resources and ensure that all classrooms have access to as many titles as possible.

Collect some nonfiction materials on the time periods the clubs will be studying.

This unit will also help you to teach children how to read across fiction and nonfiction, synthesizing information between the two. You'll teach children to turn to their nonfiction books and articles when seeking to understand more about a time period or when trying to understand a historical backdrop. Then, too, you'll teach them that after reading nonfiction, we take a fresh look at the theories we've developed about our stories, asking: "What might I have misunderstood?" or "What more do I understand about this character's experiences and actions now?"

With the support of multiple texts on the same time period, children will be able to work toward determining the meaning of academic vocabulary specific to their time periods. Many will start word banks to collect and use this newfound terminology in writing and conversation. Students will draw on all they have learned about nonfiction reading by studying the structure of informational texts, researching specific events and topics, and analyzing multiple accounts from the same time period and noting the similarities and differences in the point of view they represent.

If you have created time period text sets, you will want to add some accompanying nonfiction texts to the mix. In this way, you will be building up intertextual baskets of books for each book club. For the club that is reading *Bud, Not Buddy*, for instance, you might also hand them a basketful of nonfiction texts and articles on the Great Depression. You could also include a few images of the time period for them to study, which will ultimately help them to envision more accurately as they read.

Another option for schools that have more access to technology is to create digital baskets for students to peruse. These can be used whether students have tablets, laptops, or desktops. Some teachers take time to bookmark or simply gather a page of URLs for various online resources. These might include virtual museums, newsreel footage, powerful images, audio clips of music from different time periods, audio clips of radio shows and famous speeches, and video clips of documentaries or news broadcasts.

Across the unit, you will want to take advantage of opportunities to support students in moving across fiction and nonfiction. You will want to teach children when to consult the nonfiction books that make up their text sets. Here are a few possibilities for when to consult nonfiction:

- When we have questions about a place, event, person, or issue in our club books, we can scan the table of contents and index to see if our nonfiction books can help us get the answers to our questions.

- When hitting roadblocks trying to visualize a time or place, nonfiction video, images, and audio clips can help us make more concrete images in our minds.

- When as a club we can't understand why people are treated a certain way, rules that govern the people, or roles that certain characters in our books have, we can consult our nonfiction books to gain a deeper understanding of the context around the characters and how that might influence what is occurring in the story.

- When issues of religion, gender, race, class, and culture confuse us, we can consult our nonfiction books.

- When a character's decisions, actions, behaviors, and motivations leave us wondering, we might think that he or she is constrained by the time period in which she or he is living, so we would want to read up on these constraints.

- When we see evidence of power and we don't know why one person has more power than others, we might want to research the time period in which they are living to see if we can get information that might help us understand who has the power and why they have it.

Choose your read-aloud(s).

During this unit of study, you will want to read aloud a variety of historical fiction and informational texts. Several times throughout the unit, you'll want to provide opportunities for engaging students in studying sections of text closely, rereading key parts of the text, summarizing the text, and discussing their thinking, all while referring explicitly to the text for evidence. You will want to pose questions that ask the students to reconsider the text and move to high levels of comprehension, synthesizing and interpreting the text, and analyzing it through speaking and writing. Close reading provides the opportunity to study a shorter section of text, analyzing and discussing its nuances. This will be a perfect complement to your longer read-louds, which allows for the opportunity to discuss thinking across a broader swath of text.

In fourth grade, students engaged in a study of the Holocaust through the class read-aloud, *Number the Stars* by Lois Lowry, as well as some complementary picture books and informational texts on the time period. For the fifth-grade iteration of this unit, we recommend reading aloud *Out of the Dust* by Karen Hesse. To us, this beautiful and powerful story is the perfect choice for fifth-graders. If you have read this book before, you know that it is hard not to stop on every page, at every chapter, in awe of the character and plot development and the way Karen Hesse's subtle use of language develops themes and symbols that thread across the text. The level of interpretation that can be done with this text is limitless and the content is mature. The Guided Reading Level of this book is X and the Lexile Level is just over 700, making it a great read-aloud for the spring of fifth grade.

Of course, you might also decide that you would prefer to use a different text—whether it's because you have another favorite historical fiction novel or another reason altogether. If you decide to go with that option, make sure your chosen text includes some of the same elements as *Out of the Dust*—namely, complex characters that develop along with the historical context and plotline(s), layered meaning, and finely wrought craft and structure.

We also suggest that you might read some picture books so that students can practice comparing and contrasting how different authors approach similar themes and topics, as a class. Some picture books about the Dust Bowl that we especially recommend, and which nicely complement *Out of the Dust*, are:

- *The Dust Bowl* by David Booth
- *What You Know First* by Patricia MacLachlan
- *Rose's Journal: The Story of a Girl in the Great Depression* by Marissa Moss
- *Born and Bred in the Great Depression* by Jonah Winter
- *The Dust Bowl* by Allison Lassieur (An Interactive History Adventure; You Choose: History)
- *Dust for Dinner* by Ann Turner (I Can Read Book, Level 3)

Plan to use your read-alouds to anchor this unit. If you decide to have students reading books from a variety of time periods, your class read-aloud could also switch time periods, though most teachers find that sticking to one era in history allows for the greatest depth of work. In order to better support your struggling readers, have them read novels about the same time period you are studying as a class. This practice will give them an added boost as they venture into navigating novels set in an unfamiliar time and place.

You'll also want to seize the power of read-aloud to tackle difficult skill work head-on. Read not only historical fiction but nonfiction, urging children to make connections and talk across the two. Engage the class in close readings of critical passages, mining the author's words for ideas and new understandings. Teach children to think not just about the story but about the author's intent. You might start read-aloud with a small snippet from a book and then pause to ask, "Why did the author just do that? What does he or she want us to know, think, feel?" Alternately, you might pause to realize that you are having trouble putting together the pieces of the story (as many of your students will at the beginning of their books) and need a bit more information about the time period. In this instance, model going to a nonfiction book, image, or article for help. Some nonfiction books we've successfully paired with *Out of the Dust* are:

- *Children of the Dust Bowl* by Jerry Stanley
- *The Great Depression* by Nathaniel Harris (Witness to History)
- *Life in the Dust Bowl* by Sally Senzell Isaacs (Picture the Past)
- *Voices of the Dust Bowl* by Sherry Garland (Voices of History)
- *The Great Depression: A History Just for Kids* by KidCaps
- *Years of Dust: The Story of the Dust Bowl* by Albert Marrin
- *Children of the Great Depression* by Russell Freedman

Read-aloud is also an important time to support accountable talk. Help children talk longer and stronger about ideas, listen more intently, and cite evidence as they build theories. Use data and observations from prior units to think about what students need the most support with in this unit. In turn-and-talk you might say things like:

- "So the main character is facing a big problem. Turn and talk to your club about how you think she may try to solve it." (prediction, interpretation, intertextuality)

- "Hmm, I'm thinking that if I were this character in this situation, I might have done something different. Stop and jot what you would do. Keep in mind what you know about the time period." (interpretation, envisioning, accumulating the text)

- "So far we've gathered a lot of details about the setting. Stop and jot: How do you think the setting is affecting the main character?" (determining importance, interpretation)

- "How do you think what just happened will affect the character? Turn and tell your partner." (inference, prediction)

- "How does this situation compare to other experiences or situations we've read about?" (intertextuality)

Establish clubs prior to starting the unit.

If your students have been engaged in the Units of Study curriculum over the years, chances are they have already had several rounds of book clubs in both fiction and nonfiction reading. Some teachers decide to keep clubs consistent. This offers students the ability to get to know each other well, to learn to work as a cohesive whole, and to face (rather than run from) issues that arise. Other teachers feel strongly that students should have an opportunity to work with a variety of children in the class and therefore decide to switch the students that make up each club. Your choices will be limited by reading level (since all students in a club need to be reading approximately the same-level text), but there are generally ways in which to make clubs feel fresh and new, if that is your goal. As much as possible, we'd urge you to base these choices on data. If a club has performed well and its members have lifted the level of each other's reading work, this is certainly something you want to keep going. If the opposite has happened, you will want to seek out alternate possibilities. Partnerships and threesomes are always a possibility if you struggle to put all of your students into clubs of four or five.

Prepare to support students' abilities to handle increasingly complex texts.

Throughout this unit, you'll want to make sure you continue to bolster children's growing abilities to handle increasingly complex texts. This unit is designed to support that work—just make sure that students are in books that represent the point of opportunity for them. Matching readers to books doesn't mean that they're all reading easy-as-pie texts, nor, of course, does it mean that students are struggling through texts that are too difficult without support. It means that they're encountering that magical mix of challenge and support that ensures engagement. You will probably want to talk up the fact that reading clubs provide readers with the group solidarity that allows each member to aspire to grow, reaching toward more ambitious goals. One way to do this is to be willing to tackle texts that are more complex and nuanced than the ones read before.

If you are moving some readers into challenging texts, in addition to the support of a club, you can also provide those readers with book introductions, film versions of the start of a book, or background information on the time period given in the form of oral storytelling. Often parents are willing to help out by reading a few chapters aloud to a reader and talking deeply about them—this is very helpful at the start of a book, especially. Parents can help also simply by reading the same book, in sync with a reader, and talking with great interest about it.

Participate in an adult book club.

The unit is organized so that children are in the frequent company of friends, reading shared historical fiction from a particular era with support from a book club. In order to support your children's book club conversations, we encourage you to participate in your own adult reading club before the start or alongside this unit, giving yourself and your colleagues an insider's perspective on the work that you are asking children to do. Use this unit as an excuse to pick up that new historical fiction book you've been dying to read, whether it's Avi's latest for middle-grade readers or Philippa Gregory for adults, and gather a few friends to read and discuss it with. We promise the experience will give you new insight into the joys and challenges of being a deep, insightful member of a book club!

BEND I: DEEP COMPREHENSION AND SYNTHESIS OF COMPLEX STORY ELEMENTS

The big goal for Bend I is for readers to be able to read complex texts with deep comprehension, keeping track of multiple plotlines, many characters, and shifts in time and place. Readers will also investigate the special role setting plays in historical fiction in informing their understanding of the story. Additionally, they will learn to accumulate and synthesize details and use essential reading tools such as timelines, graphic organizers, lists of characters, and so on.

Launch this unit by studying a part of your read-aloud closely, reading and rereading for different purposes.

You might start this work by putting a part of your read-aloud book up on the document camera to study it closely, asking your students to read and reread the text with you. We suggest you teach them to notice the words the author chose to describe a character or place. Ask them to pay attention to the feeling, mood, or tone of the event and change their voices to match this, thinking about how and why the author created that mood. Parts of the text can be read and reread, pulling on information learned earlier to understand what is really happening. You will also want to show students how two parts can be studied side by side to bring out revision of thinking and that they can synthesize these parts to see a new possibility or a different perspective.

You want to select a portion of text that has descriptions that give a sense of time and place. If you are using *Out of the Dust*, the opening scene is an excellent example of this. It begins with Billie Jo being born on the kitchen floor, her mother barefoot and her father wiping his hand inside her mouth until she cries. Their home is referred to as a "panhandle shack," with mention of "tractors," the main character's "restlessness," and a grandpa with a cancer that "ate up most of his skin" (pages 3–4). The words are harsh, the life the characters are living, harsher.

You'll want students to notice these details and more, stopping to consider the fact that the author *chose* these images to share. "The author could have included any details, but chose . . ." you might say. "What might she want us to think or feel about Billie Jo's life? About this place?" If your students did similar work last year, or are simply ready for more, you might push that thinking by having them think about the relationship between all aspects of setting (place, time, mood) and themes or messages the text is putting forward. Then, too, from the start, they can be considering the title—*Out of the Dust*. What, exactly, is the role and meaning of dust in this text?

Draw readers' attention to the significance of the physical and emotional setting of the book.

Once readers progress to higher levels of text difficulty, the settings often become less familiar and more dynamic, and also more essential to the story. In more complicated texts, though, especially stories in the R-S-T band and above, the setting becomes significant. It may even function as part of the problem that a character has to overcome—Jewish people needing to escape a hostile area, impoverished families looking for a way to survive during the Dust Bowl, Japanese Americans relegated to camps during World War II in America. A natural disaster, or invasion by a hostile enemy might change the setting completely. The setting may operate at a symbolic level, too: The dust of the prairie may mean more than simply that the land is dry. In the U-V-W band and above, there might also be an expectation that readers have some literary background; some books have settings that rely on students' prior knowledge (literary or otherwise) or on their ability to look outside the text for more information.

Apart from teaching your students to be alert for clues about the physical setting, you might also want to explore the setting as an emotional space as the story progresses, particularly for those readers who are reading books at higher bands of text difficulty. Is this the kind of town where people are good to each other or where groups fear and mistrust each other? Is it a place that is on the brink of change or that has been swept up in a war? What is the mood of this place? Oftentimes different places will mean different things or have different moods, therefore prompting characters to act differently when there. At home, for instance, Billie Jo wishes for more love from her mom and feels the weight of "the dust" everywhere. At school, however, she finds outlets. Arley Wanderdale fosters her love of piano, and her class takes in a homeless family for a bit of time, tending to them with their own limited supplies.

You'll teach readers to pay attention to descriptive, transitional passages that tell about daily life—for example, about how a character gets from one place to another. You'll teach that these sections can't be bypassed because they often reveal a great deal about the world in which the story is set. Readers need to infer all that is implicit in what is given to them. Part of this involves reading with attentiveness not just to the concrete facts of the setting but to tone and mood. Readers should come to realize that nothing that happens in a story is included accidentally. If the lightning flashes and the dark clouds rumble, the impending storm is included in the story for a purpose, and readers profit from thinking, "Why might the author have made it storm just now? What am I supposed to be thinking?" These will be new questions for your readers. They'll emerge from their study of settings more prepared to tackle the complex shifts in settings in any novel. Certainly, the work you did in *Interpretation Book Clubs* and—if you've taught it already this year—in *Fantasy Book Clubs* has set up children for this intense study of author's craft. Be sure to remind students of this work.

> **"Readers, you already know what the setting is in a story. It's the place where the story, or scene, happens. But today, I want to teach you that in historical fiction, because the setting is inevitably unfamiliar to readers, they have to pay close attention not just to what the place looks like but what it feels like—not just its physical details but its emotional atmosphere."**

After modeling this work in *Out of the Dust*, you might ask students to locate a portion of their historical fiction book where there is quite a bit of setting detail. Oftentimes this is the beginning of the book or during a setting shift. Clubs can study these parts together, reading them aloud and discussing the emotional impact they have on them as readers.

As students read further in their books, they will encounter shifts in the setting, and it will be important for them to compare and contrast the physical and psychological elements of these places. This will also help students do the work of comparing and contrasting two characters, settings, or events in a story, drawing on specific details as they do, as this is work called for by global fifth-grade standards.

Coach into clubs to support high-level skill work and effective discussion.

If you spot any problems with your book clubs, you'll want to teach into them right away rather than letting them pass. Effective clubs are integral to the work students do in this unit, and you won't want high-level skillwork to pass students by because their clubs are not working particularly well. No single reader will notice as much, or synthesize as many details, as a small group of readers. So, as you did in earlier club units, you'll want to coach your students to listen carefully to each other, build on one another's comments, and honor relationships so that every club member feels valued.

You might teach this work by saying, "Readers, as we continue to strengthen our work in reading clubs, I want to also teach you that it's important in any club to take care of relationships within that club. We do that by making sure that we're creating work where each member will feel a part of something important, and where each member will always feel supported by the group." If you have already taught either of the book club units, you can always revisit lessons you taught around club behaviors. If this is students' first experience working in clubs as fifth-graders, you may need to spend more time teaching into club norms and ways to encourage strong conversations that deepen each reader's ideas about a text.

As the bend continues, teach kids to accumulate and synthesize details about the who, what, where, when, and why of their books.

As students gather key details about the setting to grow theories about the role of the places in their texts, they may overlook details about the characters. If this is the case, remind them that historical fiction, from the very first page, presents a tremendous amount of crucial information not only about the kind of place where the story is set but also about the kind of people who occupy the story. In these novels, as in all good novels, details matter. If you learn something on page two, or in Chapter One, it's because you're going to need it later in the story. Historical fiction, at the levels at which your children are likely reading, moves swiftly. Readers need to gather a lot of information quickly. And so you'll teach them to accumulate and synthesize details.

You'll want to teach your readers some strategies for quickly synthesizing details. They can pin these to an imaginary "felt board" where they can keep track of all the incoming information. You might say something like, "When the members of my book club and I began reading our historical fiction books, there was so much information flying past us as we read that a lot of our mindwork included catching the important stuff—the information we'd need to know—and tacking it up on mental bulletin boards."

> **"Today I want to teach you that when historical fiction readers begin a new book, they tack up the important information onto mental bulletin boards, sorting it so as to grasp the who, what, where, when, and why of the book."**

You may find it helpful to show a short film clip, such as the trailer for the film adaptation of *The Book Thief,* to show readers how much information is usually given at the start of a historical fiction text. Right away, authors introduce information about multiple important characters, their world and way of life, and the challenges and conflicts they face. Some readers who need extra support taking in this information find that talking about a film clip helps them visualize it and raises their engagement and attention to detail. They can then bring this experience to their books. You could also model this with the read-aloud, showing students how you begin taking notes on the different characters when the story commences, noticing various details that you think may be important. Show them how you revise and add to that initial noticing as the story progresses. Later, you can show students how these initial thoughts and jottings turn into bigger theories or interpretations.

Some questions and prompts that you might teach club members to use to support this work are:

- What ideas can you begin to develop about _____ (a character) based on what they say, do, or think?

- Which detail from the story best helps you understand why _____ (a character) displays _____ (a particular response/emotion)?

- Why does the author most likely include _____ in the story?

- What message does the author get across to readers through _____ (character's responses)?

- An important contrast in the story is between _____ (two characters).

For more ideas about the work students should be doing in relation to inference and interpretation, refer to the Narrative Reading Learning Progression, specifically the "Inferring About Characters and Other Story Elements" strand.

Remind students of the reading comprehension strategies they already have at their disposal, and teach them new strategies that will help them tackle more complex texts.

As your readers begin to discover the sort of details that matter most in their stories, they'll also begin to notice gaps in their knowledge, perhaps in parts where time moves fast or where there are flashbacks, or simply because an author has not provisioned them with specific details pertinent to the understanding of a time period. Essential reading tools such as timelines, graphic organizers, and lists of characters, which your readers may not have relied on for a time, now become important again. One thing you'll teach is that good readers don't wait for a teacher to tell them how or when to use comprehension strategies. Good readers know that as their books get harder, they have to work harder. A reading curriculum, like a writing curriculum, spirals. As students move up levels into harder books, they'll find that they need to consciously harness comprehension strategies that were helpful to them in the past.

Of course, even as you encourage students to use strategies independently, you will model this crucial reading work, demonstrating how to use multiple strategies to make sense of reading. You'll remind them to use their pencils as they read, and you'll suggest that sometimes they'll need to reread on the run (which they worked to make a habit of mind in fourth grade), so that they can more easily tackle the complicated texts that they are reading this year.

But, you will also likely need to teach them that in some of the higher levels of texts (levels R and up), rereading doesn't always help. Sometimes the only way to make sense of all that is happening in a text is by reading forward. For example, in the beginning of *Out of the Dust*, we don't fully understand why the tone is so pessimistic and dire. It isn't until later that we learn about the true nature of the family's problems—of all the town's problems. We come to realize that the setting, the weather, and other factors all contribute to a situation that is quite literally about life or death.

Timelines will be particularly important during this unit. Readers of historical fiction benefit from creating two timelines—one of historical events and one of pivotal moments for the main character. This is because in historical fiction, characters exist in a relationship with history. Creating these two timelines allows readers to analyze the relationship between the main character and historical events. They can then think, "When does history affect the main character, and vice versa?" This lens will help readers tackle any complex novel, where characters never exist in a vacuum but are always affected by the social pressures, community norms, and forces around them. Historical fiction simply requires readers to wrap their minds around a greater volume of context: the personal story of the main character, the subplots of side characters, and the historical backdrop of an era, each with its own changing timeline. It is sometimes not clear at the outset exactly *how* these different timelines connect, but it helps to know that always, they will be intertwined.

For students who are new to this genre or to texts at or above level P–Q, you may need to offer additional support as they attempt to keep track of several simultaneously unfolding timelines or plots. To convey the importance of synthesizing across a text and tracking how time works in a story, you might say, "Today I want to teach you that when skilled readers read any complex story, and especially when they read historical fiction, they are aware that time is one of the elements in the story that is often complex. Specifically, they are aware that the spotlight of the story is not always on the present. Sometimes the story recalls events that have already occurred, either earlier in the story or before the story even began."

> **"Today I want to teach you that readers try to understand the decisions characters make, knowing that characters' behavior is shaped, in part, by what is happening in the world in which they live, that is, by the historical context. When various characters respond differently to one event, it is helpful to ask 'Why?' Usually, it is because each of those characters plays a different role in the world and thus is shaped differently by the times."**

BEND II: INTERPRETING COMPLEX TEXTS

As children are now reading with attentiveness to setting, empathizing with characters, and noticing their complexity, they will be able to embark upon the heady interpretation work that happens in this second bend. You will invite them to linger in texts, alert to details that reveal themes. It's easy for children to get caught up in the action of historical fiction and the alluring settings, but you'll want to teach them that just as the realistic fiction books they've read are about more than just plot, so too are historical fiction books. Students will need to look beyond what's happening to uncover the ideas and themes that underlie the plot, especially as their books become more complex. In this part of the unit, you'll teach your students that reading is about drafting and revising ideas. The class will do this work first within one text, then across texts, and finally between texts and their lives. Students will learn to grow nuanced ideas and to allow themselves to be changed by the new worlds and characters they encounter.

As a fifth-grade teacher, you are well aware of the degree to which independence and agency are the cornerstone of all learning this year. The work in this bend is no different. It's crucial to understand that teaching interpretation does not mean getting kids to recite an idea that you give them. You will not tell students "the theme" of a book or send them off to seek evidence for an idea they did not develop themselves. Keep asking yourself, "Am I doing the hard intellectual work needed to grapple with themes, or am I having students do it?" Of course, you want the answer to be the students! We recommend your goal be that your students learn to articulate significant ideas about their books, to revise those ideas on their own, and to reconsider, elaborate on, and defend their ideas in the company of other readers. If their ideas are weak in the beginning, or not quite what you are looking for, all the more reason for them to keep practicing!

Activate students' prior knowledge about thinking, talking, and writing in interpretive ways.

We recommend beginning the interpretation work by having students recall what they have *already* learned about this skill. Ask them to flip back in their reader's notebooks, returning to entries from the beginning of the year. Point to the charts you've brought back from any previous interpretation minilessons you've done. Don't let students off the hook by starting from scratch. They have learned a lot about interpretation, and you'll want to hold them accountable to all of that learning.

You might even begin this unit by showing students a book club talking in highly interpretative ways. One video, available to you in the digital resources accompanying this series, shows four boys discussing symbolism and themes in *Out of the Dust*. This video will show students what you hope for and expect in their own book club conversations. If you do decide to show this video, make it an inquiry into which students investigate the question: "What makes for strong book club conversations about themes and symbols?" As they watch the boys talk, ask students to take notes about what they notice (with one club member taking a category from the chart above) and then share their jots with their clubs and then the class. Your end goal will be to create a class chart (or add to the one you made in the fall, if you still have it!) that details the expectations you and your students have for thinking, talking, and writing about reading in interpretive ways.

Teach kids to bring their own history to their interpretations of the books they read.

You'll begin the interpretation work in this unit, therefore, by teaching your students to author their own responses. Too often, in too many places, kids are taught that they don't matter in the curriculum. Not here. Not in your classroom. You'll teach your students that what they bring to texts matters. You'll show them that what they notice in texts is intricately related to their personal and ethical concerns, to the history they bring to the page. You may also reveal how your history informs your own reading response, showing how you sometimes read as a big sister or sometimes as a victim of bullying or sometimes as an expert on a historical time period. Your students don't need to know this, but you'll be depending on the reading response theories of Louise Rosenblatt. You'll teach that the meaning of a text lies between the book and the reader. It exists in the union of the words on the page and the mind reading those words. What really matters is that your kids learn that they matter—that what they bring to reading shapes their understanding.

> **"Today I want to teach you that each reader brings a unique perspective to a text. Readers respond to and come up with ideas about what they are reading based on their personal stories, their experiences, their histories. There is no one 'right' way to think about a story."**

As you teach this first lesson, you'll emphasize that just as no one can tell a reader what or how to think about a story, there is no "right" idea about a story. Each reader brings his or her own history to a book, so that what you might think is important, such as how Billie Jo perseveres in playing the piano even after her hands are burned, might be different than what I focus on, such as that she struggles to be close to her father after her mother dies. I might notice that because I, too, struggle to be close to my dad. It's crucial to teach your students that their own responses and feelings matter. Otherwise, they'll be waiting for you to tell them what to notice and what to think!

If you notice your students racing through their books without much thought, you'll probably want to teach a lesson in which you encourage readers to pause as they read, lingering in certain passages—usually the extra dramatic or surprising ones, where they feel as if there is a sense that what is happening now is connected to other parts of the story or could be tremendously important to the characters' development. Point out that those parts of the story seem to be written in bold. Teach them that readers linger in those parts, jot about them, reread them with their clubs, compare their thinking, connect them to other parts, and have long discussions about them again and again. Often readers come away from certain passages with big ideas that they then carry with them for the rest of the book.

As this bend continues, channel students to be alert readers, grounding their own ideas in details, and to be flexible readers, open to multiple ideas.

Once students come up with some big ideas, you can expect that they will need support grounding these in details. So again, you'll teach your readers that in good books, details matter, and that perceptive readers accumulate and string together these details. It matters, for instance, that recurring images of the elements—of water (rain, Pa's pond), fire, air—weave through *Out of the Dust*. In particular, there are recurring images of choking, suffocating dust—and of (mostly) soothing, healing rain. Each element symbolizes something key to the characters, to the backdrop, and to the story.

As your readers begin to follow ideas, they can keep track of details that support those, and as well as details that lead them to related ideas. Teach them to keep those ideas—those interpretations—in mind as they read, thinking, "Ah, yes!" or "Huh? That doesn't fit." They may jot themselves notes about the lenses they plan to read with each day. That way, clubs won't end up losing track of their ideas or losing their focus. This is a great time to again study the Narrative Reading Learning Progression, perhaps focusing on the "Determining Themes" strand. Students might jot their ideas about the larger meanings they are beginning to notice in their books and then study their responses against the progression. Partners could work together to support each other in raising the level of this work.

The main goal of this part of the unit is for students to form and embrace their own ideas about books and then hold onto these as they read, grounding them in details, deepening them, and sharing them with others. But it's important, too, that children remain open to new ideas—that they are willing to widen their thinking, not holding so steadfastly to one or two ideas that they cannot embrace changing thoughts and interpretations as they push further into their books.

> **"Today I want to teach you that although it is important to fashion ideas and to care about them, it's also important to be open to new ideas. You don't want to read, or to talk, like you are determined not to let your mind budge even an inch. One reason to talk and to read is to learn. Thoughtful readers, and thinkers, allow their ideas to be changed."**

So we suggest that you teach your students that good stories are about more than one idea and that to read a complex book well means being open to a journey of thought. You'll also want to teach students to revise their understandings as they change. Too often, young readers may reject or ignore parts of the story that don't fit an idea they came up with early on. Express that thoughtful readers keep their horizons open as they read, and they use conversation as well as their individual observations to broaden their understanding.

Channel kids to note and discuss author's craft and author's purpose.

You may want to also spend some time teaching into work you touched on during the first bend in this unit: the role of author's craft and structure. You launched this unit with a focus on how an author sets the tone or mood of an event or place, choosing his or her words very deliberately. You focused on the beginning of the book—those first few pages or chapters and how they fit into the body of the text as a whole. You may have even had conversations with students during read-aloud about why the author made the choices he or she did. Now, you can build on this to explore more about authorial decisions. For example, you might say, "We've talked a lot about the role of *beginnings* in historical fiction. Today I want to teach you that authors of historical fiction (and all fiction) make deliberate choices, not just about the first chapter but about each chapter and where it will go in the story. One way readers analyze themes in books is to notice how the text is structured—how the chapters fit together—and that the events included or not can be signposts to deeper meaning."

The interpretive work students do in this bend may parallel some of the work they do in "Social Issues Book Clubs: Applying Analytical Lenses across Literature and Informational Texts" (if you opt to teach that alternate unit)—reading to foster social justice. They can raise questions in their book clubs about why history unfolds the way it does, how individual stories bear witness to suffering and courage, and what lessons readers can take from characters' experiences. Their jottings and conversations will grow as you coach into this synthesis work, helping them place two ideas next to each other in order to form a new, more nuanced one. The book club work will be tremendously important here, as students put their heads and ideas together to extend their thinking. One of the most significant lessons of this unit, and we hope one of the most lasting, will be that children's greatest strength lies in building thoughts off their talk with one another.

You'll want to facilitate this talk by providing literary language for some of the things students see in their books but don't yet have the terminology to name. You might teach readers that authors have many tools they use to craft their stories, that they use allusions, figurative language, imagery, and symbolism to convey big ideas—ones that are not easily contained in ordinary language. You might then focus on one that will pay off for students to notice. You might say, "One tool that authors use often is symbolism—an (often ordinary) object or setting or other element that stands for something more thematically significant. Historical fiction is rich with symbolism that points readers to deeper themes, not only in the novel's time period but also in their own." Teach students that astute historical fiction readers are ever on the lookout for symbols or anything else the author used that feels significant.

Out of the Dust is rife with symbolism. The most obvious, perhaps, is the dust, which in addition to being part of the book's title, is referenced on so many pages that it is almost a character. Dust covers everything—the land, cattle, crops, people, their personal belongings, and homes; it chokes, suffocates, takes away people's farms, their livelihood, and their lives. Children should have an easy time understanding that as well as being a real-life physical problem, dust in this book stands for hardship, oppression, and struggle. From there it's a natural next step to notice that water—rain, Pa's pond—represents relief, possibility, and life. As do babies, music, and trees—Ma's apple tree, especially. This book is so rich with imagery, symbolism, figurative language, and personification that you could open to almost any page and invite children to identify one of these with success.

Another accessible way to teach higher-level interpretation skills and authorial intent is to show a clip of a television show popular among your students or a music video that you then invite students to analyze. Don't worry if it's not historical fiction. In fact, the transference will be higher if it's not. One music video we have used to great effect is "What Does the Fox Say?" by Ylvis, whose dramatic changes in costume, setting, and music are easy for students to spot. The singer starts inside a house, wearing everyday clothes, then makes a shift to a dark forest, wearing a costume. Because the changes are so sudden and extreme, they evoke a strong response in viewers. It is easy for students to see the choices of the "author" as well as name the effects these have on them, the "reader." Because of the drama, students don't simply retell what they saw. Instead, they jump right to interpretation work. "Why did this happen? What could it mean?" If you jot down students' observations and questions, a day or so later you can ask them to analyze the work they did as viewers and to consider how they might apply these same skills as readers.

BEND III: BECOMING MORE COMPLEX BECAUSE WE READ

Now that your students have some interpretation tools and practice under their belts, they will be ready to develop their critical reading skills. Specifically, in this bend, students will learn to examine texts from the lens of perspective and power. They will develop ideas across books, and they will read nonfiction to inform their reading of historical fiction. Finally, they will consider implications of reading about the past for their present lives.

Teach kids to consider the impact of multiple points of view.

You might begin this bend with a focus on point of view. Remind students that one of the first jobs a reader has is to figure out who is narrating a book. A story might be told by an impartial outsider (third-person voice) or it could be told by the main character (first-person voice). Usually, even if a story is told in the third person, readers will have access to the main character's thoughts; that is, the narration will reveal the main character's perspective. It is important for students to understand that the story they are privy to as a reader is *that* character's experience. Another character might tell the story of an event entirely differently or might act in ways that they don't understand because they do not have access to his or her inner thoughts. Therefore, as readers, they must ask, "Whose point of view am I given access to, and whose is left out?" Then, "If I step into another character's shoes, can I understand things differently?"

> **"Today I want to teach you that the voice narrating a story is a deliberate choice, with consequences. Readers can deepen their understanding of a book's big picture—what it's all about—by considering how the story might have been told otherwise if it were narrated by someone else—by a character rather than an outside voice or by a different character than the one who is narrating."**

Today's global standards expect fifth-graders to be able to compare and contrast characters within a story, describing each of them in-depth, and to discern the various perspectives of different characters within a story. You might invite your students, therefore, to look closely at a scene and imagine the various points of view that characters in that scene bring to the action. You'll be teaching into critical literacy while also building your students' empathy and imagination, observation and discernment.

In their clubs, students may also discuss how the story might have been told differently if it were being told by a different character. Building on what they already know—that texts will be told very differently when they are told by a character within the story or a removed outsider—reinforce that the choice of who tells the story is a deliberate one made by the author and for good reason

You may decide to provide students with a list of questions they could ask themselves or their clubmates when considering how the way a scene is told might be influenced by the narrator.

Analyze How Who the Narrator Is Influences the Telling of the Story

- If a different perspective was used to present this scene, what details might have been included/excluded? Why?
- If a different perspective was used to present this scene, how might the mood and tone of the scene be different? Why?
- If a different perspective was used to present the scene, how might the reader understand things differently?
- What might be gained or lost by the author choosing *this* narrator to tell the scene/presenting this scene through *this* perspective? Why might the author have made this choice?

As students begin to analyze the points of view of characters, they will take steps toward understanding the point of view of the author who crafted the story. If you have decided to use film clips throughout this unit, you might, in a share session, further explore point of view by inviting students to reconsider the camera angle of the first clip they saw. What if the camera were focused on another character? What would the viewer see? How would that change the story? Students can "direct in the air" to imagine what that film clip would look like.

Finally, you might also shine a spotlight on something you taught in past units—that a reader has to separate his or her own perspective, too, from that of the character. This is a skill emphasized in key standards for reading.

Channel students to read through the lens of power.

Another way to teach into critical literacy is through the lens of power. Students can analyze a book, thinking, "Who has power? Who doesn't? How is power visible? What forms can power take? How does power shift?" This work often leads to new thinking, especially for readers of this age, who may not have thought about power before now, even though they themselves may at times feel powerless.

> **"Today I want to teach you that looking at our books through the lens of power leads to all sorts of new thinking. When we investigate who has power, what form power takes (how you see it), and how power changes, that helps us find huge meanings in books."**

You can go on to explain that power is not always about weapons or physical strength—though it can take those forms, too. In *Out of the Dust*, nature is a powerful force, but so too are the tenacity and spirit of the people who live during the dust storms. Illness and death are resultant forces of power, but so too are community, music, and family. In the end, dust and poverty don't defeat the characters. Instead, the characters come together in powerful new ways. They heal old wounds, welcome new unions, and find ways to persevere despite adversity. This, you can point out, is its own form of power.

You might invite children to look at *Out of the Dust* and think about how various individuals, communities, and the government do and don't have power and how they react to situations in which power comes into play. You might refer to the chapters that show Billie Jo's town's response to the migrant family that seeks refuge ("Guests," pages 119–30), to the children ("Something Sweet from Moonshine," pages 125–26), and to the abandoned baby ("Baby," pages 184–85). You could read aloud "Lunch" (pages 117–18) and "Help from Uncle Sam" (pages 172–73) to consider the government's role. Or you could ask children to consider how characters like Ardley and Mad Dog use their power in this book. You might ask questions like, "What kind of power does ___ have/not have?" "How else might ___ have responded to this situation?" "How does this action affect Billie Jo/her father/the town?" Children might think about subtle versus obvious displays of power—or reactions to it—and about ways in which power shifts from beginning to end of this book.

Help students to integrate nonfiction reading into their fiction reading to spark new ideas.

If you haven't done so yet, you'll want to make sure that your students now have the opportunity to read some nonfiction alongside their fiction. This doesn't have to mean that you create enormous text sets, ravage your libraries, and do big book orders. You could simply type up some statistics or download some simple fact sheets or articles. Knowing how many people left the Dust Bowl (nearly three million), the lengths of the big droughts, and the numbers of dust storms that hit during the particularly bad years between 1931 and 1938, for example, will give children a sense of what was at stake for the characters in *Out of the Dust*.

You could begin this work by introducing *Life in the Dust Bowl* by Sally Senzell Isaacs. You might first ask students to analyze the pictures (the ones in the chapters "Black Blizzards" and "A Child's Life" are particularly powerful), asking, "What kind of place is this?" As you read the text and students put that together with the images, they will come to see that the Great Plains were a desolate and dire place during the 1930s. You might then read aloud the section called "No Jobs" on page 23 and invite a conversation about the fact that even in a state as large and removed as California, there weren't enough jobs to employ the over one million people who made the move there between 1935 and 1940. Or you could read the sections about farm life, children, and school, so that students will have real-life images and details to fill in the ones they've been reading about in *Out of the Dust*.

Images of the time periods during which children's books are set will be a valuable resource for students to reference as they envision. Even though they will have learned that the books they are reading are set during real-life events, they may experience these events and characters at a certain distance because they are reading about them against the backdrop of fiction. It is one thing to read about Billie Jo's plight and another thing to see photographs of real people who lived through the Dust Storm, the Depression, or other historical events, firsthand. If you have access to technology, encourage students to sift through digital bins filled with virtual museums, audio clips of witness accounts, and video clips of newsreels. There is a wealth of multidimensional historical records and experiences available online that can fill in gaps and bring a more current human element to their reading. You might teach children that historical fiction readers often turn to nonfiction to spark new ideas about their novels.

Teach comparison to deepen students' thinking across texts.

As your readers add in nonfiction reading, you'll guide them to talk about ideas across texts—both fiction and nonfiction. The idea that poverty, hardship, and loss teach children to grow up fast, for instance, is true not only in *Out of the Dust* but also in *Bud, Not Buddy*, *Rose's Journal*, and in countless other accounts— both real and imagined—of this period in time. The realization that an idea a reader has in one text can be true in another text is revolutionary for young readers. They'll begin to see themes everywhere. So you won't have to build text sets around themes—instead, invite your readers to imagine how each text they read can be read in comparison to other texts, as if they are making virtual text sets. Teach them to look closely at themes across texts.

> **"Today I want to teach you that historical fiction readers can deepen their thinking by comparing how a big idea or theme is explored in books about the same historical event or time period. Sometimes similar themes are addressed by authors writing about different historical events."**

As students begin to look at similar themes across their texts, they may notice the theme of strength in numbers and communities during times of hardship and of strength and bravery in individuals, too, especially when tested in big ways. They may talk about the themes of discovering new possibility, hope, and growth following suffering and loss and about the idea of making amends and seeking or granting forgiveness. Students may think about how bravery, sacrifice, and friendship often come into play during times of conflict. Children who are reading about times of war or oppression may notice that violence often leads to more violence, that power is unequal, that war and injustice can tear people apart, yet also bring them together.

As students identify these and other themes across their texts, you might steer them to discuss *how* authors reveal these themes. As they compare and contrast multiple books with similar themes, nudge them to analyze carefully, using details as evidence for their ideas. You might teach that one way to compare how authors convey themes is to study how characters respond to challenges. In *Out of the Dust*, after the accident that takes her mother's life and badly burns Billie Jo's hands, Billie Jo works hard to continue playing piano, and her father digs the hole for the pool that his wife always wanted. The author, Karen Hesse, explores themes of perseverance, growth, and hope in the face of hardship and of attempts to make amends. Meanwhile, in *Rose's Journal*, Rose's parents join various competitions to raise money so they can keep their farm. Here, too, we see the theme of perseverance in times of trouble. But whereas Billie Jo leaves home for a time, anxious to get out of the dust, Rose's family does everything it can to not abandon their home and town.

Some questions that students might ask themselves and others around this critical work:

- What theme is present in both stories?
- How have the authors approached the topic differently?
- What ideas are supported by both stories?
- How did each of the characters react differently to conflict? What messages does the author seem to be trying to convey through those reactions?

Another way to compare and contrast historical fiction authors' approaches to theme is to look across texts with similar topics, considering how each author may have made choices to comment on life today, through their books. An oft-repeated adage is that history repeats itself. Could the decision to highlight a survival against great odds in *Out of the Dust* be a message from Karen Hesse that no matter how hard our world can feel, other people throughout time have also made it through difficult times? Or, might the story mirror something that the students have read about in current events? Could there be a recent natural disaster or conflict that raises similar big ideas as the ones running through one of their novels? Could the author be using this past time period as an analogy for that? Or could the author be saying something about certain themes repeating across time?

This thinking about present-day issues can lead students to some interesting comparisons and interpretations. Of course, if you decide to explore this line of thinking, it will be important to keep students' conversations firmly grounded in their citations of texts, so that they don't lose sight of the interpretation work they are doing in reading.

Another way to use comparison to deepen thinking is through allusion. Sometimes, readers struggle to find the words that contain their thoughts. In these instances, you can teach them to draw on allusions, comparing one story or character to another story or character who is well known. You might say, "Today I want to teach you that sometimes readers have huge thoughts, for which no ordinary words will do. When that happens, they can reference a beautiful detail, significant theme, or lasting image from a story that people know well, and by doing so, they conjure up that whole story, so that people who know it say, 'Ah, yes, yes. I know what you mean.' That's called making an allusion. Literate people do this all the time."

You might then model this yourself by saying that the main character in the story you are reading is as clever (or self-sacrificing) as Charlotte in *Charlotte's Web*. Your students should know what that means—and you can point out that so will anyone else who is familiar with this children's book classic. So saying that a character is trying to find her way "out of the dust" like Billie Jo will convey huge meaning. The ability to make allusions is a key part of understanding literary traditions and archetypes—the foundations of cultural literacy.

Now that your students have begun to develop a repertoire of strategies for analyzing how authors approach themes, you might give them a list of elements that can be compared and contrasted across texts as well as questions to consider.

Analyzing How Different Authors Approach Themes by Comparing and Contrasting:

- Moments of choice
- Times when character(s) respond to trouble
- Moments when characters feel conflicting emotions
- Perspectives authors have chosen
- Physical and psychological settings
- Parts where images, objects, and more seem to resurface
- Parts where minor, seemingly unimportant characters resurface
- Choices of language (e.g., names of titles, characters, places) and how this language might connect to the themes of the story
- How life lessons are taught (some are taught through characters themselves realizing lessons while others are taught through readers seeing characters' mistakes/flaws)

And Asking:

- What can I learn from these moments?
- What does each author seem to be trying to really say?
- What might the author be trying to say about our life today?
- How is each author approaching a theme in his or her own way?

Integrate the unit with your social studies curriculum.

You might invite your students to do some writing side by side with their reading. Students will be collecting many new insights about the time period that could inform this writing. You might, then, choose to align your social studies instruction with your historical fiction reading work so students have multiple opportunities to explore this time period. For example, in social studies your students might be learning about westward expansion through discussions, trips, film clips, and primary sources—all the while collecting jottings about what they are learning about the period, talking in partnerships and clubs, and creating whole-class word walls and charts gathering their understandings. Simultaneously, in reading workshop, your students will need to read historical fiction from various time periods (so that you can keep everyone "in books"), one of which might be westward expansion. During read-aloud time, you could highlight books set within the time period.

Of course, just because you are studying westward expansion doesn't mean that your students can't take on related, but broader, topics in their book clubs—ones that focus on stories of war or oppression or change. When children read one historical fiction text after another, this provides an excellent opportunity for them to compare texts. This kind of intertextual reading work supports a richer understanding of historical fiction in general. Another way to go, if you feel your social studies materials are not broad or supportive enough, is to lean more heavily on the reading workshop work paired with your social studies unit—using historical fiction book clubs and read-alouds of picture books, short texts, or novels as points of research for your readers.

In both your content study and your reading workshop, you may use word charts, timelines, visuals, and maps to record class understandings of the concepts, events, places, and vocabulary. You will likely also decide to make a variety of nonfiction texts available so that students can supplement their reading of historical fiction with informational texts. It's helpful to have nonfiction texts with lots of images, so that students can use these as references while they envision. If there are any crucial historical events in the stories your students will be reading, try to include some texts that explain these events and give some background information on them. Include maps as well, so students get an idea where the stories they are reading take place.

Social studies is also a perfect time to teach children to write quick essays about the time periods their clubs are reading about. Begin by showing readers how to generate several big ideas as they read about a time period, then pick one idea to fast-draft into an essay.

We believe these quick essays will help students to learn to develop and support their thinking, not only strengthening their skills in opinion writing but also deepening the reading work they do. The current standards emphasize the importance of comparing and contrasting, integrating information for multiple sources, and supporting ideas with key details, all of which students will need to do as they craft these fast essays.

CELEBRATION

Close this unit by inviting students to consider the meaning these books hold for their own lives and for the world at large.

As you bring this unit to a close, invite children to step back a little from the historical worlds they've stepped into, and from the heady interpretation work they've been doing within and across texts, to think more largely about the meaning these tales bear for their own lives—and for the world at large. What does it mean to them, for example, that Mama in *Roll of Thunder, Hear My Cry* covers up the offensive notations in her seventh-grade students' texts so that they do not have to be humiliated by seeing these every day? How are we affected by that decision and by the school's response of firing her? What can we learn from Annemarie's decision, in a moment of high stakes, to rip off her best friend's Star of David necklace, which identifies Ellen's Jewishness and now potentially marks Annemarie, too? What's the significance of Billie Jo's decision to return home to her father, the farm, and the dust? There are lessons in these defining choices that characters make, and you'll want your students to think deeply about them, to be affected by them, and to live differently because of them.

You might then invite children to share this thinking—or any other important insights they've had over the course of this unit—with the class at a small celebration. They could do this in small groups made up of members of different club. Alternatively, children could put their thinking into writing and maybe even illustrate this and display it around the room. Then, you could set up a museum walk, so that students can admire each other's thinking. No doubt they will notice that there are overlapping themes and lessons, even in historical fiction that spans different time periods and events.

POSSIBLE TEACHING POINTS

BEND I: DEEP COMPREHENSION AND SYNTHESIS OF COMPLEX STORY ELEMENTS

- "Today I want to teach you that authors carefully choose words to describe a character or place. Readers need to pay attention to the feeling, mood, or tone of the event and change their voices to match this, thinking about how and why the author created that mood."

- "Readers, you already know what the setting is in a story. It's the place where the story, or scene, happens. But today, I want to teach you that in historical fiction, because the setting is inevitably unfamiliar to readers, they have to pay close attention not just to what the place looks like but what it feels like—not just its physical details, but its emotional atmosphere."

- "Today I want to teach you that it's common for shifts in setting to occur as you read further into a book. When readers encounter a shift, it's important to compare and contrast the physical and psychological elements of these places."

- "Readers, as we continue to strengthen our work in reading clubs, I want to also teach you that it's important in any club to take care of relationships within that club. We do that by making sure that we're creating work, where each member will feel a part of something important, and where each member will always feel supported by the group."

- "Today I want to teach you that when historical fiction readers begin a new book, they tack up the important information onto mental bulletin boards, sorting it so as to grasp the who, what, where, when, and why of the book."

- "Today I want to teach you that strong readers take charge of their reading lives. They don't wait for a teacher to tell them how or when to use comprehension strategies. Good readers know that as their books get harder, they have to work harder."

Use this list as a menu of possibilities, selecting only the teaching points that meet the needs of your students. Use your assessment data (conferring and small-group notes, observations, responses to read-alouds, and other information) to decide on a plan that is tailored to the needs of your class. These teaching points may be used as whole-class minilessons, as mid-workshop teaching, or for conferences and small-group work. You need not use every teaching point. See the unit overview for guidelines on how much time to spend in each bend.

- "Readers, today I want to teach you that as texts become more complex, rereading doesn't always help. Sometimes the only way to make sense of all that is happening in a text is by reading forward."

- "Today I want to teach you that readers of historical fiction can use timelines to help them make sense of what they are reading. It helps to create two timelines—one of historical events and one of pivotal moments for the main character. Then you can analyze the relationship between the main character and historical events, thinking, 'When does history affect the main character, and vice versa?'"

- "Today I want to teach you that readers try to understand the decisions characters make, knowing that characters' behavior is shaped, in part, by what is happening in the world in which they live, that is, by the historical context. When various characters respond differently to one event, it is helpful to ask 'Why?' Usually, it is because each of those characters plays a different role in the world and thus is shaped differently by the times."

BEND II: INTERPRETING COMPLEX TEXTS

- "Readers need to think, talk, and write in interpretive ways. Today we will investigate the question 'What makes for strong book club conversations about themes and symbols?'"

- "Today I want to teach you that each reader brings a unique perspective to a text. Readers respond to and come up with ideas about what they are reading based on their personal stories, their experiences, and their histories. There is no one 'right' way to think about a story."

- "Today I want to teach you that readers pause as they read, lingering in certain passages—usually the extra dramatic or surprising ones, where they feel as if there is a sense that what is happening now is connected to other parts of the story or could be tremendously important to the characters' development. Readers sometimes jot about them, reread them with their clubs, compare their thinking, connect them to other parts, and have long discussions about them again and again."

- "Readers know that details matter! Today I want to teach you that readers accumulate and string together details as they read. Readers ground their big ideas in the details, and as they read, they keep track of details that support their ideas and as well as details that lead them to related ideas."

- "Today I want to teach you that although it is important to fashion ideas and to care about them, it's also important to be open to new ideas. You don't want to read, or to talk, like you are determined not to let your mind budge even an inch. One reason to talk and to read is to learn. Thoughtful readers, and thinkers, allow their ideas to be changed."

- "Readers, we've talked a lot about the role of *beginnings* in historical fiction. Today I want to teach you that authors of historical fiction (and all fiction) make deliberate choices, not just about the first chapter but about each chapter and where it will go in the story. One way readers analyze themes in books is to notice how the text is structured—how the chapters fit together—and that the events included or not can be signposts to deeper meaning."

- "Authors have many tools they use to craft their stories, such as allusions, figurative language, imagery, and symbolism—all can be used to convey big ideas. One tool that authors use often is symbolism—an (often ordinary) object or setting or other element that stands for something more thematically significant. Historical fiction is rich with symbolism that points readers to deeper themes, not only in the novel's time period but also in their own. Today I want to teach you that historical fiction readers are ever on the lookout for symbols that feel significant."

BEND III: BECOMING MORE COMPLEX BECAUSE WE READ

- "Today I want to teach you that the voice narrating a story is a deliberate choice, with consequences. Readers can deepen their understanding of a book's big picture—what it's all about—by considering how the story might have been told otherwise if it were narrated by someone else—by a character rather than an outside voice or by a different character than the one who is narrating."

- "Today I want to teach you that it is important for a reader to separate his or her own perspective from that of the characters or narrator of the story."

- "Today I want to teach you that looking at our books through the lens of power leads to all sorts of new thinking. When we investigate who has power, what form power takes (how you see it), and how power changes, that helps us find huge meanings in books."

- "Readers, today I want to teach you that historical fiction readers often turn to nonfiction texts to spark new ideas about their novels as well as fill in gaps in their knowledge."

- "Today I want to teach you that historical fiction readers can compare how a big idea or theme is explored in books about the same historical event or time period, to deepen their thinking. Sometimes similar themes are addressed by authors writing about different historical events."

- "Readers, authors reveal themes in a variety of ways. Today I want to teach you that one way to compare how authors convey themes is to study how characters respond to challenges."

- "Today I want to teach you that sometimes authors comment on life today through the theme of their books. Readers can look across texts and consider how themes convey messages on current times or perhaps how certain themes repeat across time."

- "Today I want to teach you that sometimes readers have huge thoughts, for which no ordinary words will do. When that happens, they can reference a beautiful detail, significant theme, or lasting image from a story that people know well, and by doing so, they conjure up that whole story, so that people who know it say, 'Ah, yes, yes. I know what you mean.' That's called making an allusion. Literate people do this all the time."

Learning through Reading
Westward Expansion

RATIONALE/INTRODUCTION

This unit offers students an opportunity to use their nonfiction reading skills to research a historical time period. This also means that it offers you the ability to align your teaching of history or social studies and your teaching of reading, so that you are able to immerse your students in a particular topic. Most teachers who choose to teach this unit align their social studies, reading, and writing instruction at this time of the year. You will probably want get your social studies and reading instruction underway before beginning the accompanying writing unit, *The Lens of History: Research Reports* (a Units of Study in Opinion, Information, and Narrative Writing unit book for grade 5, by Lucy Calkins and Emily Butler Smith), because students will need to have some background knowledge of the time period before they begin to write research reports.

You'll note that this unit is devoted to reading to learn about westward expansion. This is a broad time period that may or may not be part of your social studies or history curriculum. If this time period is not one that you study, you don't need to worry; you can still make use of this unit by using the overarching plan for the unit as well as the teaching points and inserting your own content. The texts mentioned and the examples given in this unit will not transfer to your classroom, but the skills and strategies absolutely will. You'll simply need to choose your own time period and texts to demonstrate with.

The first bend of the unit is devoted to students reading about the time period in general ways, building background knowledge and practicing the nonfiction reading skills they have learned this year and in previous years. The second bend focuses students' attention on a particular aspect of the time period in order to give them a chance to become true experts on a subtopic that they will also teach others about through their report writing. In the third and final bend of the unit, students read to build theories and think more critically. The goal is for students to be seamlessly transferring and applying their learning from one subject to another.

A SUMMARY OF THE BENDS IN THE ROAD FOR THIS UNIT

Essential Question: How can I use all that I know about nonfiction reading and research to learn about westward expansion?

- **Bend I: Reading Nonfiction about Westward Expansion and Summarizing with Structure in Mind**

  How can I understand what I read, aware not just of the content but also of the structure and of reasons why that structure is a good one for carrying the content?

- **Bend II: Learning about an Aspect of the Westward Expansion through Reading**

  How can I organize a learning life that allows me to read across multiple texts, studying an aspect of westward expansion from multiple perspectives?

- **Bend III: Building Theories and Reading Critically**

  How can I build theories from studying multiple perspectives on a topic? How can I start to see how various authors approach the same topic differently, swaying their readers to think in particular ways? How do I want to sway people learning from me?

In Bend I (Reading Nonfiction about Westward Expansion and Summarizing with Structure in Mind), students will spend about a week and a half reading nonfiction texts about westward expansion—focusing on text structures and summarizing as they read, as well as building background knowledge on the topic. When you start conferring with students and looking at the data you collect, you might find that some children have difficulty organizing the information that they are learning. You might teach some lessons on using text structure as a way to help organize new information.

In Bend II (Learning about an Aspect of the Westward Expansion through Reading), students will form research teams on subtopics of interest related to westward expansion and set forth on an inquiry. They will survey their materials, drawing on all they know about going through a research project in order to organize their learning lives. Students will use a variety of note-taking strategies to hold onto and organize information as well as teach others what they have learned so far. Plan to spend about a week and a half in this bend.

In Bend III (Building Theories and Reading Critically), you will charge students to raise the level of their work to new heights. As they begin to learn what is most important about a subtopic relating to westward expansion, they will come to see that different authors have chosen to present information in sometimes similar and sometimes different ways. You will support them in continuing to look more closely at how authors present information, including helping students to see how the point of view of an author influences how the information is presented. It will take about a week and a half for this portion of the unit.

ASSESSMENT

For this unit, as for all units, we recommend that you identify two or three aspects of reading on which you'll predominantly focus. In this unit, for example, you may want to focus on students' abilities to grasp what is most important about the texts they read, seeing what information is most key to supporting main ideas of the text. You may also want to focus on their abilities to compare and contrast information across texts as well as the ways that authors are presenting that information (their points of view, for example).

We suggest you draw upon the "Main Idea(s) and Supporting Details/Summary," "Cross-Text Synthesis/ Cohesion," and "Analyzing Perspective" strands of the Informational Reading Learning Progression.

Another option would be to embed some questions in your read-aloud text and collect students' jottings. The text *The Oregon Trail and Westward Expansion: A History Perspectives Book* by Kristin Marciniak offers different points of view on this event. You might decide to read parts of this text to your students, ask them the embedded questions, and collect their jottings in response in order to give you data to inform your teaching of this unit. You might also repeat part of this assessment at the end in order to study growth.

Another option to do this assessing and gathering of data includes collecting and studying student work from their independent reading. You might make a child-friendly rubric out of the Informational Reading Learning Progression and assess how well students are doing this sort of work in their independent reading.

GETTING READY

Gather texts on westward expansion (both print and digital, if possible).

It is impossible to overstate the value of engaging your students by making sure they have materials to read that feel interesting and exciting and that they can read well. You'll need to look at the texts you have and assess your needs. You may find that you have many titles available, and you really just need to spruce things up a bit. Placing a dusty basket of books in the classroom library will probably not do the trick, but if you organize the books in an enticing way and present them to your students with a bit of fanfare, you'll be more likely to generate excitement. You can also seek out magazines, like *Cobblestone*, and series that energize students, like the You Wouldn't Want to Be . . . series or the True Book series. Of course, it is usually not possible to purchase tons of new materials each year so as to address the topics that are especially interesting to that year's class, but we do recommend you make a trip to your school or public library to gather as many books on the topic as you possibly can. You might also seek out digital texts and audio informational texts for students who are continuing to develop their fluency and vocabulary skills. This will be especially helpful for your ELLs and speech and language students, as these recordings provide models for fluent reading of nonfiction texts. Audio books also give students the opportunity to access topics and text levels that they may not have otherwise read on their own. (We recommend students listen to the audio books at the same time as they are following along with a print version.)

A word of advice: Especially if you do not have enough within-reach texts for students to maintain their volume of reading during this unit, we strongly suggest that you reserve time every day (at least fifteen to twenty minutes in school and more time at home) for students to continue reading literature at their levels. And, in any case, be sure readers continue to maintain their reading logs so that you are able to monitor the total volume of reading they do during this unit. You should expect that readers are reading an appropriate number of chapter books each week—probably anywhere from one to four, more for the readers who are reading at lower levels and, therefore, shorter books. That volume of fiction reading will be in addition to the reading they do of information texts. You may question this, thinking that every minute of a reader's time should go toward reading information texts, but most literate people read a balance of fiction and nonfiction. Then, too, if you are accountable for your students' results on your state's high-stakes test, keep in mind that at least until now, there is a tremendous alignment between the level of text complexity that a child can read and his or her results on high-stakes tests. The single most important way to accelerate students' progress up the ladder of text complexity is to be sure they are reading a high volume of texts they can read with high levels of comprehension and engagement.

Plan for the work students will do in reading workshop and during content area instruction.

The ideal setup for this unit is that students study the topic of westward expansion during social studies or another time outside of reading workshop. During reading workshop, they should mostly be *reading* books, articles (digital or print), book excerpts, and so on. In social studies, they have the opportunity to bolster their content knowledge by studying video clips and maps, lists of statistics, images, and more. Then, students bring all of the knowledge and thinking they do in social studies to their reading work. During reading workshop, you can emphasize volume, stamina, and nonfiction reading skills rather than content knowledge.

Study *The Lens of History: Research Reports* from Units of Study in Opinion, Information, and Narrative Writing, Grade 5 (if you have it) to note how the reading and writing units are aligned.

This study of westward expansion has been designed to unite three subject areas in your curriculum, but it can also be self-standing. The units in reading and writing have been developed as companion units. Thus, we highly encourage you to familiarize yourself with the grade 5 *Lens of History: Research Reports* unit from the Units of Study in Opinion, Information, and Narrative Writing, so that you take full advantage of the opportunities for interdisciplinary work.

Here's how we envision the different units working together and the bends of each lining up.

Content Area	Reading Workshop	Writing Workshop
Begin studying westward expansion (getting at least a basic orientation to the topic)	Bend I: Reading Nonfiction about Westward Expansion and Summarizing with Structure in Mind	alternate work/wrap up preceding unit
Continue studying westward expansion	Bend II: Learning about an Aspect of the Westward Expansion through Reading	Begin Bend I of *The Lens of History*
Continue studying westward expansion	Bend III: Building Theories and Reading Critically	Bend II of *The Lens of History*

Form research teams in the first bend of this unit.

In the days leading up to this unit, you might talk up the teamwork aspect of it, letting students know that they are about to embark on an exciting research project and that they will have the opportunity to work in teams. During Bend I, you may want to post topics of interest and let students begin to choose which one they want to research. Some teachers let students pick their top three choices and then make a final decision, doing their best to take student interests into account but also attending to students' academic needs. You'll want the research teams to be balanced so that each team will be productive within the workshop and will have the materials they need. The point is that you might have to engage in a little "behind-the-scenes engineering" before teams launch to give the impression that readers have had some hand in forming the teams. In the second bend of this unit, you'll want students to be in research clubs.

Some possible topics of inquiry might include:

- Pony Express
- Erie Canal
- Lewis and Clark
- Oregon Trail
- Gold Rush
- Trail of Tears

Of course your list may look longer or different. The important part is to have the resources to support inquiries on whichever topics are chosen.

Choose your read-aloud(s).

Your read-alouds should allow you to mirror the work your students are doing, so choose a few different texts about westward expansion. We suggest that you might read from *The Split History of Westward Expansion in the United States* by Nell Musolf. This book is actually part of the Perspectives Flip Book series (each of which show an aspect of American history through two perspectives). In this instance, one part of the book tells the story of the time period from the perspective of the white settlers. When you flip the book over, the next part tells the story of westward expansion from the perspective of the American Indians. We have chosen the book for many reasons, but primarily, we suggest it as a central read-aloud because it will offer a nuanced understanding of westward expansion—and the sense that any version of history is just that—one version. As you move into Bend II of the unit, you can show students how you are purposefully choosing which sections you read so that you can learn more about a specific aspect of westward expansion (say the transcontinental railroad). You'll note that this subtopic becomes the focus of the teacher's demonstration text in the second bend of *The Lens of History*. In addition to this text we also suggest that you might read parts from *Who Settled the West?* by Bobbie Kalman and *The Story of America: Westward Expansion* by Greg Roza.

If you want to read aloud texts that are just on the transcontinental railroad, we suggest the following:

- *Ten Mile Day: And the Building of the Transcontinental Railroad* by Mary Ann Fraser (890L/No Guided Reading Level)
- *Coolies* by Yin (picture book—historical fiction) (660L/Guided Reading Q)
- *True Books: The Transcontinental Railroad* (910L/No Guided Reading Level)

BEND I: READING NONFICTION ABOUT WESTWARD EXPANSION AND SUMMARIZING WITH STRUCTURE IN MIND

Across this bend, students will be working to determine importance and summarize, all while considering text structures. But another goal for this bend is to support students in approaching their reading of informational texts with as much agency and independence as they approached reading fiction in previous units. One of the key ways to approach an informational text with this sort of agency is to set expectations before reading through previewing.

Even though they have been taught about the importance of previewing in earlier years, for many students, this may not have yet become a habit of mind, something they do no matter what. Students may also need support in figuring out how to preview more complex texts. Previewing and setting expectations (along with confirming and revising expectations) is some of the most important work a reader of informational texts can do. It is important that students do not skip over this aspect of reading.

So, on your first day of this unit, you may want to remind your readers that it's important to rev up their minds to read information texts and that the way most informational texts are structured will help them to do this well. You can raise the level of what students have done in prior years by placing an emphasis on previewing to look at how authors have chosen to organize information. You might put up a chart of text structures (compare/contrast; pro/con; problem/solution; chronological; cause/effect) along with the signal words that indicate these structures might be used.

> "Today I want to remind you that revving up your mind to read nonfiction is some of the most important work you can do as nonfiction readers. One way to set stronger, more focused expectations from the start is to look not just at *what* information you are going to learn but also at *how* that information is being presented. Then you can ask, 'What do I expect this will be about? What ideas and information will I learn?'"

Engage students in an inquiry to practice previewing a nonfiction text.

You might take an article or section of text from *The Split History of Westward Expansion* and involve students in studying the text with you, revving up their minds to read it. Rather than demonstrate this work, you could involve students in studying the text, asking them to study not just the content of the information presented but also how it is being presented, constantly asking, "What do I expect this will be about? What ideas and information will I learn?" You can listen in and correct misconceptions as well as extend thinking. If you hear the students just talk about what they will learn about traveling west, you might direct their attention to the way the section of text has been organized. "I hear you all saying how it will be probably be about how challenging it was to travel west," you might say. "Try to set more focused expectations. One way to do this is to look at some of the structures used to present and organize information."

You could point out the headings. "Hmm, . . ." you might say. "The headings seem to be organized in a cause-and-effect structure. Turn and talk about how that might help you to set a more focused expectation. You could say to your partner, 'Maybe the text will unfold like this. . . . Maybe it's the kind of text that . . .'" Channel students to discuss what they think they will learn in the text based on some of the choices the author has made about how to organize and present information.

As you listen in again, you might hear some students talking only about the print on the page and, if so, ask them to pause, and voice over to the whole class, "What about the illustrations? The way the text has been organized does not only include the print. Let's look at this photo." You might zoom in on a photo so that students can see even the smallest details. "How does this photograph fit with what you think this section might be about?"

Instead of a photograph you could ask students to look more closely at and discuss other aspects of the text: a map, the timeline at the end of the entire section, and so on. Each time, push students to think about how this new feature and the ideas and information presented fit in with what they were thinking (or change it) and help them to set expectations for what this section of the text might be about. You might also read a little bit from the beginning of the text to think about some of the other organizational choices. You can ask students to share some of their ideas, and you might want to record these on chart paper.

Remind students that the important thing is that they are approaching their own reading with the same kind of intensity and agency that the class just showed in previewing this text and setting expectations. You might even involve them in setting some expectations for their own reading right in the meeting area, asking them to dive into previewing and perhaps jotting down some initial ideas or questions. Then they can begin reading, always alert to information that might help them confirm or revise their expectations. As you see students immersed in this work, you can send them off to continue reading.

As students go off to work, this is a good time to pull a partnership or small group of students who are ready to move to a new level of reading and support them in getting there. You might give them a book introduction, which helps them to see some of the new challenges this level of text will offer, and involve them in reading the start of the text with a lens. "What are the different ideas this text is starting to convey?" or "What information seems most important to understanding what the author really wants the reader to know, and what seems interesting but not as critical?" You can leave these students to work and then return, involving them in constructing a shared summary, and then perhaps asking them to reread the beginning, this time with a new lens, such as: "What are the different perspectives that are being introduced on this issue?"

Teach students how to determine importance, discerning the main ideas and supporting evidence in what they are reading.

As students work, you may see that they still need support in discerning importance, particularly as their texts are getting more complicated. So you may decide that you need to remind students how expository informational texts often contain main ideas followed—or surrounded—by supporting evidence. This boxes-and-bullets structure will allow students to determine main ideas and key details. If this is true for these readers, it may be true for others in your class. Do a quick check of reader's notebooks and sticky notes to see how students are doing when they are determining importance. If needed, you may decide that you will need to teach a whole-class lesson on this work.

You might start by offering a teaching point that might sound something like, "Today I want to remind you that nonfiction readers read with a pencil. We don't just use a pencil to jot down fun facts. We use a pencil to help us pay attention to the main ideas, to note the way those ideas are developed, and to make those thoughts and ideas visible."

> **"Today I want to remind you that nonfiction readers read with a pencil. We don't just use a pencil to jot down fun facts. We use a pencil to help us pay attention to the main ideas, to note the way those ideas are developed, and to make those thoughts and ideas visible."**

Here, of course, you can remind students that the texts they read could be about multiple ideas. "I'm also starting to think that maybe this article is about . . ." Understanding that texts do not just convey one idea is a key expectation for fifth grade—a major shift from the work of fourth grade—and you will want to come back to this work again and again. Students should start to notice that different parts of the text can convey different ideas. You can send students off to continue to read the article you used for the minilesson, determining key details and summarizing the text as they read. Or they could go back to their own texts to try this work.

For students that seem to need further support, you might continue to coach them to think about what each section is mostly about. What idea(s) does each section seem to be trying to convey? Some main ideas will be contained in topic sentences, but as students read more complex texts, they will need to continue to apply this same work (even when sections are not clearly set apart and labeled—even when ideas are subtle and multiple within a single section). Helping them to do this work now is important. You will also need to continue to support students in doing this work as their texts get more challenging.

For students who grasp this work fairly well, you might show them the next step of laying out various main ideas and asking, "How do these fit together? What new theories can I grow from studying them?" As students' texts become more complicated, you may find that you need to help them to move from summarizing a text by stating what seems to be its most obvious main idea and supporting details to now discussing its central idea and the supporting smaller main ideas that underlie that central one.

In what is likely to be the share that day, you can involve students in constructing a shared summary of the text and then they can go off and write their own summaries (if your students learned to write summaries last year, hopefully you will find that they can write a nice summary quite easily).

Reading what students have written will offer you insight into how well they are grasping this work. Students can assess their own work against the "Main Idea(s) and Supporting Details/Summary" strand of the Informational Reading Learning Progression and consider how to improve their work. (See the fourth-grade nonfiction unit for more support on teaching summarizing, if needed.)

Over the next few days, you will want to continue to support students' working to determine importance. You may find that some still do not seem to be alert to the different types of text structures or the way information is presented as a means to help them hold onto ideas and information (even though they likely learned this in fourth grade). If this is the case, you may want to remind them that recognizing the way a text (or part of a text) is structured can help readers to know what is most important to hold onto.

> **"Today I want to remind you that figuring out how a text (or part of a text) is structured can help you to figure out what ideas and information are the most important to hold onto."**

To teach this, you might show them a snippet of text and involve them in thinking along with you as you demonstrate how knowing the way that section is structured can help you to figure out what is most important to hold onto. Then you might put up another snippet of text, ask students to figure out the structure of this section, then let that lead them to discuss what seems most important.

As the days go on, you may find that you need to continue to support students in the notion of a text forwarding multiple main ideas. You will want to keep reminding them how as texts get more complicated, they can have multiple main ideas within one section.

> **"Today I want to remind you that texts are not only about one main idea. As texts get more complicated, so do the ideas they are forwarding. Readers need to stop often and ask, 'What does this part seem to be mostly about? How does it fit with what I have already read?'"**

All the while, encourage students to take notes on their reading. You might suggest they take notes on only one side of the paper, so they can scissor apart and categorize what they have learned. Some teachers have stapled loose-leaf paper together to make little research booklets for students.

Engage students in determining main ideas and supporting details during read-aloud.

During read-aloud, you might engage students in studying the text along with you, considering how you might determine the main ideas and key details as well as summarize a portion of the text. You may want to choose a section of text that has no headings, so students are forced to do the heavy lifting of determining central ideas without the scaffolding of text features.

In addition, you might choose to spend some read-aloud time studying and reading articles together as a class. We suggest articles from magazines, such as "Orphan Trains: Traveling West to a New Life" (from *Cobblestone*). Students will see that they need to approach this text with an enormous amount of energy, from understanding how the text boxes and features fit into the ideas of the text, to grasping the shifts in time through the main text, to interpreting maps. Your read-aloud time is a valuable chance to read a variety of texts, exposing students to a variety of text structures and supporting the range of work that a nonfiction reader needs to do.

Use small-group work and conferring to continue to support students who may need more work with main ideas.

Across the next few days, you may need to use your small-group work and conferring to continue to address main idea work. Here are some other ways that readers determine main ideas and key details in nonfiction that students might try (and note that any of the following could be full class minilessons, if necessary):

- Readers ask themselves, "What is a big idea or ideas that this text is conveying, and how do the other details connect with it?"

- Readers can be on the lookout for a "pop-out sentence" as they read, knowing that often one sentence summarizes the content of a paragraph or a passage. This sentence will often be broad and sweeping and feel like it needs key details to support it. Sometimes this sentence is the first or last sentence—but not always!

- Readers read, always pushing themselves to think about how new information fits with what the text has taught them so far. They read, pausing to ask themselves "What is the big thing this part teaches me? How does this fit with what's been said so far?"

- Readers sometimes identify key details first. They pay attention to what important details they are learning and then ask, "What is the big idea these details are trying to show or support?" To help them do this work, readers might mentally or physically cut up an article and study the different parts to ask themselves what those parts add up to show (_____ + _____ + _____ = ?).

- Readers consider the structures of the text, asking, "How is the way this is structured helping me to know what is most important to hold onto?"

You might also introduce the following questions that students can ask each other or themselves to support this work:

- How would you summarize this (paragraph, section, part) of the text?
- What are the main ideas of this entire text?
- Which detail would be most important to include in one of the main ideas of the text?
- What is a main idea of the first three paragraphs of this text? The final section?

As students are beginning to determine importance and figure out main ideas and key details, you will want to give them opportunities to synthesize what they have learned. You might ask them to prepare for partner talk by rehearsing how they'll explain important information they've jotted on their Post-its—they might use the text's pictures and charts, an explaining voice, an explaining finger, and gestures. This will support their work on summarizing as well. Remind readers that summaries are meant to be concise versions of the text. That means that a summary should contain the most important ideas and information so that anyone who read or heard the summary would have a good grasp of the text's most crucial ideas and information. If a detail is interesting but does not help to get across what matters most in understanding this text, it should not be included.

Move students beyond thinking about text structures on a surface level to thinking about *why* and *how* authors use structure to convey meaning.

All of this work on determining main ideas and summarizing texts takes place only across the first week or so of the unit. Ensure that students also have time to move to thinking more deeply about text structures, comparing and contrasting these and thinking about why an author may have chosen them. You will want to move your students from seeing structures only as tools for them to know what to hold onto and start to see that the way sections are structured is also a tool for authors to help convey larger ideas. You will want them to now start thinking about the way that structures can relate to larger purposes. Help students to see that authors deliberately organize their texts to convey ideas and make points.

> "Today I want to teach you that each part of a text has a job to do in helping an author show or develop his or her ideas. Figuring out the structure of a part can help you to think about why an author might have included it and how it helps to show or develop the main ideas of the text."

To begin this work, you might put up two different sections of text and let students think about what the author wanted the reader to know in each section and how the structure chosen helped to make the purpose clear. For example, if you flip between the two versions of *The Split History of Westward Expansion*, you'll see contrasting perspectives on the same events.

As students go off to read today, you can push them to go back to study texts they have already read and look at different text structures authors have chosen for their texts or parts of their texts. Students can continue to draw on what they have learned about describing text structures to notice what structures have been used.

You might guide students to consider questions such as

- What best describes the main text structure of the entire article?
- What best describes the structure of the paragraph? The sentence?
- Why does the author start/end the article with a question, quote, and so on?
- What best describes the text structure used to connect the events told in this text?
- What does each author want us to know? How does the structure help the author to present that information?
- What structure has each author chosen? Why might they have used these different structures?
- How does this part contribute to the overall structure?

As students are doing this work, you may also see that you need to help them deal with other kinds of vocabulary. When reading books on unfamiliar subjects, as is often the case when children take on informational texts, especially those about an era of history, they will encounter many unfamiliar words. It is wise for a unit of study on informational reading to contain several minilessons designed to help readers tackle challenging words. Students need to notice the vocabulary that is specific to the topic on which they are reading, determine the meaning of terms, and transfer and apply this learning by using the terms themselves when writing or speaking about the topics. In addition, they need to transfer academic words across units and across the curriculum. Tier 2 words such as *concise*, for example, can be carried across and discussed in each area of the curriculum.

BEND II: LEARNING ABOUT AN ASPECT OF WESTWARD EXPANSION THROUGH READING

As students have spent a week or so revving up their minds before reading and reading alert to the structures of texts and their implications, you'll want to now support them in transferring and applying all of their nonfiction reading strategies as they undertake reading to research on a particular subtopic related to westward expansion.

The main goal of this bend is to support students in independently creating a research project, taking notes and organizing information, and paying attention to when different sources give different information. This bend is intended to last for about a week or so before students move on to the final portion of the unit where they will be building theories and reading more critically.

Orient students to the work of the bend, form research teams, and launch the team research projects.

To start this work off, on the first day of this bend, you might gather students in the meeting area and ask them to sit with their teams. You'll want to issue a generous invitation, welcoming students into the worthy work of research. You might say something like, "A few days ago, I asked you to choose an aspect of westward expansion that you wanted to study more, and you got into teams. You're sitting in those teams now, and today is the day you get started digging deep, working with your team to learn as much as you can about your subtopic so your team can teach others about it." After a connection like that, you could name your first teaching point: "So today I want to teach you that when readers get started on a research project, they figure out how to get themselves set up for reading in ways that let them learn all they can about their topic. One way they do that is by getting a lay of the land of their texts and making a plan for what to read." Then you might demonstrate this work to students by using the topic that will become the class research topic.

> **"Today I want to teach you that when readers get started on a research project, they figure out how to get themselves set up for reading in ways that let them learn all they can about their topic. One way they do that is by getting a lay of the land of their texts and making a plan for what to read."**

We suggest that you engineer things so that the topic the whole class studies (the transcontinental railroad, for example) is also the topic that readers who need the most support also research. That way, your demonstration can scaffold their work. Begin by laying out the texts you have gathered for the class demonstration set, and show students how you take a broad survey of them. "So I've decided that we as a class might study the transcontinental railroad. Let's look through these books to decide what parts we should read that will help us to learn more about that event."

You might leaf through a few of the books and then put a table of contents up from *The Split History of Westward Expansion* (settlers' perspective side) on the document camera. "Hmm, uh oh . . . no chapters called 'The Transcontinental Railroad.' Okay, so, one option is to go to the index and look for 'railroad' or 'Transcontinental Railroad' there, but let's just take a minute to look at these chapter titles again and see where the transcontinental railroad might be mentioned in this book." You could continue to muse about where to locate the information you want, tucking in tips about skimming and scanning as you go. "So I know that often, history books are set up in chronological order, so that means the railroad probably wouldn't be mentioned in the beginning chapters. Hmm, . . . well, look here how one of the chapters is called 'Connecting the East and the West.' That seems like it might mention the transcontinental railroad, right? I mean, that's one of the purposes for the railroad—to connect the east and the west." You might flip to that chapter and skim a bit to confirm that this section will be about the transcontinental railroad. "Let's see, it's about the Erie Canal, so far. Wait, the bottom of this page mentions railroads. Let's flip to the next page—Aha! Here's a photo of the transcontinental railroad being built, and the section is called 'A Massive Undertaking.' Yes, it's definitely about the transcontinental railroad. That feels like it will be really important to read. Maybe I should even start making a plan for what to read, jotting book titles and page numbers that have information about my topic."

After you model this for a bit longer, you might give each club the chance to do some preliminary work in the meeting area. Give them the opportunity to start leafing through the books and articles in their bins and making a plan for what to read. You might keep students on the rug for a bit longer than is typical (be sure to explain that you are doing this) so that you can ensure each team is getting itself readied for a strong start. After you listen in and coach teams, you might call students back and highlight some of what you heard. You could emphasize that readers are making plans for what to read so that they learn the most they can about their topics. As part of that, they're looking for texts that will be easy for them to read, knowing that after reading the easier texts, they'll be more informed on their topic and able to tackle the harder ones. You might pick up *The Story of America: Westward Expansion* by Roza and show students.

"This one seems a bit easier than the others so maybe I'll start with that. That way I think I can get some basic background and maybe learn some of the vocabulary. Then I'll move to some of the harder books." You can send readers off to begin this work.

As readers get working with their teams they will have already made some decisions, so you can expect them to start moving immediately into their reading. You'll want to watch how students get themselves started and how they hold onto the information they are learning. You'll expect to see them using what they know of note-taking strategies from previous content area and informational reading units they did in fourth grade, though you may also find it necessary to review some strategies and techniques. Students should be accustomed to looking through texts, laying out a plan for research, and getting themselves started. You'll want to take some time to watch them work and consider what they are holding onto from previous units and years. Are they getting themselves started, creating a plan for reading, and then choosing what seems like slightly easier and perhaps broader texts first? Do they automatically set up their notebooks for note taking? Do they jot the title and author of the book they are reading? This is all previous learning, and if you don't see it happening, you'll want to coach into this work right away. A series of whole class voice-overs and table compliments will go a long way for helping you touch base with as many members of the class as possible while ensuring that all are getting started.

You might also compliment a child at a table, making sure the rest of the members of the table are within earshot. "I love that I see you looking back at the timeline we made in social studies. I hope that everyone is also thinking about what resources we used in social studies that can help with this new work!" In this way, you'll help all of the students get on track and start working.

Highlight for students all the resources they have available to them, including those used in social studies.

In what is likely to be the share on the first day, you'll want to help students recall their previous learning about westward expansion in social studies and from their reading in the first bend, and remind them that all of that learning can help them with this new work. You might point to all of the charts you have out about westward expansion and remind students that these resources can help them now. You might demonstrate looking at a timeline: "So, if I am studying the transcontinental railroad—I am looking at this timeline to see where in the course of events related to westward expansion the transcontinental railroad fits in. Wow, so late in the timeline! One of the last events considered part of westward expansion. Actually, the last major event. Hmm, . . . this is making me think more about the completion of the building of the transcontinental railroad's relationship to other events on the timeline. It seems like it was sort of a culmination—that means it is the result of many events—but it's the start of something too. It's the start of a new era of American history—what comes after westward expansion. I'm starting to think that maybe I'll need to do a bit of reading about the events that came before *and* after the transcontinental railroad to really think more deeply about its causes, consequences, and significance in history. I'm going to try to read the sections in my books that have to do with events that come right before the transcontinental railroad, for example, to try to figure out what led to it happening."

You can give students some time to think about their own topics in light of the class's timeline—and then nudge them to scan the room for other charts that could help them. Of course, there are other resources students have available, including their own prior knowledge. Another teaching point could be: "Readers think about *all* they know when they are learning about a topic. If you are learning about penguins, you review all you know about birds because that can help you think about penguins. And if you are learning about Lewis and Clark, you think of all you know about westward expansion, because that all relates to Lewis and Clark." You might, then, channel children to pull out their social studies notebooks and scan old notes, asking how to code the old notes (perhaps about westward expansion in general) that are also relevant to their new subtopic. Another day you might have students pull out their social studies notebooks to look back at their old notes and ask them to decide what they want to include in their new notes.

Coach into predictable problems that sometimes befall students as they work on research projects.

Students will find it to be a heady and sometimes daunting endeavor to research a subtopic with their small group. You'll want to find ways to help them keep their energy high throughout the process. So you might teach students, saying, "Today I want to teach you that it helps for researchers to think not only about their topic but also about their work, talking together about questions such as, 'How can we keep our energy high during this process?'"

Over the next few days, as students research and take notes, you'll likely see there are predictable ways that you'll need to teach into this work. Chris Lehman reminds us in his book *Energize Research Reading and Writing* (Heinemann, 2012) that one such concern might be that you see students copying large sections of text. If this is the case for your students, you'll want to teach a lesson in which you teach students some tips about notetaking.

> **"Today I want to teach you that researchers choose only what seems most important to jot down, and they jot mostly in their own words, quickly, without full sentences."**

You might model this by showing students how you read a chunk of text, then look up from the book and try to summarize what you read by listing the major points (you can hold up your hand and list the points on your fingers as a model for students to follow), then come up with an idea those points support. You might then show students how you quickly jot down what you wrote and then decide on a heading for the points you have listed. So you might read the first few paragraphs of the section "A Massive Undertaking" in Nell Musolf's *The Split History of Westward Expansion* (pages 22–23) and might model listing these major points.

The Split History of Westward Expansion by Nell Musolf (pages 22-23)

<u>Building the railroad was a huge undertaking</u>

- Work started in two places (Omaha, Nebraska—Union Pacific Company//Sacramento, California—Central Pacific Company)—would meet in the middle and make one line
- Would have to be built over all types of land—prairies, through mountains, over rivers and gorges (Promontory Trestle in Utah—450 feet high)
- 1000s of workers needed (12,000 Chinese worked for Central Pacific//10,000 men worked for Union Pacific—(including Irish Immigrants + African Am.)
- Harsh conditions—blizzards, windstorms, "blazing sun and the bitter cold," accidents, illnesses, death, fear of attacks by Native Americans

You can then offer students a chance to try this work with another chunk of text—pushing them to decide whether they need to create a new category to record the new information or whether it can be incorporated into the notes you have already taken. You can also talk with students about whether to include details that seem tangential in your notes. (For example, on these pages, you might talk about the textbox about the Mormon settlement in Utah. While interesting, this detail doesn't seem to be as important to helping you understand how the transcontinental railroad was a huge undertaking.) As students go off to work, you may also need to remind them to read over their notes to see if they have included the names of key people, key places, and key events.

You might now add onto your notes so they look like this:

The Split History of Westward Expansion by Nell Musolf (pages 22-23)

<u>Building the railroad was a huge undertaking</u>

- Finished in 1869—so took 6 years to build—seen as "transforming the United States"
- Anyone could go West—if they could afford a ticket—no more wagons

You'll want to point out to your students how you quote within your notes, using quotation marks when you do so that you can then go back to incorporate quotes into your writing and conversation about your topic. Remember, that fifth-graders need to quote accurately.

Students will also likely need help categorizing their notes on their subtopics. You may see a student, for example, taking down notes from one book on one page, then moving to another book and starting a new page for those notes. If that is the case, you'll want to intervene and help that reader see that he or she can incorporate new learning into old notes. You might demonstrate how you can read a new text section on the transcontinental railroad and add your new notes to the ones you have already taken from another text.

Another strategy is to have students cut up their notes so they can practice grouping notes that seem similar together and then tape these into their notebook (or a booklet). Or, you might provide index cards and let students take notes on these, then sort and categorize them.

Provide students with opportunities to teach others about their topics.

To support students in synthesizing their learning right away, you can involve them in teaching others about the importance of their subtopic. Students will need to see that they can integrate all that they have learned about their topic across their texts. You might ask them to take a minute and consider questions like the following:

- Why was my topic significant to American history? Why do we still care about this topic today? Why have authors taken the time to write books on it?
- How does my topic change American history or life in America?

Children might first talk about the class topic, the transcontinental railroad. You might overhear them saying (or coach them to think about) how the railroad connected two sides of America and helped food, clothes, tools, animals, and even people travel faster from one side of the country to the other. They might discuss how the building of the railroad meant that people no longer had to head west in wagon trains. Students might also start to think about how the railroad could help America rely on its own natural resources more—it didn't have to buy stuff from other countries as much. The railroad also helped more people to communicate: Letters were put on the railroad, and people could hear from each other much faster! Big cities popped up around railroad stations. And the railroad helped create the "wild west" towns where railroad workers stayed while they were building. Students might also talk about the different groups of people who helped to build the railroad—Chinese and Irish immigrants and African Americans, among others.

Then students might now take some time to consider what they have learned about their own topics across the books and articles they have been reading. In this discussion, you may notice that students are not using the domain-specific vocabulary they are encountering in their texts. If that is the case, then you'll next want to show students that they can use the "lingo of experts" when talking and writing about their topics. Your teaching point could be: "Today I want to teach you that when you become an expert on a topic, it is important to begin using the technical vocabulary of that subject. Even if you are just really beginning to learn about a subject, you can accelerate your learning curve by 'talking the talk.'"

You might even have each team begin to invent ways to record new terms that seem important to their topic. Students could make mini word walls or glossaries and keep these in the middle of their tables when they teach each other.

You can also help students to see that while the names of people, places, and events matter, other terms matter as well. One way to know a term is important is if the author repeats it. So if one author has repeated a term like *grueling* or if a few different authors have pointed out that the journey west on a covered wagon was *grueling*, then students should try to use the word *grueling* in their own speaking and writing. Encourage them to use the term and then unpack it and analyze its significance to what they are learning. So, students might explain why the journey west was grueling and what motivated settlers to go despite the grueling conditions. Helping students to acquire academic vocabulary is as essential as helping them to acquire domain-specific terms. You'll want them to notice and begin to lift terms like *disregard*, *progress*, *perilous*, *terrain*, *resentment*, *distributed*, *expansion*, *commerce*, and *exploited* in addition to terms like *settlers*, *pioneers*, *Union Pacific Company*, *Sacajawea*, *Manifest Destiny*, and so on.

Guide students to move beyond simply gathering information about a topic to growing ideas about a topic.

Another session in this part of the unit will likely be about helping students to see that note-taking can involve not only recording information but also growing ideas. To support this work, you might remind them of the prompts they have used to grow their thinking in other units and help them to see that they can do that same work here.

> "Today I want to remind you that readers don't only use writing to record information; readers also write to grow ideas. And to do that, readers sometimes rely on the same 'thought prompts' as they use to grow ideas when talking."

Some prompts that might help include

- I used to think . . . but now I realize . . .
- At one point I thought . . . and now I think . . .
- My ideas about . . . are complicated. One the one hand, I think . . . while on the other hand, I think . . .

Students can also ask themselves and others questions of the information they are learning to push themselves to consider causes, consequences, and the relationships of events in history.

- Does that remind you of anything you have already learned?
- What might be a result of ____?
- What might that lead to?
- What do you think caused ____?

Encourage students to constantly go back to research further to find the answers to these questions and to jot these questions in their notes.

Model a variety of strategies for notetaking.

Your read-aloud will be of key importance during this part of the unit. Use your read-aloud to model taking notes and growing ideas. During your read-alouds, you'll demonstrate going back to notes you have already taken to include new information. Show students how you add headings to your notes to organize them. You can also model taking notes using different text structures, showing students how you consider which structure of note-taking will best help you hold onto the information in a section. Students will continually see an exemplar model of this work, which can give them a vision for what they should be doing in their teams.

As you watch students take notes and teach each other, you will likely see ways that students can make better use of their notebooks. You might see, for example, that students seem to put their notes aside when they begin teaching others about their topics. If this is the case, you'll want to help students see their notes as tools that can help them teach others. You can coach them to quote from their notes as well as from other texts when they teach. In addition, students can quote facts they have jotted down and their own ideas after they hear another student's teaching session and want to extend or challenge that student's ideas.

Students can also raise their work to new heights by seeing their notes as a living document that can be revised and strengthened. They can do more with their notes than simply add on to them. Here a few ways you might raise the level of note-taking and thinking about notes in your room:

- Researchers are interested in each other's studies. They sometimes swap notebooks and take notes on each other's notes. That helps not only the person reading and learning from someone's notes but also the note-taker, because the note-taker can learn what others find interesting.

- Researchers find it interesting when a different researcher has different information or ideas on a topic. Researchers stop and challenge other researchers. "Right here, you wrote . . . I'm just not sure about that, because that wasn't my understanding of it. In my notes, I wrote . . . Let's go back to that section of text and look at it again together." In this way, by challenging each other, researchers can help each other revise information that may be inaccurate or misleading and can also think about why different sources might include different information on a topic.

- Researchers can also notice that when reading the same book or listening to the same videotape, different things will seem important to different researchers. It is helpful to talk about why one person or another thinks something is especially important.

As students gain a stronger background on their topics, you might teach them that they will often find they can progress to harder texts. Say to students: "Readers, once a researcher has read a bunch of easier texts on a topic and started knowing more about that topic, it is often possible to read and understand texts that would at first have seemed too hard. Also, tackling the hard texts with another person sometimes leads to more success."

Teach students multiple strategies for tackling complex texts and synthesizing their learning.

You might also teach students that there are particular strategies they can use when tackling harder texts. For example, show students how right at the start of a text, it helps if you preview quickly and then—even before reading the text—try making a quick summary of the text. Then, as you read on, when parts get confusing, it can help to push yourself past them, continuing to summarize what you are able to glean, even if you know you aren't grasping everything. By channeling students to continue to summarize, you help them hold onto the major points of a text. To show students how to do this you might put a super complex text on the document camera and show students how, even when a reader doesn't know every word, the reader can still continue to summarize what he or she does know and hold onto the gist of a text.

There are other strategies that some reading researchers recommend for helping students tackle complex text, and you can try them out and see if they work for your students. For example, some people think it helps to suggest that when reading a text that is a bit overwhelming, it works to read the first and last line of every paragraph, summarizing what you can from just those lines in an effort to figure out main idea(s) and key details as you go. No matter what, you will want to help students recognize when they feel a text is too hard—when they start to feel overwhelmed or lose focus, for example—so they don't just plow along but instead try to alter their reading so they work hard to hold onto understanding. You can also continue to teach small-group lessons on dealing with unfamiliar terms and on decoding throughout this bend and throughout the unit, if you find your students need this.

Likely, before this bend is over, you'll teach students to synthesize what they are learning across texts.

> **"Readers, today I want to teach you that researchers push themselves to draw on all they have learned from anywhere about the topic they are researching, and they read across texts, thinking, 'How are the lessons I am learning from these texts the same and different?'"**

As the bend ends, students can again take some time to consolidate their notes and prepare to teach others. You can teach them by saying, "Researchers and writers need to think, 'What are the most important idea that I want to forward?' and then think, 'How can I pop out the really big ideas, maybe by writing or saying more about them, maybe by using text features to help make those ideas more important to people reading and listening to me.'"

Help students to think about why the subtopic they have focused upon seems interesting and important to them. Why should people care about this subtopic? How does it change or add to a person's understanding of westward expansion?

Some essential questions to consider could be

- What were the wants and needs of the new nation?
- How did these needs and wants lead to conflict among groups? What were the troubles experienced in the new nation? What were the perspectives of conflicting groups?
- What were the results of the movement west?

As students are reading through texts and taking notes, you might teach them that one way readers synthesize their learning is by talking through—and teaching—what they are learning to others. Then you can channel students to teach the other members of their group what they are learning. This work can support students' abilities to summarize and help them to determine importance. (Remember that the Informational Reading Learning Progression can help students self-assess and set goals for this work.) As you listen, you may need to coach students into moving away from just reading parts of the text to each other. It will help immeasurably if you give students a few minutes to plan their teaching session before they teach, deciding on the most important information to share with group members and collecting ways to elaborate on each of those points. Students can then teach each other some key points, making sure to provide supporting evidence, details, and also to reflect on the significance of their content by developing an idea or two about that information. As part of this you can teach students that one way to develop a key point is to quote from one of their texts in ways that highlight the key point, or support it. Remind them that it is important to explain why that quote seems important.

You can also encourage them to make connections between their learning by offering them some conversation prompts.

- That fits with what I'm learning because . . .
- That's different from what I read because . . .
- What you just said is making me realize that . . .
- Now I'm starting to have a new idea . . .
- This is helping me to understand why . . .
- This connects to what we learned in social studies because . . .
- Now, I'm wondering . . .

Students will be filling the pages of their research booklets with information and their ideas and teaching each other what seems most important to know about their topics.

BEND III: BUILDING THEORIES AND READING CRITICALLY

As the unit enters the third and final bend, students will draw on what they have already learned in order to build theories and interpret the historical texts they are reading with greater independence. Students will synthesize their thinking about their texts and push themselves to develop big ideas that they can support with inferences they have made earlier. As students are building theories, they will be considering questions such as "Who benefited? Who lost? What were the consequences of these events?" and by doing so, they will be raising the level of their work from fourth grade.

Guide students to look across the work they have done for the last few weeks and develop theories and themes about their topics.

Your students' notebooks and books will be bursting with jottings and Post-its. You might want to begin with a session on pausing in the midst of reading to organize one's thoughts. Children might sort Post-its into piles that are about one particular subtopic they have studied so far. You might then remind your students that they can look for patterns and new ideas within this stack of related Post-its.

> **"Today I want to teach you that when readers look at a series of ideas about a book (or set of books) they can ask themselves, 'What do these have in common? What is different about these ideas?' Then they use the answers to create a theory."**

Once children have developed a few theories about their topics, they can revisit earlier parts of the text in light of their theories. They can also read forward, gathering more evidence to support their theories and making individual theory charts. If you are teaching the connected writing unit, you'll want to remind students to do the work that they learned there: to speculate and hypothesize, using tentative language— "Maybe it was . . . ," "It might have been the case that . . . ," and so on.

You may want to demonstrate sorting and building theories based on these notes. As you look at Post-its together, first help students to sort their lists further, looking for ideas that go together. Then, you can coach your students to think about what these combined ideas are showing us about the topic. You can craft an example about the subtopic of the westward expansion that the class has been studying, the transcontinental railroad. Students might build a theory such as

It may have been the case that the building of the transcontinental railroad depended largely on groups of people who faced discrimination.

Students can also begin to question and consider what larger lessons each book might be teaching about history and power and human nature and the economy and so on. They can ask, as readers do,

"What lessons might this book be teaching not just about westward expansion but about American history?" Students can, by building on their inferences, begin thinking about big lessons readers can learn from the text. In this, they will be very close to studying themes.

Examples include:

- Progress seems to mean only progress for some; other groups lose out.
- Throughout American history, it seems that one way of being powerful was to get more land.

Now that they have grasped some of the content related to their research and begun to grow ideas and build theories, this last part of the unit aims to help them to go back to some of those sources and reread them, this time more critically. You'll want to show students that sometimes when you start to put pieces of information together, some of those sources say different things.

To demonstrate this, you might show students the pages about the transcontinental railroad from *The Split History of Westward Expansion*. You can remind them of some of the important points this author has made and new theories the class has grown by showing them the class notes.

The Split History of Westward Expansion by Nell Musolf (pages 22-23)

<u>Building the railroad was a huge undertaking</u>

- Work started in two places (Omaha, Nebraska—Union Pacific Company//Sacramento, California—Central Pacific Company)—would meet in the middle and make one line
- Would have to be built over all types of land—prairies, through mountains, over rivers and gorges (Promontory Trestle in Utah—450 feet high)
- 1000s of workers needed (12,000 Chinese worked for Central Pacific//10,000 men worked for Union Pacific—(including Irish immigrants + African Am.)
- Harsh conditions—blizzards, windstorms, "blazing sun and the bitter cold," accidents, illnesses, death, fear of attacks by Native Americans
- Finished in 1869—so took 6 years to build—seen as "transforming the United States"
- Anyone could go west—if they could afford a ticket—no more wagons
- It may have been the case that the building of the transcontinental railroad depended largely on groups of people who faced discrimination.
- Progress seems to mean only progress for some; other groups lose out.
- Throughout American history, it seems that one way of being powerful was to get more land.

Then, you might display part of *The Split History of Westward Expansion* (American Indian side). You can display pages 18–19 on the document camera and engage the class in close reading of just the first paragraph, asking students what new information or what conflicting information they have gained from this text that the other text did not say. Students might notice, for example, that this paragraph of *The Split History of Westward Expansion* tells the reader that the railroad led to the end of a key part of the existence of the tribes living in the Great Plains. You might give students a second active involvement by reading the rest of these pages and letting students talk again. Students may notice that the author has mentioned the role of the buffalo and the killing of the buffalo during the construction of the transcontinental railroad. There was no mention of the buffalo in the settlers' side of the story. Students might talk about how details that are so major to one group's story are ignored by another group. You can also push them to consider how both sides of this book were written by the same author, so she is trying to convey ideas about westward expansion through telling both sides of the story. Students can go back to think about what larger ideas the author might be trying to convey and what new theories they have. As they go off to work independently today, encourage them to think about what details the authors of their texts have included, what details may have been left out, and what details might conflict with what other authors have written.

You can also provide some prompts for students to help them do more of this compare-and-contrast work.

- This text says but this text (does not say/also says) . . .
- This text conflicts with what the other text has said by . . .
- This text builds on what the other text has said by . . .

Students might even go back to look at some of the texts they have already read to more closely compare the information they provide. You can coach into this work by asking them to notice what each author has made most important. "Readers, after you have read a couple of sources on a topic, it is helpful to compare and contrast those sources, noticing how the texts portray the topic in similar ways—and how the texts are different. Then you can to try to figure out why the authors may have made different craft decisions, thinking, 'Does this relate to the different central ideas they are trying to get across?'" *The Split History of Westward Expansion* (settlers' side) seems to most want readers to know that the building of the railroad was a huge and difficult undertaking, for example, while *The Split History of Westward Expansion* (American Indians' side) seems to most want readers to know that the killing of the buffalo during the construction of the transcontinental railroad led to the destruction of a major part of American Indians' way of life. Students might ask each other the following:

- What information is in this account that is not in the other account?
- What major points is the author making? What are the key details each includes?

As your students look for discrepancies or similarities in their sources, you'll also want to remind them that it's important to continue to be able to summarize or synthesize the major points and idea(s) related to your topic.

You might now show students how you do your best to summarize what you know on the topic, across all of your texts. When information conflicts, you can acknowledge that conflict in your summary. So, for example, your own summary of the building of the transcontinental railroad might include the acknowledgment that the event is fraught with conflict. "The building of the transcontinental railroad led to progress for some; loss for others. What is clear is that it changed America."

As the unit heads toward the final days, students will reread previously read material, this time considering not just the information the author wanted to teach but also the emotion or opinion about that information the author wanted to convey and how he or she conveyed this. You'll gather students and rally them toward this point-of-view work.

> **"What I want to teach you today is that readers don't just think about the information in a text, they also figure out the point of view of the author of that text and how he or she might be swaying you to think a certain way about the topic."**

Offer students entry points for determining and analyzing an author's point of view.

You might then teach students that one way to figure out the author's point of view on a topic is to look for places where the author's opinion is coming through. You might show them two sentences:

- Many settlers went west in covered wagons.
- Boldly, full of courage and determination, settlers set forth on the journey west.

You can let students know that the first statement is a fact. There are records to show that many settlers did go west in covered wagons. The second statement is an opinion. It is a feeling about the event. The words *boldly* and *full of courage and determination* in the second sentence are clues to the author's opinion. You can tell the author supports the settlers.

You might now provide an active involvement and give students a chance to try this work with multiple sources. You might keep students on the rug a bit longer for this lesson. It is likely that when they go off to work, they will not find such clear examples of overt point of view in their own texts, and so the work at the rug is providing a chance to practice with supportive examples. We have found that this kind of point-of-view work is sometimes easier when texts are laid side by side. So you might now provide an active involvement where you type up three texts on the transcontinental railroad and show these to students.

"On May 10, 1869, the first transcontinental railroad in the United States was completed. The line connected the east and west, making travel easier, safer, and quicker. It sped up the rate at which the west was populated, bringing more and more settlers every year. Soon travelers could reach just about any location in the United States on newly built railroads" (pages 28–29 of *The Story of America: Westward Expansion* by Roza).

"Despite all the anti-Chinese attacks, snow and rock avalanches, fierce weather conditions, and blasting accidents, the Chinese laborers worked harder and harder. Their achievement—hammering a railroad out of hundreds of miles of treacherous and unexplored country—remains an incredible feat" (author's note from *Coolies* by Yin).

"When railroads were built in the west, travel became faster and easier for the settlers. But for the American Indians, especially the tribes living in the Great Plains, the railroads spelled the end to a vital part of their existence" (page 18 from *The Split History of Westward Expansion* [American Indians' side] by Musolf).

Likely students will notice that while one author has taken what seems to be a more "neutral" position, not mentioning any of the conflict and portraying the railroad as wholly good, another author is more nuanced, allowing for some of the complications that came along with the building of the railroad.

Additionally, lead students to discuss the kinds of language choices that the authors have made and what those language choices show about the authors' points of view on topics and events. Then, set up students to practice this using multiple accounts of the same event (including first-person and third-person accounts and in different types of text structures).

You might also give each group of students a primary source document they have already studied in social studies and let them try this point-of-view work with these documents. Some questions they might ask themselves and others:

- Suppose the _____ (person involved) wrote about the _____ (event). How would his account most likely be different than the account given by the _____ (outside observer)?

- What are the differences in focus between the two accounts?

- What is the purpose of each of the documents? How does that help you to think about the author's point of view?

- What words or phrases best show the author's point of view?

- How does the point of view in _____ (text 1) differ from the point of view in _____ (text 2)?

- The points of view in both texts are similar because both authors . . . ?

Teach students to analyze author's craft by paying attention to structure.

Another lesson you might teach is to help students to look at how authors have chosen to structure their texts and what reasons and evidence they give to support their points. One has started with a photo of the Golden Spike Ceremony; another has started by providing statistics of how workers crossed from China to come build the railroad and how much their passage cost. Students can think about why authors chose to organize their texts in these ways and how these choices help to support their points. In this way, you will be helping students to see how authors use reasons and evidence to support points. In fifth grade, students need to figure out which reasons and evidence support which points, so you'll want them to consider: "What points is the author making? Why is that illustration included? What point does it support? What point does that example support?" Some other questions students might ask themselves and others follow:

- The author seems to be making the point that. . . . Which sentence has evidence supporting that point?

- Why does the author most likely say this?

- What reason does the author give to support her point that . . . ?

- What text structures has each author used? Why do you think those text structures were chosen to develop the accounts? Are there other text structures that could have been used?

Students might now return to their notes and reread these with a more critical lens. Now they can return to the questions they asked before and add some additional, more critical questions.

- Why was my topic significant to American history? Why do we still care about this topic today? Why have authors taken the time to write books on it?

- How does my topic change American history or life in America?

- What are the benefits and consequences related to my topic? Who benefited? Who did not? How were different groups of people affected?

You can model this by returning to your own notes on the transcontinental railroad and showing how you might write long in response to these.

The author goes out of her way to point out certain groups of people who helped to build the transcontinental railroad (Chinese, Irish immigrants + African Am.). I'm wondering why she has done that. Why those three groups? What do they have in common? I guess Chinese and Irish are both immigrants, but African Americans are not. I'm starting to think of what those three groups might have in common, and I'm wondering if maybe the author wanted to point out groups of people who faced discrimination. Maybe she's trying to show that the building of the railroad for rich Americans was done by the very people who were likely excluded and discriminated against by those same rich Americans. This book doesn't mention what the workers were paid, but I'm betting it wasn't that much. This makes me start to realize that so much of the history of America is about exploiting those who are in minority groups.

As students work independently, you may want to remind them that a text can offer more than one idea. You might model this by looking back at your notes and thinking about what other ideas some of these key details might support.

I'm wondering about why Native Americans wanted to attack the people who were building the railroad. I'm thinking they were probably so angry that their land was being destroyed even further by this construction. This is another detail that the author has mentioned that is making me start to realize how many conflicts were involved with the building of this railroad. I'm thinking that another idea this text might be trying to convey is that change and progress will always include conflict and it will not be progress for everyone, only some groups. Other groups will lose.

As the unit ends in reading workshop, students can take all of the writing they have done on their subtopics and bring it to writing workshop to help them develop and add more pages to their informational books.

CELEBRATION

You might hold a joint reading/writing/social studies celebration to wrap up the work of this unit. We recommend holding an expert fair, in which you invite students from other classes, and ideally, parents and caregivers, to attend the fair and learn from your students' hard-won expertise.

To prepare, ask students to create an introduction to their topics and their work, and to organize some visuals that they might display to invite visitors to learn more about their topics. Then, consider how you will group students. You may place students with similar topics together and ask them to plan their introductions together as well. If your students were engaged in writing informational texts all about westward expansion during writing workshop, those texts will make perfect items to display. Students might choose certain key pages they would really like to show visitors, as time will likely be too tight for visitors to read each book in its entirety.

Organize your classroom so that your students are set up in "booths" around the periphery of the room. When visitors arrive, you might give a short welcome speech, explaining a bit about the trajectory of work students undertook, then inviting them to mingle from booth to booth, to listen to each group's introduction and to take in the visuals.

When the celebration is over and visitors have left, you might gather your students in the meeting area, to toast their hard work with a celebratory glass of seltzer. Give them an opportunity for reflection as well. You might ask them to jot a few key pieces of learning that they plan to carry with them each time they engage in research. This step is especially important if you are sending your students off to middle school next year.

POSSIBLE TEACHING POINTS

BEND I: READING NONFICTION ABOUT WESTWARD EXPANSION AND SUMMARIZING WITH STRUCTURE IN MIND

- "Today I want to remind you that revving up your mind to read nonfiction is some of the most important work you can do as nonfiction readers. One way to set stronger, more focused expectations from the start is to look not just at what information you are going to learn but also at how that information is being presented. Then you can ask, 'What do I expect this will be about? What ideas and information will I learn?'"

- "Today I want to remind you that nonfiction readers read with a pencil. We don't just use a pencil to jot down fun facts. We use a pencil to help us pay attention to the main ideas, to note the way those ideas are developed, and to make those thoughts and ideas visible."

- "Today I want to remind you that figuring out how a text (or part of a text) is structured can help you to figure out what ideas and information are the most important to hold onto."

- "Today I want to remind you that texts are not only about one main idea. As texts get more complicated, so do the ideas they are forwarding. Readers need to stop often and ask, 'What does this part seem to be mostly about? How does it fit with what I have already read?'"

- "Today I want to teach you that each part of a text has a job to do in helping an author show or develop his or her ideas. Figuring out the structure of a part can help you to think about why an author might have included it and how it helps to show or develop the main ideas of the text."

BEND II: LEARNING ABOUT AN ASPECT OF WESTWARD EXPANSION THROUGH READING

- "Today I want to teach you that when readers get started on a research project, they figure out how to get themselves set up for reading in ways that let them learn all they can about their topic. One way they do that is by getting a lay of the land of their texts and making a plan for what to read."

- "Readers think about *all* they know when they are learning about a topic. If you are learning about penguins, you review all you know about birds because that can help you think about penguins. And if you are learning about Lewis and Clark, you think of all you know about westward expansion, because that all relates to Lewis and Clark."

- "Today I want to teach you that it helps for researchers to think not only about their topic but also about their work, talking together about questions such as, 'How can we keep our energy high during this process?'"

Use this list as a menu of possibilities, selecting only the teaching points that meet the needs of your students. Use your assessment data (conferring and small-group notes, observations, responses to read-alouds, and other information) to decide on a plan that is tailored to the needs of your class. These teaching points may be used as whole-class minilessons, as mid-workshop teaching, or for conferences and small-group work. You need not use every teaching point. See the unit overview for guidelines on how much time to spend in each bend.

- "Today I want to teach you that researchers choose only what seems most important to jot down, and they jot mostly in their own words, quickly, without full sentences."

- "Today I want to remind you that readers don't use writing only to record information; readers also write to grow ideas. And to do that, readers sometimes rely on the same 'thought prompts' as they use to grow ideas when talking."

- "Readers, today I want to teach you that once a researcher has read a bunch of easier texts on a topic and started knowing more about that topic, it is often possible to read and understand texts that would at first have seemed too hard. Also, tackling the hard texts with another person sometimes leads to more success."

- "Readers, today I want to teach you that researchers push themselves to draw on all they have learned from anywhere about the topic they are researching, and they read across texts, thinking, 'How are the lessons I am learning from these texts the same and different?'"

BEND III: BUILDING THEORIES AND READING CRITICALLY

- "Today I want to teach you that when readers look at a series of ideas about a book (or set of books) they can ask themselves, 'What do these have in common? What is different about these ideas?' Then they use the answers to create a theory."

- "What I want to teach you today is that readers don't just think about the information in a text, they also figure out the point of view of the author of that text and how he or she might be swaying you to think a certain way about the topic."

- "Today I want to teach you that readers often think about why an author has chosen to organize a text in a certain way and how structural choices help to support the author's points."

- "Today I want to teach you that researchers often celebrate their learning by sharing it with others."